W9-AMX-701

The American Magazine

The American Magazine

Research Perspectives and Prospects

Edited by DAVID ABRAHAMSON

IOWA STATE UNIVERSITY PRESS / AMES

For Barbara

© 1995 Iowa State University Press, Ames, Iowa 50014

This work was originally published in the *Electronic Journal of Communication/La Revue Electronique de Communication* (EJC/REC), volume 4, numbers 2, 3, and 4, December 1994.

∞ Printed on acid-free paper in the United States of America

First edition, 1995

Library of Congress Cataloging-in-Publication Data

The American magazine: research perspectives and prospects/edited by David Abrahamson.—1st ed.
    p.   cm.
    Originally published electronically as a special issue of: Electronic journal of communication/La revue electronique de communication.
    Includes bibliographical references.
    ISBN 0-8138-2484-2
    1. American periodicals.   I. Abrahamson, David.
PN4877.A475   1995
051—dc20   94-29798

Contents

Contributors, xi

Editorial Board, xv

Introduction
  Brilliant Fragments: The Scholarly Engagement with the
  American Magazine, xvii
    David Abrahamson

I. Perspectives on Magazine Research

1. Research Review: Issues in Magazine Typology, 3
      Marcia Prior-Miller
   Abstract, 3
   Introduction, 3
   Background: Magazine Type and the Theory of Typologies, 4
   Method, 7
   Findings, 8
       The General-Specialized Dichotomy, 9
       Editorial Interest Area Approach, 10
       The Information Function Approach, 11
       The Multiple Characteristics Approach, 11
   Discussion, 13
       General-Specialized Dichotomy, 13
       Editorial Interest Area Approach, 14
       Information Function Approach, 15
       Multiple Characteristics Approach, 17
   Summary and Conclusions, 18
   Notes, 19

2. Research Review: Quantitative Magazine Studies, 1983-1993, 24
      Mark N. Popovich
   Abstract, 24
   Introduction, 24

Literature Review, 25
>Magazine Advertising Sudies, 25
>Magazine Photo Coverage, 27
>Magazine Minority Coverage, 28
>Magazine Content Studies, 29
>Magazine Effects, 30
Conclusions, 31
Notes, 32

3. An Overview of Political Content Analyses of Magazines, 37
>*Lawrence J. Mullen*
Abstract, 37
Introduction, 37
History, 37
Recent Studies, 38
>Who Says..., 39
>...What..., 40
>...To Whom in Which Channel..., 40
>...How..., 41
>...With What Effects..., 43
>...Conclusion..., 44
>Notes..., 44

II. Professional Issues in Magazine Publishing

4. Research Review: Magazine Editors and Editing Practices, 51
>*Lee Jolliffe*
Abstract, 51
Introduction, 51
The Biographical Emphasis, 52
Effects of the Biographical Form on Magazine Editing
>Research, 53
Biography When Broadened, 54
>Editors in the Editing Role, 54
>Editors as Authors, 56
>Editorship as a "Platform", 57
>Editors and Societal Influences, 58
Editorial Practices, 59
>Surveys and Interviews, 59
>Content Analyses: Ethical Tests versus
>>Relationship Tests, 61
>Qualitative Studies, 63
>Quantitative Studies, 64
New Directions, 64

Notes, 65

5. Research Review: The Specialized Business Press, 72
     Kathleen L. Endres
    Abstract, 72
    Introduction, 72
    Research Review, 73
    Future Possibilities, 80
    Notes, 81
6. Research Review: Magazine Management and Economics, 84
     Robert Worthington
    Abstract, 84
    Introduction, 84
    Background, 85
    The Magazine Publishing Process, 86
    Magazine Management Research, 87
    A Review of Research in Magazine Management, 89
        Trend Studies, 89
        Case Studies, 91
        Specific Topic Studies, 92
    Discussion, 93
    Suggestions for the Future, 94
    Notes, 95

7. *Ms*.ing the Free Press: The Advertising and Editorial
    Content of *Ms*. Magazine, 1972-1992, 98
     Lori Melton McKinnon
    Abstract, 98
    Introduction, 98
    Literature, 100
    Research Hypotheses, 102
    Methodology, 103
    Summary of Findings, 104
    Discussion, 105
    Notes, 106

III. Pedagogical and Curricular Perspectives

8. Research Review: Laboratory Student Magazine Programs, 111
     Tom Wheeler
    Abstract, 111
    Introduction, 111
    General Parameters, 112
        Curricular Structure, 114
        The First Amendment, 114
        Ethics, 115

Funding, 115
The Role of Faculty Advisers, 116
Critiques, Suggestions for Further Research, 117
Notes, 118

9. Research Review: Issues in Magazine Journalism Education, 122
   Elliot King
   Abstract, 122
   Introduction, 122
   The Theory of Magazine Journalism Education, 124
   The Composition Revolution Meets Journalism Education, 126
   Other Empirical Research and Teaching Tips, 128
   Future Directions, 129
   Conclusion, 131
   Notes, 131

10. Magazine and Feature Writing Unbound: A Critique of
    Current Teaching Paradigms and a Case for Rhetoric, 134
    Monica Johnstone and Andrew Ciofalo
    Abstract, 134
    Introduction, 134
    News Influences in Feature and Magazine Courses, 135
    The Challenge of the "New" Journalism, 140
    The Case for Rhetoric, 140
    Notes, 145

11. Preaching Our Practice: On Sharing Professional Work
    with Students, 147
    Paul Mendelbaum
    Abstract, 147
    Introduction, 147
    Interview Preparation Demonstrated, 149
    Hearing the Interviews, 150
    Cutting and Revision, 152
    Rewards, 153
    Notes, 154

IV. Global and Local Issues in Magazine Journalism

12. Research Review: An International Perspective on
    Magazines, 159
    Leara Rhodes
    Abstract, 159
    Introduction, 159
    Methodology, 160
    The Study: Part One, 160
    The Study: Part Two, 165

Discussion, 167
Notes, 169

13. Research Review: City and Regional Magazines, 172
   Ernest C. Hynds
   Abstract, 172
   Introduction, 172
   Evolution of City Magazines, 174
       Renaissance Begins in the 1960s, 175
       Emphasis Patterns Emerge and Persist, 176
   Review of Research on City Magazines, 177
       Scholarly Contributions, 178
       Papers, Dissertations, and Theses, 179
       Books, Trade Journals, Consumer Magazines,
           Newspapers, 181
       Other Sources for Research Information, 182
   Suggestions for Future Research, 182
   Notes, 184

14. Regional Consumer Magazines and the Ideal White Reader:
   Constructing and Retaining Geography as Text, 186
       Katherine Fry
   Abstract, 186
   Introduction, 186
   Geographic Place and Power Relations, 187
   U.S. Regionalism and Representation, 188
   U.S. Magazine Industry, 189
   Patterns of Regional Representation, 190
   Representations of Nature and Culture in Identity
       Construction, 191
       The Rugged Frontier West, 191
       The Agrarian Midwest, 194
       The Old/New South, 196
   Regional Identity and Race, 199
   Notes, 201

V. Magazines as Literature, Magazines as History

15. Research Review: Magazines and Literary Journalism, an
   Embarrassment of Riches, 207
       Thomas B. Connery
   Abstract, 207
   Introduction, 207

Uncovering Riches, 209
Notes, 214

16. The Reform Years at *Hampton's*: The Magazine Journalism
   of Rheta Childe Dorr, 1909-1912, 217
      Agnes Hooper Gottlieb
   Abstract, 217
   Introduction, 217
   Historical and Biographical Review, 218
   Conclusion, 227
   Notes, 228

17. The Women's Movement in the 1920s: American Magazines
   Document the Health and Progress of Feminism, 231
      Carolyn Ann Bonard
   Abstract, 231
   Introduction, 231
   Method, 232
   Results, 232
      Social and Economic Aspects of the Women's Movement, 232
      Political Aspects of the Women's Movement, 236
      Controversy over the Equal Rights Issue, 237
   Conclusion, 239
   Notes , 239

Contributors

David **Abrahamson** is associate professor of Journalism in the Medill School of Journalism at Northwestern University. He is the former research chair of the Magazine Division of the Association for Education in Journalism and Mass Communication, the former coordinator of the magazine publishing program at New York University, and the author of *Magazine-Made America: The Cultural Transformation of the Postwar Periodical* (forthcoming, 1994).

Carolyn Ann Bonard is a B.J. (Magazine) and A.B. (History) candidate in the School of Journalism at the University of Missouri, Columbia. She is the winner of the 1993 Top Undergraduate Paper Prize awarded by the Magazine Division of the Association for Education in Journalism and Mass Communication and a free-lance writer, photographer, and publication designer.

Andrew Ciofalo is associate professor of Writing and Media and media coordinator in the Department of Writing and Media at Loyola College in Maryland. He is the former head of the Magazine Division of the Association for Education in Journalism and Mass Communication and the editor of *Those Years: Recollections of a Baltimore Newspaperman* (1990) and *Internships: Perspectives on Experiential Learning* (1992).

Thomas Connery is associate professor of Journalism and Mass Communications and chair of the Department of Journalism and Mass Communications at the University of St. Thomas. He is the book-review editor of *American Journalism*, the journal of the American Journalism Historians Association, and the editor of *A Sourcebook of American Literary Journalism: Representative Writers in an Emerging Genre* (1992).

Kathleen L. Endres is associate professor of Communication in the School of Communication at the University of Akron. She is the 1994 head of the Magazine Division of the Association for Education in Journalism and Mass Communication and the editor of *Trade, Industrial, and Professional Periodicals of the United States* (1994) and the co-editor of *Women's Periodicals in the United States: Consumer Magazines* (forthcoming, 1995).

Katherine Fry is assistant professor of Television and Radio in the Department of Television and Radio at Brooklyn College, City University of New York. The scholarly study of regional magazines was the subject of her doctoral dissertation, recently completed in the Mass Media and Communications Program at Temple University.

Agnes Hooper Gottlieb is assistant professor of Communication in the Department of Communication at Seton Hall University. She is the winner of the 1993 Top Faculty Paper Prize awarded by the Magazine Division of the Association for Education in Journalism and Mass Communication, a former Associated Press reporter, and the former editor of the English-language monthly, *Commerce in Belgium*.

Ernest C. Hynds is professor of Journalism and Mass Communication and head of the Department of Journalism in the Henry W. Grady College of Journalism and Mass Communication at the University of Georgia. He is a former editorial writer and the author of *American Newspapers in the Nineteen Eighties* (1980).

Monica Johnstone is assistant professor of Rhetoric in the Department of Writing and Media at Loyola College in Maryland. She is the author of an interpretive essay included in the edited volume, *Keeping Company: Rhetoric, Pluralism, and Wayne Booth* (1994).

Lee Jolliffe is assistant professor of Journalism at the School of Journalism at the University of Missouri, Columbia. She is the former head of the Magazine Division of the Association for Education in Journalism and Mass Communication and a member of this publication's Editorial Board.

Elliot King is assistant professor of Media Studies in the Department of Writing and Media at Loyola College in Maryland. He is the co-author of *The Book of FAX: An Impartial Guide to Buying & Using Facsimile Machines* (1990) and *The Online Journalist: Using the Internet and Electronic Information Sources* (forthcoming, 1995).

Paul Mandelbaum is managing editor of *Story* Magazine. He has taught magazine journalism at the University of Iowa and at Drake University, and is the editor of a critical anthology, *First Words* (1993).

Lori Melton McKinnon is a Ph.D. candidate in the Department of Communication at the University of Oklahoma. She is the winner of the 1993 Top Graduate Paper Prize awarded by the Magazine Division of the Association for Education in Journalism and Mass Communication and a member of the executive committe of the AEJMC Interest Group on Graduate Education.

Lawrence J. Mullen is assistant professor of Telecommunications in the Greenspun School of Communication at the University of Nevada, Las Vegas. The scholarly study of news images was the subject of his doctoral dissertation, recently completed in the Department of Communication Studies at the University of Iowa.

Mark Popovich is professor of Journalism and former chair of the Department of Journalism at Ball State University. He is the former head of the Mass Communications and Society Division of the Association for Education in Journalism and Mass Communications.

Marcia Prior-Miller is associate professor of Journalism and Mass Communication and head of the magazine emphasis in the Department of Journalism and Mass Communication at Iowa State University.

Leara Rhodes is assistant professor of Journalism and Mass Communication in the Henry W. Grady College of Journalism and Mass Communication at the University of Georgia. She was awarded a Fulbright Fellowship to Haiti in 1990, and has worked extensively with various Caribbean newspapers and publishers.

Tom Wheeler is associate professor of Journalism in the School of Journalism and Communication at the University of Oregon. He is the former editor of *Guitar Player* Magazine and the author of two encyclopedias on musical instruments, *The Guitar Book* (1978) and *American Guitars: An Illustrated History* (1992).

Robert Worthington is associate professor of Journalism in the Department of Journalism and Mass Communications at New Mexico State University. He is the teaching standards chair of the Media Management and Economics Division of the Association for Education in Journalism and Mass Communication and the co-author of *Staffing a Small Business: Hiring, Compensating & Evaluating* (1987) and *People Investment: How to Make Your Hiring Decisions Pay off for Everyone* (1993).

Editorial Board

Abe Peck is professor of Journalism and chair of the magazine program in the Medill School of Journalism at Northwestern University. He is the 1995 head-elect of the Magazine Division of the Association for Education in Journalism and Mass Communication and the author of *Uncovering the Sixties: The Life and Times of the Underground Press* (1991).

Norman Sims is professor of Journalism in the Department of Journalism at the University of Massachusetts, Amherst. He is the editor of *Literary Journalism in the Twentieth Century* (1990) and the co-editor of the second edition of *The Literary Journalists* (forthcoming, 1995).

David E. Sumner is assistant professor of Journalism and coordinator of the magazine program in the Department of Journalism at Ball State University. He is the 1994 co-chair of the Membership Committee of the Association for Education in Journalism and Mass Communication, the 1994 research chair of the AEJMC Magazine Division, and the author of *The Episcopal Church's History* (1987).

INTRODUCTION

Brilliant Fragments:
The Scholarly Engagement with
the American Magazine

David Abrahamson

ABSTRACT

The editor of this volume discusses the origin of the work's underlying concept—an attempt to suggest a schema through which the larger corpus of magazine scholarship can perhaps be viewed as a coherent whole—and introduces the interrelated themes addressed by the various contributors to the volume.

Introduction

Like most projects of some complexity, this volume was born, in roughly equal measure, of both synergy and serendipity. The original idea emerged in the fall of 1992 at the mid-year meeting of the Magazine Division of the Association for Education in Journalism and Mass Communication. Convened on a beautiful, brisk November weekend at Northwestern University, some forty scholars of the magazine form assembled to do what professors always do at such occasions. Research papers were presented, teaching methods were examined, and issues of professional responsibility were explored. Also as always, there was a great deal of less structured talk and discussion—which, as anyone familiar with such academic rituals will readily attest, are often the most stimulating and productive aspects of such meetings.

It was in just such a conversation that a number of attendees concluded after considerable reflection that the existing body of scholarly knowledge about magazines seemed to lack a larger coherence. As the discussion progressed, an informal but fervent consensus was reached that, should the sum of magazine research ever be assembled into a rational corpus of knowledge, it would then be possible to identify important theoretical and/or methodological issues and perhaps even to suggest promising new directions for further research. Further than that, it was agreed that such an effort, in addition to its potential to advance magazine scholarship, might also prove a valuable teaching tool.

There are perhaps a number of reasons that the scholarly engagement with the magazine form has long suffered from a degree of fragmentation. In the absence of any overarching intellectual structure, many researchers have often pursued their studies in relative isolation. As a result, they have often produced what might be characterized as "brilliant fragments"—worthy research of clear merit, but, it might be argued, occasionally unconnected to any larger framework.

Moreover, there has long been an element of confusion regarding the magazine's place in the journalistic pantheon. In the view of some, the magazine form itself is strangely suspect. Even though as celebrated an authority as George Washington might call them "such easy vehicles of knowledge,"[1] a certain lack of conventional *gravitas* may have consigned magazines and their study to the status of second-tier subject and activity. As a generalization about journalism scholarship, magazines as a research subject certainly have drawn less attention than either newspapers or television. A study covering twenty years of issues of the profession's research journal, *Journalism Quarterly* found that magazine subjects represented only six percent of the articles, and more than half of them were narrowly focused on journalistic "content analyses."[2] A similar survey of *Communication Abstracts* found that scholarly articles about magazines accounted for less than one percent of the content; in comparison, research concerning newspapers represented more than five percent of the articles, and television, more than twenty percent.[3]

Part of the reason for this inattention might be the small number of University departments that offer magazine research instruction, but a larger, more systemic consideration is also a possibility. "Much magazine study has been limited to the discussion of magazine publishing as a branch of the craft of journalism, or to the analysis of the content of particular magazines because of some editorial or authorial prominence," wrote Dorothy Schmidt, a cultural historian. "Academic disciplines have almost routinely concentrated on the other legs of the print triad [i.e. newspapers and books]...but scant attention is given to the continuing role of magazines as reflectors and molders of public opinion and political and social attitudes."[4]

The vast preponderance of historical scholarship related to American magazines, moreover, can be characterized as "chronicle," for much of it includes neither broad historical interpretations of the sociocultural contexts nor detailed insights into the defining—and often competing—editorial and economic realities of the medium. The principle reason for this approach is that in most instances media scholars have generally chosen to study magazines as isolated journalistic artifacts, rather than as interesting products and catalysts of social, cultural, and economic change. Though often commendable as examples of extraordinary archival rigor, the results have rarely been able to connect magazines to their larger social role.[5]

One last possible explanation for the fragmentation of magazine research might, at least in part, be the responsibility of magazine scholars themselves. We are certainly no more immune than our colleagues in other disciplines from either the temptation of trendy topics or the curse of tunnel vision. Fashions in magazine scholarship rise and fall in concert with those in the rest of the academy, and often the animating principle may be something other than a desire to make a substantive contribution to the accepted body of existing knowledge.

As the November 1992 conference drew to a close, participants agreed that there was a need to survey and organize the field of magazine scholarship. And it was this synergistic consensus which soon intersected with a serendipitous opportunity. Less than three months after the conference, a fortuitous circumstance materialized in the form of an offer from the *Electronic Journal of Communication/La revue electronique de communication* to devote an entire special issue to a broad consideration of precisely this subject. It is that electronically produced journal's kind permission that has made this hard-copy version possible.

In ensuing consultations with many of the most prominent magazine scholars, the form and content of the volume were quickly reified. Many of the researchers had in fact attended the Northwestern meeting; others were easily reached through a wide network of collegial contacts. Some graciously agreed to author essays which would be included in the work, while others kindly consented to referee the submitted contributions as members of the volume's Editorial Board.

The underlying schema of work is readily apparent from a quick glance at the contents. The articles fall into two broad categories. A majority are "research reviews" of the sort occasionally found in journals serving the physical sciences. Addressing a particular subfield of magazine scholarship, each identifies and organizes the important literature on its topic, discusses any relevant theoretical or methodological matters, and suggests cogent avenues for possible future study. Each, in effect, attempts to address a series of interrelated questions: What do we know? What questions have been asked? How well were they asked? How well were they answered? What questions have yet to be posed? And how can they perhaps best be approached? The balance of the essays are more conventional scholarly articles which serve to illuminate the broader topics.

For purposes of organizing the entire realm of magazine research this volume employs a subdivisional scheme comprised of five broad areas. The first, something of an overview, addresses three broad themes which have been the foci of much scholarly attention. Marcia Prior-Miller of Iowa State University explicates the recurrent problem of magazine typology; Mark N. Popovich of Ball State University reviews the occasionally conflicting mass of quantitative studies; and Lawrence J. Mullen of the University of Nevada, Las Vegas surveys the research centered on the political content of magazines.

The second major area concerns professional issues in magazine publishing. Lee Jolliffe of the University of Missouri, Columbia analyzes matters related to editorial theory and practice; Kathleen L. Endres of the University of Akron reviews the scholarship related to the specialized business press; and Robert Worthington of New Mexico State University discusses magazine management and economic issues. In addition, Lori Melton McKinnon of the University of Oklahoma examines the advertising and editorial content of *Ms.* Magazine.

Pedagogical and curricular issues comprise the third major area. Tom Wheeler of the University of Oregon considers the extant research on laboratory student magazines, and Elliot King of Loyola College surveys the scholarship related to magazine journalism education. Additionally, Monica Johnstone and Andrew Ciofalo of Loyola College suggest a new rhetorical approach to magazine-writing instruction, and Paul Mandelbaum of *Story* Magazine explores the benefits and drawbacks of sharing one's own professional work experiences with students.

The fourth major area addresses the peculiar geographic dimension of magazine journalism on both the local and global scales. Leara Rhodes of the University of Georgia reviews scholarship related to the international aspect of magazines, while Ernest C. Hynds of the University of Georgia analyzes the research on city and regional magazines. In addition, Katherine Fry of Brooklyn College investigates the class and race assumptions inherent in many consumer regional magazines.

Consideration of magazines in both literary and historical terms constitute the last major area. Tom Connery of the University of St. Thomas assays the subfield of literary journalism. Agnes Hooper Gottlieb of Seton Hall University provides insights into the magazine journalism of Rheta Childe Dorr, a social reformer, while Carolyn Ann Bonard of the University of Missouri, Columbia uses American magazines to document the progress of feminism.

Viewed both as a whole and separately, it is our intention that the detailed scholarship in these five areas which make up this volume will serve a variety of purposes. The nature of the subjects has in all cases dictated the method, and readers will find some chapters notably specific and bounded, others quite broad and inclusive. An esteemed colleague once playfully referred to the particular labor required to bring such collaborative works into being as "dancing with a partner of unknown dimension." During the course of editing this volume, the veracity of the comment was clearly demonstrated. Now that the dance is complete, one can only hope that the efforts prove useful to a number of new, unseen, likely-never-to-be-met partners, the readers of this volume. It is our fondest hope that, for all students of the academic literature of the American periodical, this work may in some way prove a useful tool to orgainize and further the scholarly engagement with the magazine form.

Notes

[1] Lyon N. Richardson, A History of Early American Magazines, 1741-1789 (New York: Thomas Nelson and Sons, 1931), 1.

[2] Between 1964 and 1983, 116 of 1,917 articles published concerned magazines; fifty-three percent were content analyses, twenty-two percent were historical in nature, and eleven percent dealt with economics. See Peter Gerlach, "Research About Magazines Appearing in Journalism Quarterly," Journalism Quarterly 64.1 (Spring 1987): 178- 182. See also J. Jacobson, "Research Activity in Magazine Publishing," Journalism Quarterly 65.2 (Summer 1988): 511-514.

[3] Communication Abstracts from 1978 (its first year of publication) to 1991 were analyzed by the author, using the index headings of Magazine, Magazine Readership, and Magazine History (but not Magazine Advertising). Magazine research represented 151 of 15,900 articles (0.95 percent) and averaged just under eleven articles per annual issue. Newspaper research averaged over sixty articles per issue; TV, over 200.

[4] Dorothy S. Schmidt, "Magazines," in M. Thomas Ingre, ed., Handbook of American Popular Culture (2nd ed.; New York: Greenwood Press, 1989), 648-649.

[5] The two most widely cited works of magazine history are Frank Luther Mott, A History of American Magazines, 5 vols. (Cambridge: Harvard University Press, 1938) and Theodore Peterson, Magazines in the Twentieth Century (Urbana: University of Illinois Press, 1956). Other narrative histories include Lyon N. Richardson, A History of Early American Magazines, 1741-1789 (New York: Thomas Nelson and Sons, 1931); Roland E. Wolseley, The Magazine World: An Introduction to Magazine Journalism (New York: Prentice-Hall, 1951); Walter Davenport and James C. Derieux, Ladies, Gentlemen, and Editors (Garden City, NY: Doubleday, 1960); James L.C. Ford, Magazines for Millions (Carbondale, IL: Southern Illinois University Press, 1969); John W.Tebbel, The American Magazine: A Compact History (New York: Hawthorn Books, 1969); James Playstead Wood, Magazines in the United States (New York: Roland Press, 1971); William H. Taft, American Magazines for the 1980s (New York: Hastings House, 1982); John W. Tebbel and Mary Ellen Zuckerman, The Magazine in America, 1741-1990 (New York: Oxford University Press, 1991); and Amy Janello and Brennon Jones, The American Magazine (New York: Harry Abrams, 1991). Though newspapers rather than magazines are its principal focus, see also Michael Emery and Edwin Emery, The Press and America: An Interpretive History of the Mass Media (7th ed.; Englewood Cliffs, NJ: Prentice-Hall, 1992).

Acknowledgements

The author would like to express his gratitude to Teresa Harrison and Lucien Gerber of Rensselaer Polytechnic Institute, the Managing Editor and French Editor, respectively, of this project. Special thanks are also due the members of this issue's Editorial Board: Sharon Bass of University of Kansas; Maurine Beasley of University of Maryland; Doug Covert of University of Evansville; Vicki Hesterman of Point Loma Nazarene College; Jeffrey Alan John of Wright State University; Sammye Johnson of Trinity University; Lee Jolliffe of University of Missouri, Columbia; Abe Peck of Northwestern University; Norm Sims of University of Massachusetts, Amherst; and David Sumner of Ball State University.

I

Perspectives
on
Magazine Research

1

Research Review:
Issues in Magazine Typology

Marcia R. Prior-Miller

ABSTRACT

This article explores how magazine type has been defined and on what criteria categories of magazines have been based in published reports of communication research. Four definition strategies were observed in 223 research
reports published from 1977 through 1991. The approaches are critiqued on
their apparent ability to meet five generally accepted standards for the usefulness of scientifically designed typologies. Recommendations for future
research follow the analysis.

Introduction

Communication scholars generally agree that the universe of magazines,
journals and other non-newspaper periodicals can be clustered by titles with
shared characteristics. However, they differ on category criteria, on definitions for commonly used labels and on relationships between characteristics.
These differences hold even when scholars appear to be classifying magazines
for similar purposes. Among the consequences of this confusion is a lack of
clarity about how to draw cross-sectional samples of the universe of magazines for systematic, empirical studies of communication behavior. Johnson
and Schmidt also noted the negative impacts for designing magazine research.[1]

The ability to clearly identify trait patterns that distinguish one group of
magazines from another is basic to systematic studies of magazines. Yet there
are no published analyses of the competing classification schemes. Neither is
the problem addressed in the research methods literature.[2]

3

Because positioning new studies within the body of literature is the first step in designing new research, one starting point is to identify how past researchers have classified magazines. The purpose of this chapter is to investigate how the concept of magazine type has been defined and magazines categorized in published studies. From that inquiry, suggestions for future research will be made.

Background: Magazine Type and
The Theory of Typologies

The lack of a clearly defined and empirically tested method for classifying non-newspaper periodicals is a problem that has theoretical and methodological implications central to the study of magazines as a medium of communication.

It can be argued that there is no single method of defining and classifying magazines that will apply to all research questions.[3] Reynolds said that "any set of concepts can be used to organize and classify the objects of study." However, he also suggested that some classification methods are more useful than others. He argued that naming, organizing, and categorizing the "things" being studied are the first tasks of science and the most basic roles of scientific knowledge. Building on this base, the scientific enterprise can move forward to the higher level tasks of explaining and predicting.[4] Conversely, if no agreement can be found on how objects are to be named and classified, explanation and prediction cannot occur.

This study is based on the assumption that the importance of how magazines are categorized does not lie in determining a single "right" way to categorize titles or in identifying a method against which other methods can be measured as "wrong." Two needs exist: a framework within which the existing body of research can be understood and new research designed, and a means to determine valid sampling frames for cross-sectional magazine studies.

Clarifying definitions and building classification systems for scientific study are processes nearly as old as the scientific enterprise. Developing typologies and taxonomies has been traced to Aristotle.[5] Contemporary social scientists disagree on the value of taxonomic research as a science in its own right, but generally agree on the role typologies can play in developing and testing theory. Bailey called the typology a form of nominal measurement used to "delineate meaningful social types" and to be based on one or more dimensions or variables. Babbie recommended using typologies only as independent or predictive variables for interpreting data.[6]

The third function of typologies, to define groups for sample designs, is indirectly related to building theory. Lowry asked:

If a content analysis study shows a highly significant decrease in sexual stereotyping in a sample of full-page ads taken from two women's magazines
during the last 30 years, a natural question is: To what other magazines or
types of content might this result be generalized?[7]

Lowry's question was one of several designed to illustrate the importance
of sample population validity in communication research, regardless of medium. He wrote:

The degree of population validity of a research study, or of an entire field of
research, is largely a function of the types of samples studied, and how similar those samples are to the types of populations to which one would like to
generalize. However, the crucial point is: It is impossible to determine to
what populations a study can be generalized unless the sampling procedures
used and the basic characteristics of the people or objects studied are *clearly
specified*. To put it another way, if this important information is not clearly
specified in a research article, then such an article has *no demonstrated population validity*.[8]

Reynolds outlined three criteria for typologies: The first, exhaustiveness,
is the ability to place every object into the scheme: in this case, magazines.
The second, mutual exclusivity, requires that there be no ambiguity about where
each periodical is to be placed in the scheme. The third criterion, theoretical
relevance, requires that a typology be consistent with other concepts used press
the purposes of science. These include questions of parsimony, a common level
of abstraction, explanatory and predictive capability, and language with descriptive relevance for building theory. Tiryakian also noted that the dimension or dimensions that are "differentiated into types must be explicitly
stated."[9] Of these criteria, Reynolds suggests that the first two are the more
obvious but the third is the "most important."[10]

Media professionals and scholars have long recognized the need to classify media into groups, both to simplify information processing and to conduct
systematic studies. Cannon and Williams observed that the most common and
"most obvious level of simplification" has been to divide the media into general classes: radio, television, newspapers and magazines.[11] The communication literature almost universally assumes the existence of magazine subgroups. However, there are few systematic explorations of the underlying characteristics for classifying magazines or how differences in these characteristics affect communication behaviors.

Exceptions can be found in the marketing and advertising literature, which
provides examples of multiple efforts to subdivide the media beyond the primary levels. Cannon and Williams concluded from their review of this literature that efforts to classify television had been relatively unproductive, but

efforts to classify magazines had identified "relatively stable classifications based on editorial appeal."[12] However, the usefulness of classification systems identified from these studies is somewhat limited. Marketing and advertising studies have focused almost exclusively on magazines that carry advertising for consumer products. Adless magazines are absent from the studies, as are magazines that carry only regional or local advertising. Also missing are studies of a wide range of business, scholarly and organization publications.[13]

Compaine argued for a relationship between audience size and the active-passive orientation of editorial content in magazines.[14] He laid out his argument using a range of titles, but used only consumer titles to illustrate the framework. He did not test the framework or reconcile it with other approaches to classifying magazines. It would seem reasonable to expect textbooks that focus on the magazine publishing industry to provide empirically tested typologies. But they do not. Comparing three of the texts illustrates the conflicting perspectives available to researchers. In 1965 Wolseley divided the universe of magazines into two editorial "appeal" groups, based on audience size: (a) consumer or general interest, and (b) specialized. He then subdivided these two groups into 11 and 13 subgroups, respectively.[15]

More recently, Mogel divided the universe of magazines into four groups: consumer magazines (of which, he said, there are both general and specialized interest titles), business, scholarly or literary, and newsletters.[16] Mogel thus placed business and scholarly publications in separate categories on an equal conceptual level with consumer magazines. Wolseley included business, scholarly and literary in the specialized, or limited circulation, subgroup. Mogel used the term "specialized" only to differentiate between two consumer magazine subgroups.

Click and Baird divided the universe of magazines first into two circulation groups: mass and specialized. They then identified consumer, business, farm, public relations, and one-shot magazines as subgroups, and further subdivided these five subgroups into an additional thirteen groups.[17] The relationships between the five subgroups and the mass and specialized groupings are not stated. Readers of their text might conclude that the specialized category has eight subdivisions and the public relations category, five, for a total of twenty magazine types.

Click and Baird placed organization magazines in a separate category. Wolseley placed "industrial or company" magazines in a subgroup of specialized, limited circulation publications. Mogel did not include the category, and neither Wolseley nor Click and Baird included newsletters.

Introductory mass media textbooks, the majority of which are industry oriented,[18] also give conflicting perspectives. An examination of thirteen mass communication texts[19] and twelve magazine texts[20] revealed only two that used the same classificatory scheme: Gamble and Gamble used Click and Baird's framework. Reynolds said developing a method of organizing and categorizing the objects of study is "the easiest [task of science] to achieve."[21] Nonetheless, five authors described the difficulty of defining the population of magazines.[22] Because systematic, empirically tested typologies based on clearly delineated dimensions are not present in the literature, one can conclude that the existing classification methods are best described as "commonsense" typologies.[23]

Because the emphasis on empirically based inquiry in communication research has increased in recent years,[24] and because scientifically designed research requires carefully defined concepts and terms to be operationalized for sampling and measurement, it is expected that an exploration of the research literature might provide clarity where textbooks do not. However, reviewing the body of communication research on magazines is beyond the scope of the typical literature review.

Faced with similar problems of reviewing sizable bodies of literature, scholars in social and communication sciences have used several strategies to compare and synthesize findings in order to establish baselines for future research. Among these are meta-research techniques and integrative literature reviews. The meta-analysis has been defined and applied primarily with quantitative procedures to provide data points for statistical studies. The integrative literature review, on the other hand, is a method more suited to integrating theory and concepts.[25]

To study the concept of magazine type, an integrative literature review of published studies was conducted to find answers to the following questions: (a) How do investigators define the universe, or population, of magazines? (b) If investigators subdivide the universe of magazines, on what characteristic(s) are categories based?

Method

Investigators' direct and implied definitions of the "magazine type" concept were examined in 223 reports of communication research on magazines indexed in Volumes 1 through 14 of *Communication Abstracts*. The studies were published in the 14 years from 1977 through 1991, the most recent available when data were collected. Hereafter referred to as "magazine research," these reports included studies on the visual and verbal elements of magazine editorial and advertising content, as well as studies of the history and social order of magazines and investigations of communication problems and structure.

Following Cooper's protocol, the *CA* volume, issue, and abstract numbers, author, and journal were recorded for each research report.[26] Abstracts were copied and reviewed. Duplicate and book abstracts were removed, leaving a total of 228 articles. Also removed was a study of the temporal variable indexed under the keyword "Time." The remaining articles were located and copied. Four additional reports were deleted because they were not reports on magazines, though they had been indexed as such. The study sample totaled 223 research reports.

Each study was examined to identify how researchers identified the universe and categories of periodicals in that universe. Descriptive terms and titles assigned to categories of magazines were recorded, as were statements about the magazine dimension(s), or characteristic(s), on which category(ies) were based. Sampling frames and units of analysis were noted as controls to prevent confusing authors' statements about the universe of periodicals with sample populations. No further analysis of these dimensions was conducted.

Descriptors were clustered twice: First, by the specific terms investigators used to describe the universe of periodicals or study population. Any deviation in terms was treated as a unique descriptor. Thus, "consumer magazines," "general consumer magazines," and "general magazines" were categorized as unique descriptors, as were "large mass circulation" magazines and "wide circulation and appeal" magazines. Two or more descriptors used in a single study to describe a population and its subcategories were treated as a conceptual unit, or a descriptor set. Descriptors and descriptor sets were then grouped by 1) authors' stated definitions, and when stated criteria were not available, 2) the characteristics that underlay assigned labels. Descriptor and descriptor set frequencies were computed within and across clusters.

Findings

Analysis of author descriptions in 223 studies identified 140 unique descriptor sets used to designate the universe of periodicals or the population that was the focus of the study. The most frequently used unique descriptors were "news magazines" (in 11 of 223 studies); "women's magazines" (9 studies); "consumer magazines" (8 studies); "general audience [magazines], men's [magazines] and women's magazines" (5 studies). In 37 studies (16.6 percent of 223), no population or universe of magazines was named or implied.

In the remaining 186 studies, the population of magazines was primarily defined as the sampling frame. The majority, 97 of 186, based population categories on a single characteristic (i.e., "magazines that serve general audiences"). The remainder used clusters of characteristics (i.e., "magazines with large mass circulation and a large spectrum of genres").

Similarly, the majority of investigators defined the study population without stating how the selected magazine group fit into the universe of periodicals. In only three (1.4 percent) of the 223 studies did authors state a goal of designing the study within a framework of the universe of periodicals. In only one of the three studies did the author position the study within competing classificatory perspectives.

Descriptors used in both qualitative and quantitative research literature were less carefully defined than expected. In general, they were similar to and somewhat more specific than textbook descriptors. As a result, research-based definitions highlighted subtleties less easily discerned in textbook definitions.

Three primary approaches to categorizing magazines were identified from the analysis of descriptors and descriptor sets: (a) general-specialized dichotomy, (b) interest area, and (c) information function approaches. Also identified was a fourth approach, (d) the multiple characteristics approach, which cut across the first three approaches and further expanded the dimensions used to identify magazine populations.

The General-Specialized Dichotomy

The terms general and specialized were used without definition in two studies. In the remaining 223 studies approximately one third (N=65) operationalized this dichotomous division of the magazine universe in one of three ways: scope of the audience, scope of the editorial content (or editorial appeal), and audience size. Although these three characteristics are highly interrelated, they are distinctly different. The first is medium based, the second and third, audience based.

Audience Scope. The general-specialized dichotomy most frequently referred to the nature of the audience. In 47 of the 65 studies that used the general-specialized perspective, the term "general" referred to audiences that are geographically and/or demographically diverse; "specialized" referred to more narrowly focused audiences and was based on audiences' shared interest in a specific subject area or one or more demographic or psychographic characteristics. In 32 of the 47 studies that used the audience scope definition, investigators selected magazines that appealed to widely diversified audiences, but did not use the "general" and "specialized" descriptors. However, these studies were placed in the same group because they used both the dichotomous breakdown of magazines and one of the general or specialized operational definitions. Some authors in this second group defined audience scope as geographic diversity, equating national or international circulation with general, and regional or even formal organization circulations with general and specialized, respectively. Both Mott and Fink used geographic and demographic criteria for defining "general audiences."[27]

Editorial Scope. The terms "general" and "specialized" were also used to refer to a magazine's editorial content, scope, or appeal, where general and specialized refer to the breadth or diversity of topics included in the magazine's editorial content.[28].

Audience Size. A few scholars divided magazines into "general and special publications" based on the criterion of audience size. Although one author cited Wolseley as source for the approach,[29] in another 9 studies researchers used magazine circulation as the criterion but did not cite a source. These also did not use the general-specialized terms.

Some scholars who used the general-specialized terminology for designating a population of magazines interchanged terms and definitions, adding the terms "mass"[30] and "popular"[31] as apparent synonyms for general magazines, and limited size as a synonym for specialized. Strickland et al compared "largest circulation" magazines with "magazines targeted to selected audiences."[32] If a distinction is made between editorial appeal, audience scope and audience size, the terms "popular" and "mass" can also be defined with greater precision.[33] Both terms are primarily audience based, but have connotations of audience identity that transcend audience size.

Several sources differentiated between editorial scope, audience scope and audience size. Hayes defined city magazines as having a general editorial orientation but geographically restricted target audiences.[34] City and regional magazine audiences can also be defined as demographically diverse for periodicals with geographically specialized editorial orientations.[35]

Editorial Interest Area Approach

Competing with the general-specialized dichotomy as the most frequently used method for categorizing periodicals is the editorial interest area approach. Using the editorial subject or area of interest as the organizing criterion, investigators in approximately one-third, or 61, of the 223 research reports studied women's magazines, news magazines, farm, fashion, student interest, children's, and science magazines, among others. Included in this group of studies were only those studies for which authors used interest area as the highest level descriptor for the universe or population of magazines: "major magazine genres," or "city magazines."

The single most studied group of magazines was the news magazines, identified in 22, or a third, of the 61 interest area studies. Women's magazines were second, with 10 studies. Both news magazine and women's titles were also frequently included in cross-category studies.[36] Of the 61 interest based studies, more than half were designed to focus on titles within a single interest area. The remaining studies crossed interest areas, comparing, for example, magazines for blacks, whites, men, and women.

The Information Function Approach

In the third most commonly used approach to classifying magazines, authors based categories on information functions for editorial or advertising content. A wide variety of descriptors were identified in the 33 studies that used this approach. Additional strategies were found in mass communication textbooks. Analysis of category criteria suggests this method was used in two ways: First, to classify magazines according to the advertising purpose and second, by editorial purpose or function.

Advertising Information Function. Of the two criteria, advertising function was the more popular: magazines that carry advertising for consumer products were categorized as "consumer magazines," and magazines that carry advertising for products and services to businesses and occupational groups, as "business magazines." A third group, "farm" magazines, carry advertising for agriculture-related products. The categories are drawn from the standard directories for magazine advertising rates.[37]

Although authors of advertising and marketing studies typically used this approach, the strategy was also used for studies of nonadvertising communication phenomena. The term "consumer magazines" was used as a unique descriptor in 8 studies; variations were used in an additional 16 studies, for a total of 24 studies. An additional 8 studies used the business magazine descriptor or a combination of business and consumer, for a total of 32 studies.

Editorial Information Function. Editorial information function approaches were used less frequently and with less clarity in the research literature than advertising information approaches. In 3 studies the approach was clearly identifiable as a criterion for classifying magazines: Investigators studied "muckraking" and "public relations" magazines. Other studies might appropriately have been placed in this category, but too little information was available to make a call.

In general, investigators who used the editorial function approach did not define categories in relation to a universe of periodicals. Textbook authors, whose clearly stated purpose was to categorize the universe of periodicals, used a broader range of labels to categorize editorial functions: escape and entertainment, news and information, advocacy and opinion, public relations. Textbook authors also introduced various synonyms for advertising and information functions and interest areas (e.g., lifestyle, trade, technical, religion, literary and academic, organization magazines).[38]

The Multiple Characteristics Approach

When examined apart from the findings of this study, research that used the multiple characteristics approach tended to further cloud the issue. Examined as part of this study, however, the choice of descriptor sets that fell into this category also began to evidence usage patterns.

Of the 223 studies that were examined, 63 could be classified as using a multiple characteristics approach. In these studies, investigators combined as many as two, and sometimes a dimension of all of the three strategies described above. The majority of mass media and magazine textbook authors use this approach to classifying magazines. Several strategies emerged from the analysis.

Comparison Groups Definition. Using Boolean logic, investigators used multiple characteristics to define samples for comparative study of a variable: That is, characteristics were used to define title clusters.The investigator then compared variable treatmentswithin and between the clusters. Lysonski, for example, compared how men and women were differentially portrayed in advertising that was carried in magazines with content designed to appeal to general, men's, and women's audiences, respectively.[39]

Sample Definition. Alternatively, and again using Boolean logic, investigators used multiple characteristics to carve out a group of magazines for study. Thus, for example, a cluster of magazines might be defined to include only "general consumer magazines with circulations over 130,000."

Hierarchy of Characteristics. In this strategy, investigators presented characteristics hierarchically. That is, one characteristic or set of characteristics established a first-level division of the universe. Then a second set of criteria further divided the categories that resulted from the first division: "general magazines: women's and family titles," or "consumer magazines, categories by content area." The hierarchical approach had three primary manifestations. The first two used two tiers, for which the general/specialized dichotomy or information function was combined with interest area categories. The third strategy used a three-tiered hierarchy: The universe of periodicals was first divided by information-function, then by audience scope, size, or editorial scope, and then by interest area. Both magazine and mass communication textbooks suggested the hierarchical approach, but with the exception of Compaine's analysis of mass-limited, active-passive framework, no one described the relationships between the dimensions.

As was true in textbooks, researchers introduced additional characteristics to define magazine clusters and to target titles germane to a particular question. The characteristics in these studies were unique; other studies did not use the same strategies. Hynes, for example, contrasted the fiction and nonfiction in "general and quality" magazines.[40] Thus both textbook authors and researchers identified characteristics that highlighted a title or group of magazines that more common descriptors failed to emphasize. Among these were (a) publication; (b) distribution method; (c) economic base (alternative media; adless magazines); and (d) writing style and information treatment (opinion, news, etc.). Other characteristics found in textbooks were format and information purpose, e.g., entertainment, education.

Discussion

Four strategies for defining magazine populations were identified from the analysis of 223 research reports. The evaluation of these strategies, using Reynolds' and Tyriakian's five-point test for the usefulness of typologies, suggests that no one strategy fully meets the requisite tests of exhaustiveness, mutual exclusivity, parsimony, common level of abstraction, and explanatory and predictive power. However, of the four strategies, a carefully defined multiple characteristics approach appears to offer the most potential for future research.

General-Specialized Dichotomy

The general-specialized dichotomy appears at first glance to meet each of the usefulness tests: Using terms that are on the same conceptual level, the schematic appears to subsume all periodicals into one of two groups, making the strategy exhaustive, mutually exclusive, and highly parsimonious. At the most basic level, the strategy suggests that all magazines that are not general are specialized. Thus, a sufficiently large sample drawn from each group would allow for a high level of explanatory and predictive capability. However, appearances deceive: The findings from this study suggest otherwise.

Because authors used several different operational definitions of these terms, the number of magazine categories in a given study that uses the general-specialized approach would be determined by whether audience scope, editorial scope, audience size, or some combination of these criteria were used to define the universe of periodicals. A researcher might divide the universe into two categories, or add several variables and thereby multiply the number of categories several times, as did Compaine.

Textbook authors and researchers differed on which publications would be classified as general or specialized. Defleur and Dennis said about 800 publications were general-interest magazines. Agee et al said that no more than 600 could be classified as general interest publications. Some authors defined all consumer magazines as "general" and all other publications as specialized. Other scholars defined a select group of consumer magazines as general magazines and both the remaining consumer and all other magazines as specialized. Still others divided the universe of magazines into three or four groups and subdivided consumer magazines into general and specialized sub-categories.[41] When these problems are combined with the fact that, over time, a change in a magazine's audience size might result in that title's being shifted from one category to the other, replicating studies that use the audience size criterion is rendered virtually impossible.

There is also lack of clarity about whether the general-specialized approach is exhaustive. Would all non-newspaper periodicals be included? An argument can be made that public relations magazines and academic journals are not magazines. Working from this premise, a researcher who wants to replicate Gerlach's 1987 study of research on magazines published in *Journalism Quarterly* would need to know whether the replicated data base would include studies of organizational magazines and scholarly publications. Wolseley listed scholarly journals as a subdivision of specialized periodicals in his 1965 text, but did not mention them in the 1977 analysis from which Gerlach drew on his definition of general and specialized publications. Replicating Gerlach's study might thus logically exclude research that had been conducted on these journals.[42]

Editorial Interest Area Approach

The interest area strategy has several strengths that commend it to the research enterprise. Based on the single criterion of specific editorial content, or subject area, the approach allows for matching the content of one or more magazines with the subject of the question to be studied. Thus, for example, if a scholar wishes to look at fiction it is both intuitively accurate and methodologically sound to select fiction published in magazines that are targeted to female audiences.[43] Of the four approaches, the interest area strategy provides the greatest explanatory and predictive capability within the scope of a given study.

However, in its strength lies its weakness: The ability to match a periodical's subject area with a substantive research question results in categories of magazines with limited explanatory and predictive power outside the interest area. Used without a hierarchical context, the strategy suggests that scholars who seek answers to questions of broad theoretical interest might need to replicate studies on every interest group in the universe of magazines.[44]

Obviously this could be a daunting, if not impossible, task. Although the criterion for clustering magazines is simple, the strategy has mixed results. Sources suggest as few as 19 and as many as 300 or more editorial interest areas. The interest area approach can meet the exhaustiveness test if a scholar is persistent in identifying all possible editorial magazine groups. Having done so, however, the strategy still does not easily meet the mutual exclusivity test.[45]

Not only do sources differ on the number of interest areas that result from this approach, but investigators also placed the same title in different interest areas.[46] The difficulty of determining the interest area category into which a magazine might fall appears to derive in part from the failure of the approach to meet the common level of abstraction test. Investigators who selected the interest area approach appeared uniformly to use editorial subject area criterion. However, the disparities in title placement suggest that a second dimension, nature of audience, frequently entered into the determination.

Using the interest area approach, a magazine might be categorized on the basis of either (a) editorial subject area, or (b) the nature of the primary audience which the magazine serves. The term "editorial appeal" itself has a decided audience orientation. Two magazines with very different editorial content can appeal primarily to female audiences without having been specifically targeted to women. The extent to which these two dimensions entered into researchers' categorizations could not be determined.

An analysis of sampling strategies was beyond the scope of this study. However, it appeared that advertising and marketing research tended to sample across interest groups, while research on non-advertising communication phenomena tended to sample within both single interest areas and advertising information functions.

Information Function Approach

Used alone, the information function approach appears to have greater capacity for meeting the exhaustiveness and mutual exclusivity tests than either the general-specialized dichotomy or the interest area approach. This is true because labels used for information function categories were typically more descriptive than the "general-specialized" terms; and they are typically on a higher level of abstraction than the majority of editorial interest area labels.

Many studies that used this approach sampled vertically within a single information function category. A few researchers drew samples that crossed two or more categories. Bearden et al compared the ability of consumer and trade publications to reach media buyers; Payne et al found statistically significant differences in media use motives for consumer magazine and trade publication readers.[47]

A single criterion frequently underlies the information function strategy. As was true with each of other single-criterion strategies, disparate numbers of categories result. In general, advertising function approaches result in fewer categories than editorial function approaches. Unlike authors of magazine and mass media texts, researchers tended to identify only those categories that were directly related to a study. So, for any given strategy, it was not possible to determine the intended range of categories for the universe of publications.

Without this information, exhaustiveness, mutual exclusivity and parsimony could not be determined.

No identifiable patterns emerged in the number of categories, the labels or the criteria used for editorial function approaches. In general, the range of categories was narrower than those found in the interest area approach. Authors of mass media and magazine texts used as few as three and no more than eight categories, regardless of which information function approach was used.

Researchers who used information function strategies frequently used terms that were not on a common level of abstraction and provided no dimension definition beyond the category label. Several text authors combined labels from the advertising and editorial information function approaches within a single classificatory scheme. Researchers tended to use more uniform terminology, drawing heavily on the advertising information labels, consumer and business. However, even those terms were used interchangeably to refer to (a) type of advertising in the publications and (b) audiences served.

If the editorial and advertising information functions are defined strictly as single-criterion categories, several interesting dimensions of their respective abilities to meet the exhaustiveness and mutual exclusivity tests can be observed. First, the advertising function approach suggests two magazine groups: magazines with ads and adless magazines. Few researchers refer to adless magazines as a counterpoint to magazines that carry advertising. Only one study of adless magazines was identified in the sample of research literature.[48]

Researchers who used the advertising function approach did not typically account for magazines funded by sources other than advertising revenues. Textbook authors frequently separated adless magazines or magazines for which advertising is a limited source of funding from consumer and business magazines. They typically labeled the resulting category according to one of several primary funding sources: company, association, or, more generically, sponsored publications.[49] However, this strategy did not account for adless magazine differences in editorial functions and target audiences. Some of these magazines parallel the purposes and audiences of "consumer" magazines, some cover occupational concerns. Still others are designed to serve organizational goals. Each of these is logically excluded if the primary criterion for inclusion is the use of consumer product advertising.

Authors who used the advertising function strategy typically appeared to include in their categories publications that carry consumer, business, or farm advertising even if the editorial purposes or audiences differ markedly from other publications in the category. For example, *SRDS Agri-media* listings include both scholarly and organization publications,[50] and some scholars follow this lead. Audiences that typically use academic publications recognize that these periodicals serve very different functions and audiences than business and trade journals, even though they occasionally carry advertising for occupation related products. Some scholars refer to academic journals as "professional journals" to distinguish them from "trade or technical" publications.[51] The editorial function approach would place these periodicals in a separate category.

A similar problem can be observed for agricultural publications. Click and Baird describe these publications as "virtually the same as business publications."[52] Using an advertising function definition for the "farm" category fails to account for magazines that deal solely with rural lifestyles.[53] The "farm" and "agriculture" labels would appear conceptually to be topical, or interest based, as is *Medical*, a more recent *SRDS* directory breakout.

Multiple Characteristics Approach

Perhaps more than any one of the other approaches, the multiple characteristics approach highlighted definition and sampling problems that result from researchers' failure to clarify definitions and state category criteria. The multiple characteristics approach appears at first glance to be the weakest of the classificatory methods. However, depending on how characteristics and dimensions are defined and used, and what relationships are established between the characteristics, it also appears to have the greatest conceptual strength.

Typologies have been defined as "classificatory schema composed of two or more ideal or constructed types that provide abstract categories" that are useful to social scientists for organizing data, guiding research, and developing theory. Howard Becker suggested that ideal types can be regarded primarily as tentative formulations regarded as the result of research.[54] As noted earlier, typologies can be based on one characteristic. However, it appears that single criterion approaches to classifying the universe of periodicals are too simple, too parsimonious. A single criterion provides insufficient descriptive power to determine how the broadest range of titles fit into a classificatory scheme. Recognizing this, the majority of researchers and text authors used multiple characteristics.

Yet, in the absence of carefully defined and empirically tested frameworks, and given the multiple meanings acquired by some of the most commonly used terms, it was difficult to determine the extent to which multiple characteristic frameworks met the typology tests. The schematics were ambiguous; terms used to label groups of magazines frequently appeared to mix levels of abstraction. Schweitzer, for example, combined two dimensions of the general-specialized framework (editorial scope and audience size) with the interest area and information function approaches when he compared "general editorial" magazines with five categories of magazines: business, news, women's service, science, and beauty/health. Magazines selected in each category were further screened for high circulations. Schweitzer did not clarify the extent to which the sample was designed to represent the universe of publications.[55]

Given the confusing array of options available to researchers, selecting a multiple characteristics scheme from the existing literature can be a daunting intellectual exercise. Without a generally accepted framework with empirically tested, relatively stable criteria on which to base magazine samples, the present use of multiple criteria results in fragmentation of the research literature.

A desire to establish explanatory and predictive capability accentuates the problem. Using multiple characteristics to define a purposive sample provides greater clarity about which periodicals might logically fit into a given cluster, but less clarity about how to categorize the excluded publications.

The 223 research reports analyzed for this study evidenced a bias toward studying consumer magazines, to the exclusion of other publications. Furthermore, there were few studies for which researchers developed samples that crossed information function categories, although a few scholars have moved in that direction.[56]

Summary and Conclusions

This study was designed to determine how investigators define the universe of non-newspaper periodicals and the criteria on which they categorize periodicals. Four definition patterns using 10 different criteria were identified from a total of 193 descriptors, descriptor sets, and the criteria on which the descriptors were based on 223 published reports of communication research using magazines.

Three dimensions defined the general-specialized dichotomy: audience scope, editorial scope, and audience size. Two dimensions, advertising and editorial, were used to define the information function approach. Researchers also used interest area strategies, based on the editorial content, or subject area. Investigators also developed categories of magazines based on multiple dimensions, by developing single clusters, comparison groups and hierarchies of categories to draw samples.

Terms used in the research literature to define populations of magazines were consistent with terms used in magazine and mass communication texts in two ways: They reflected the spectrum of classificatory approaches and category criteria. Second, definitions of terms differed from one study to the next. Researchers either assumed common definitions or defined terms within the context of the study. Few investigators cited source definitions; neither did they reconcile their classification systems with other approaches to classifying periodicals. The study findings suggest that the majority of researchers assume that commonly used terms have single-valued, unambiguous meanings, when, in fact, the terms carry multiple meanings.

Contemporary methodologists argue that researchers should use typologies primarily as independent variables, to organize and build theory. However, magazine classifications were used primarily to develop purposive samples. Few researchers positioned samples in a context of carefully defined typological frameworks.

Assessing sample appropriateness was beyond the scope of this study, as was analyzing the quality of samples and sampling frames. However, sampling strategies in the magazine research appeared to reflect the problems with population validity described by both Liebert and Schwartzberg, and Lowry.[57]

Researchers who design research using magazines need to give careful attention to reconciling and defining typological frameworks. As they do so, they will increase the external validity of samples. They will develop ideal types that can serve as starting points for research on magazines that will lead to empirically based, constructed types that provide explanatory insights into how communication occurs through the medium.[58]

From this work, researchers can also begin to build a body of knowledge that is theoretically integrated and that will provide empirically based knowledge about magazine dimensions that have theoretical significance for inquiry and practice.[59]

Notes

[1] Sammye Johnson, "Magazines: Women's Employment and Status in the Magazine Industry," in Women in Mass Communication: Challenging Gender Values, ed. Pamela J. Creedon, Sage Focus Editions, No. 106 (Newbury Park: Sage, 1989), 196; Dorothy Schmidt, "Magazines," in Handbook of American Popular Culture, ed. M. Thomas Inge (Westport, CT: Greenwood Press, 1981), 137.

[2] Stuart W. Showalter, "Sampling from the Readers' Guide," Journalism Quarterly 55:2: 346-348; Vincent P. Norris, "Consumer Magazine Prices and the Mythical Advertising Subsidy," Journalism Quarterly 59 (Summer 1982): 208; Lawrence Soley and R. Krishnan, "Does Advertising Subsidize Consumer Magazine Prices?" Journal of Advertising 16:2 (1987): 6; Earl Babbie, "The Logic of Sampling," in The Practice of Social Research, 4th ed., (Belmont, CA: Wadsworth Publishing, 1986), 136-176; Kenneth D. Bailey, "Survey Sampling," in Methods of Social Research. 2nd ed. (New York: Free Press, 1982), 83-108; Guido H. Stempel, III, and Bruce H. Westley, "Survey Research," and "Statistical Designs for Survey Research," in Research Methods in Mass Communication (Englewood Cliffs: Prentice-Hall, 1981), 144-166, 167-195.

[3] Robert Bierstedt, "Nominal and Real Definitions in Sociological Theory," in Llewellyn Gross, ed., Symposium on Sociological Theory (Evanston, IL: Row, Peterson, 1959), 121-144.

[4] Paul Davidson Reynolds, "Introduction" in A Primer in Theory Construction (Indianapolis, IN: Bobbs-Merrill Educational Publishing, 1971), 4-5.

[5] Marguerite Louis Deslauriers, "Aristotle on Definition," (Ph.D. diss., University of Toronto, 1987); Paul F. Lazarsfeld and Wagner Thielens, Jr., "Comments on the Nature of Clas-

sification in Social Research," and Paul F. Lazarsfeld, "Some Remarks on Typological Proce-dures in Social Research," in Continuities in the Language of Social Research (New York: The Free Press, 1972), 99-105; A. M. Andrews, J. N. Morgan, J. A. Sonquist and L. Klem, Multiple Classification Analysis (Ann Arbor: The University of Michigan, Institute for Social Research, 1973); Paul F. Lazarsfeld and Allen H. Barton, "Classification, Typologies, and Indices," in The Policy Sciences, eds., D. Lerner and H. D. Lasswell (Stanford: Stanford University Press, 1951), 155-192; Herschel C. Hudson and Associates, Classifying Social Data, (San Francisco: Jossey-Bass Publishers, 1982); Ernst Mayr, Principles of Systematic Zoology (New York: McGraw-Hill, 1969). See also: John C. McKinney, Constructive Typology and Social Theory, (New York: Appleton-Century-Crofts, 1966); Ramkrishna Mukherjee, Classification in Social Research (Al-bany: State University of New York Press, 1983); Tiryakian; Charles K. Warringer, "Empirical taxonomies of organizations: Problematics in Their Development," Paper prepared for the an-nual meeting of the American Sociological Association, Boston. (Lawrence, KS: University of Kansas, 1979).

[6] Bailey, "Nonsurvey Data Collection Methods," and "Data Reduction, Analysis, Inter-pretation, and Application," 262-264, 382-383; Babbie, "Indexes, Scales, and Typologies," 381-382; Edward A. Tiryakian, "Typologies," in International Encyclopedia of the Social Sciences, ed., David L. Sills, Vol. 16 (New York: Macmillan, 1968), 177-186. See also: Fred N. Kerlinger, Foundations of Behavioral Research, 2nd ed., (New York: Holt, Rinehart and Winston, 1973), 315; Robert C. Rowland, "On Generic Categorization." Communication Theory, 12 (May 1991): 128-144.

[7] Dennis T. Lowry, "Population Validity of Communication Research: Sampling the Samples." Journalism Quarterly 56 (Spring 1979): 63; Hubert M. Blalock, Jr., An Introduction to Social Research (Englewood Cliffs, NJ: Prentice Hall, 1970).

[8] Lowry, 63. Emphases in the original.

[9] Tiryakian, 178; Kenneth W. Thomas and Walter G. Tymon, Jr., "Necessary Properties of Relevant Research: Lessons from Recent Criticisms of the Organizational Sciences," Academy of Management Review 7 (July 1982): 343-352 ; Walter L. Wallace, "Theories," in The Logic of Science in Sociology (New York: Aldine Publishing, 1971), 87-119.

[10] Reynolds, 5, 67-81.

[11] Hugh M. Cannon and David L. Williams, "Toward a Hierarchical Taxonomy of Maga-zine Readership," Journal of Advertising 17 (November 1, 1988): 15-25.

[12] Cannon and Williams, 15.

[13] Frank M. Bass, Edgar A. Pessemier, and Douglas J. Tigert, "A Taxonomy of Magazine Readership Applied to Problems in Marketing Strategy and Media Selection," Journal of Busi-ness, 42 (July, 1969): 337-363; Susan P. Douglas, "Do Working Wives Read Different Maga-zines from Non-Working Wives?" Journal of Advertising 6 (Winter 1977): 40-43, 48; Charles W. King and John O. Summers, "Attitudes and Media Exposure," Journal of Advertising Research 11 (February 1971): 26-32; Joseph O. Rentz and Fred D. Reynolds, "Magazine Readership Pat-terns," Journal of Advertising 8 (Spring 1979): 22-25; Douglas J. Tigert, "Life Style Analysis as a Basis for Media Selection," in William D. Wells, ed., Life Style and Psychographics (Chicago: American Marketing Association, 1974), 173-201; Christine Urban, "Correlates of Magazine Readership," Journal of Advertising Research 20 (August 1980): 73-84; Christine Urban, "Edi-torial and Program Choices of Heavy Media Users," Journal of Advertising 9 (Winter 1980): 32-43; Alladi Venkatesh and Clint B. Tankersley, "Magazine Readership by Female Segments," Journal of Advertising Research 19 (August 1979): 31-38; Charles E. Swanson, "The Frequency Structure of Television and Magazines," Journal of Advertising Research 7 (June 1967): 8-14.

[14] Benjamin M. Compaine, "The Magazine Industry: Developing the Special Interest Audience," Journal of Communication 30:2 (1980): 98-103.

[15] Roland Wolseley, Understanding Magazines (Ames: Iowa State University Press, 1965), 9-10.

[16] Leonard Mogel, The Magazine, 3rd ed. (Boston: Globe Pequot, 1992), 4 -11.

[17] J. William Click and Russell N. Baird, Magazine Editing and Production, 6th ed. (Dubuque: Wm. C. Brown, 1994), 1-27.

[18] Pamela J. Shoemaker, "Mass Communication by the Book: A Review of 31 Texts," Journal of Communication 37:3: 109-131.

[19] Warren K. Agee, Phillip H. Ault, Edwin Emery, "Magazines," in Introduction to Mass Communications, 9th ed. (New York: Harper & Row, 1988), 151-178; Shirley Biagi, "The Magazine Industry," in Media/Impact: An Introduction to Mass Media, Updated First Edition (Belmont, CA: Wadsworth Publishing, 1990), 63-76; Jay Black and Frederick C. Whitney, "Magazines," in Introduction to Mass Communication, 2nd ed. (Dubuque: Wm. C. Brown, 1988), 126-165; Melvin L. DeFleur and Everette E. Dennis, "The Print Media," in Understanding Mass Communication (Boston: Houghton Mifflin, 1988), 163-171; Joseph R. Dominick, "Structure of the Magazine Industry," in The Dynamics of Mass Communication, 3rd ed. (New York: McGraw-Hill Publishing, 1990), 133-150; Ronald T. Farrar, "Magazines," in Mass Communication: An Introduction to the Field (St. Paul: West Publishing, 1988), 161-181; Conrad C. Fink, "The American Magazine Industry," and "Inside the American Magazine," chapts. in Inside the Media (New York: Longman, 1990), 133-156, 157-169; Michael W. Gamble and Teri Kwal Gamble, "Magazines: Forms, Functions, Audiences," in Introducing Mass Communication, 2nd ed. (New York: McGraw Hill, 1989), 125-151; James D. Harless, "The American Magazine: A Range of Reading," in Mass Communication: An Introductory Survey, 2nd ed. (Dubuque: Wm. C. Brown, 1990), 148-180; Ray Eldon Hiebert, Donald F. Ungurait, Thomas W. Bohn, "Magazines and Periodicals" in Mass Media VI: An Introduction to Modern Communication (New York: Longman, 1991), 304-326; John C. Merrill, John Lee, Edward Jay Friedlander, "Books and Magazines," in Modern Mass Media (New York: Harper & Row, 1990), 138-169; Thomas M. Pasqua, Jr., James K. Buckalew, Robert E. Rayfield, and James W. Tankard, Jr., "Magazines," in Mass Media in the Information Age (Englewood Cliffs: Prentice Hall, 1990), 66-83; Stan LeRoy Wilson, "Magazines: The Specialized Medium," in Mass Media/Mass Culture: An Introduction, 2nd ed. (New York: McGraw-Hill, 1992), 121-145.

[20] Click and Baird, 1-27; Anthony Davis, Magazine Journalism Today (Oxford: Heinemann Professional Publishing, 1988); James L. C. Ford, Magazines for Millions (Carbondale: Southern Illinois University Press, 1969), 2-12; Betsy P. Graham, "The Market for Magazine Articles," in Magazine Article Writing (New York: Holt, Rinehart and Winston, 1980), 19-27; Jim Mann, "Which Comes First: Market or Magazine," in Magazine Editing (New Canaan: Folio Magazine Publishing, 1985), 5-18; Mogel, 4-11. Theodore Peterson, Magazines in the Twentieth Century (Urbana, IL: University of Illinois Press, 1964); William L. Rivers, Free-Lancer and Staff Writer: Newspaper Features and Magazine Articles, 5th ed. (Belmont, CA.: Wadsworth Publishing, 1986), 56-64; A. Clay Schoenfeld and Karen S. Diegmueller, "Keeping Your Eye on the Market," Effective Feature Writing (New York: Holt, Rinehart and Winston, 1982), 41-56; William H. Taft, American Magazine Publishing of the 1980s (New York: Hastings House, 1982); Wolseley, Understanding Magazines; Frank Luther Mott, A History of American Magazines, 1941-1850, Vols. 1-5 (Cambridge: Harvard University Press).

[21] Reynolds, 4.

[22] Agee et al, 156-159; Dominick, 134; Farrar, 180; Gamble and Gamble, 138-139; Hiebert et al, 309.

[23] Charles K. Warriner, "Organizational Types: Notes on the 'Organizational Species' Concept," [Mimeographed copy] (Lawrence: Department of Sociology, University of Kansas, 1980).

[24] W. James Potter, Roger Cooper, and Michel Dupagne, "The Three Paradigms of Mass Media Research," Paper presented to the Communication Theory and Methodology Division, Association for Education in Journalism and Mass Communication, Boston, 1991).

[25] John E. Hunter and Frank L. Schmidt, Methods of Meta-Analysis: Correcting Error and Bias in Research Findings (Newbury Park: Sage, 1989); Everett M. Rogers, "Importance of Meta-research," International Communication Association News 9 (Summer 1981): 6-7, 12; Kenneth W. Wachter and Miron L. Straf, eds., The Future of Meta-Analysis (Newbury Park: Sage, 1990); W. Paul Vogt, Dictionary of Statistics and Methodology (Newbury Park: Sage, 1993), 138; Harris M. Cooper, Integrating Research: A Guide for Literature Reviews Vol. 2, 2nd. ed., Applied Social Research Methods Series (Newbury Park: Sage, 1989).

[26] Citations on research about magazines were identified by tracing research indexed under all keywords listed in each volume's cumulative index that related to magazines: Magazines, Magazine Advertising, Magazine Content, Magazine History, Magazine Industry, Magazine Management, Magazine Readership, Black Magazines, Children's Magazines, City Magazines, Company Publications, News Magazines, Periodicals, and Periodical Indexes. All magazine research indexed by specific countries or magazine titles was also included: British Magazines, Japanese Magazines, Korean Magazines, Ladies' Home Journal, and Time.

[27] Mott, Vol. 1, 121, 339-347; Vol. 5, Index to the Five Volumes, 421-4 22); Fink, 137.

[28] Cathy Meo Bonnstetter, "Magazine Coverage of Mentally Handicapped," Journalism Quarterly 63 (Autumn 1986): 623-626; Dennis W. Jeffers, "Using Public Relations Theory to Evaluate Specialized Magazines as Communication 'Channels,'" in James E. Grunig and Larissa A. Grunig, eds., Public Relations Research, Vol. 1 (Hillsdale, N.J.: Lawrence Erlbaum Associates, 1989): 115-124; See also: Agee et al, 156-157; Wilson, 135-139; Graham, 20-21.

[29] Peter Gerlach, "Research About Magazines Appearing in Journalism Quarterly," Journalism Quarterly 64 (Spring 1987): 178; Roland Wolseley, "The Role of Magazines in the U.S.A.," Gazette 21 (June 1977): 20-26; Understanding Magazines, 9.

[30] Sharon Bramlett-Solomon and Venessa Wilson, "Images of the Elderly in Life and Ebony, 1978-1987, "Journalism Quarterly 66 (Spring 1989): 185-188; Marcel C. LaFollette, "Eyes on the Stars: Images of Women Scientists in Popular Magazines," Science, Technology, & Human Values 13:3-4 (Summer, Autumn 1988): 262-275.

[31] LaFollette; Bonnie Orr and John H. Murphy, "Alcoholic Beverage Advertising: 1964-1983, A Longitudinal Analysis," in N. Stephen, ed., Proceedings of the 1986 Conference of the American Academy of Advertising (Provo: American Academy of Advertising, 1985), R23-R27.

[32] Donald E. Strickland, T. Andrew Finn, and M. Dow Lambert, "A Content Analysis of Beverage Alcohol Advertising" Journal of Studies on Alcohol 43:7 (1982): 655-682.

[33] Robert Escarpit, "The Concept of 'Mass'," Journal of Communication (Spring 1977): 44-48.

[34] John P. Hayes, "City/Regional Magazines: A Survey, Census," Journalism Quarterly 58 (Summer 1981): 294-296.

[35] Merrill et al, 158-159.

[36] Because these totals include both unique designators and designator sets, they differ from earlier numbers.

[37] Standard Rates and Data Service directories, (Wilmette, IL: Standard Rate & Data Service, Monthly, 1992).

[38] Black and Whitney, 137; Dominick, 138; Click and Baird, 7-8.

[39] Steven Lysonski, "Female and Male Portrayals in Magazine Advertisements: A Reexamination," Akron Business and Economic Review 14:2 (1983): 45-50; "Role Portrayals in British Magazine Advertisements," European Journal of Marketing 19:7 (1985): 37-55.

[40] Terry Hynes, "Magazine Portrayal of Women, 1911-1930," Journalism Monograph

No. 72.(Minneapolis: Association for Education in Journalism, 1981).

[41] DeFleur and Dennis, 165; Agee et al, 156.

[42] Gerlach; Wolseley, Understanding Magazines, 8; Role of Magazines, 20-26.

[43] Muriel G. Cantor and Elizabeth Jones, "Creating Fiction for Women," Communication Research 10:1 (1983): 111-137.

[44] David H. Weaver and G. Cleveland Wilhoit, The American Journalist: A Portrait of U.S. News People and Their Work (Bloomington: Indiana University Press, 1986).

[45] Taft, 19 categories; Ford, 9; Black and Whitney, 27, 137-139; Gamble and Gamble, 100, 138-139; SRDS, 300 or more.

[46] Richard W. Pollay, "Twentieth-Century Magazine Advertising: Determinants of Informativeness," Written Communication 1:1 (1984): 56-77; Jae-Hyun Choe, Gary B. Wilcox, and Andrew P. Hardy, "Facial Expressions in Magazine Ads: A Cross-Cultural Comparison," Journalism Quarterly 63 (Spring 1986): 122-126; Consumer and Agri-Media SRDS.

[47] William O. Bearden, Jesse E. Teel, Richard M. Durand and Robert H. Williams, "Consumer Magazines—An Efficient Medium for Reaching Organizational Buyers," Journal of Advertising 8 (1979): 8-16; Gregg A. Payne, Jessica J. H. Severn, and David M. Dozier, "Uses and Gratifications Motives As Indicators of Magazine Readership," Journalism Quarterly 65 (Winter 1988): 909-913, 959.

[48] Vincent P. Norris, "Mad Economics: An Analysis of an Adless Magazine," Journal of Communication 34 (1984): 44-61.

[49] Farrar, 167-169; Wilson, 135; DeFleur and Dennis, 166; Dennis W. Jeffers and David N. Bateman, "Redefining the Role of the Company Magazine," Public Relations Review 6:2 (1980): 11-29. Some organizations that fund magazines are not comfortably labeled "companies." See, for example, Catherine C. Mitchell and C. Joan Schnyder, "Public Relations for Appalachia: Berea's Mountain Life and Work," Journalism Quarterly 66 (Winter 1989): 974-978; Elmo Scott Watson, "The Organization Press: Methods of Administration," Journalism Quarterly 23 (September 1946): 302-306.

[50] See, for example, the Alumni and Airline magazine categories 1, 9B; Consumer SRDS; Quill, category 75, Business SRDS; Spokesman, category 2, Agri-Media SRDS; current directories.

[51] Taft, 85-99; Click and Baird, p. 7.

[52] Click and Baird, 8.

[53] Country and Country Woman, published by Reiman Publications (5600 S. 60th St., Greendale, WI).

[54] George A. Theodorson and Achilles G. Theodorson, A Modern Dictionary of Sociology, (New York: Barnes & Noble, 1969), 74-75, 445; Howard Becker, in Twentieth Century Sociology, eds. Georges Gurvitch and Wlbert E. Moore, (New York: Philosophical Library, 1945), 21.

[55] John C. Schweitzer, "How Valuable to an Advertiser Are Secondary Audiences?" Journalism Quarterly 63 (Winter 1986): 279-288; Black and Whitney, 137-139; Mann, 8.

[56] Stephen R. Barley, Gordon W. Meyer, Debra C. Gash, "Cultures of Culture: Academics, Practitioners and the Pragmatics of Normative Control," Administrative Science Quarterly 33 (1988): 24-60.

[57] Robert M. Liebert and Neala S. Schwartzberg, "Effects of Mass Media," Annual Review of Psychology 28 (1977): 142; Lowry.

[58] Becker.

[59] This paper is drawn from "Toward an Empirically Based Typology of Magazines and Non-Newspaper Periodicals," presented to the Association for Education in Journalism and Mass Communication, Montreal, Canada, 1992.

2

Research Review:
Quantitative Magazine Studies, 1983-1993

Mark N. Popovich

ABSTRACT

This literature review examines quantitative magazine research studies published in various journals during the period 1983-1993. The results of this examination echo the findings of previous studies which questioned the heavy reliance on content analysis techniques by magazine researchers to study the role of magazines in American society. The investigator draws on the comments of mass media investigators to call for a redirection in magazine research techniques which will combine media content studies with media effects studies.

Introduction

In a 1987 article in *Journalism Quarterly*, Peter Gerlach announced that magazine research over a 20-year period (1964-1983) had accounted for only six percent of the articles which appeared in *Journalism Quarterly*. He asked why this field of research is so underdeveloped and why its treatment is so unbalanced. He found a strong emphasis on content analysis in *JQ* magazine articles and too few studies making use of earlier research. Only 28 percent of the magazine articles turned out to be quantitative studies.[1] A similar study in 1992 of *Communication Abstracts* found that scholarly articles about magazines accounted for less than one percent of the contents, compared to five percent for newspaper research and more than 20 percent for articles about television.[2]

In the past ten years, the percentage of published magazine research articles has grown ever so slightly (from six to eight percent) in *Journalism*

Quarterly, and authors have made better use of previous research. However, quantitative magazine studies cited in this study, from *JQ* and other sources, still rely heavily on content analysis techniques; roughly 76 percent. As a body, those research studies remain fragmented and unrelated to the forces or systems from which they emanate. The majority of magazine studies have been descriptive in nature and magazine investigators have made little effort to conceptualize and integrate magazine research with a growing body of media effects studies. But more on that later.

This literature review is devoted to quantitative studies and findings concerning magazines which have appeared in various journals over the past ten years. The review is by no means exhaustive, but enough studies are discussed here to give the reader a strong sense of the direction in which magazine quantitative research has moved since 1983. In the conclusions, the author will attempt to provide some new directions for magazine investigators.

Literature Review

The quantitative magazine studies included here have been informally organized into five areas: magazine advertising, magazine photo coverage, minority coverage (including women and blacks), magazine content studies, and magazine effects. The largest number of studies are devoted to magazine advertising research, and the smallest number of articles focus on magazine effects.

Magazine Advertising Studies

By far the largest single focus of magazine studies in the past ten years, magazine advertising studies included here reflect a tradition of print advertising studies which go back to the 1950s. This tradition has evolved some sophisticated research techniques which build on content analysis. Magazine advertising studies have been concerned with whether ads are more informative or more persuasive, whether female and black models affect ad readership, and whether magazine advertising mirrors cultural trends, among other topics.

Stern, Krugman and Resnik found that the majority of magazine ads they content analyzed were more informative than persuasive.[3] Harmon, Razzouk and Stern found that comparative ads contained more information cues than did noncomparative ads.[4] Chou, Franke and Wilcox looked at the same question over a 15-year period and they found similar results for comparative ads.[5] They found that comparative ads made up 20 percent of ads examined in their study. Sarel found that the majority of ads he examined contained factual claims, so he rejected claims which said that advertising copy was becoming increasingly more nonfactual.[6]

Research concerning blacks in advertising began in the 1950s, and during the last decade magazine researchers were creating research variations on that same theme. Soley found that the use of black male models in magazine advertisement did not negatively affect the attention level of magazine advertising consumers.[7] He found that the presence of male models, no matter what race, did not enhance magazine ad readership. Humphrey and Schuman found the proportion of magazine ads which portrayed blacks increasing over time, a similar proportion of black males to black females depicted in ads, and the work roles of blacks depicted in ads changing over time.[8] Zinkhan, Cox, and Hong duplicated two previous studies and found that the number of magazine ads with blacks increased over three time periods.[9] Zinkhan, Qualls, and Biswas conducted secondary analysis on television and magazine ad data collected in 1986 and determined that use of black models had increased dramatically on television, and that the low representation of blacks in magazine advertisements had been increasing in recent years.[10]

Reid and Soley found that male readers "noted" magazine ads more frequently if women were in the ads, but the existence of any gender of models had little effect on male readership of ads.[11] Pokrywczynski found more sexual suggestiveness in black vs. white ads in magazines directed toward black and white readers, but no differences in the degree of nudity; he found that, no matter what race, sexual suggestiveness worked better for non-durable products.[12] Soley and Reid found over a 20-year period that women had become more sexy in magazine ads.[13]

Another group of magazine advertising studies examined the role advertising plays in American culture by evaluating cross-cultural advertising differences. Wilcox and Moriarty evaluated humor in *Saturday Evening Post* ads over a 20-year period and discovered that humorous ads became more frequent in the 1930s than in the 1920s, although the number of ads during the 1930s declined.[14] Belk and Pollay examined ads in 34 magazines over seven decades and found that advertisements were moving away from emphasizing products for the good life toward product scenes which were more hedonistic and materialistic in nature.[15] Gross and Sheth determined that magazine advertisers, up until World War II, had appealed to consumers' increased concern for time, but since then those themes had fluctuated and become stabilized in the 1970s.[16] Stout and Moon found that celebrity endorsers were becoming more popular over time, and that the content of magazine ads did not change with the kind of person endorsing the product.[17] Busby and Leichty found that while the feminist movement had made inroads in traditional and nontraditional women's magazines' advertising the movement had lost ground in other important areas.[18]

In cross-cultural advertising studies, Pittatore analyzed the images of Italy in American magazine ads and found that the most popular image of Italy focused on its sophistication.[19] Choe, Wilcox, and Hardy found that American magazine advertising models smiled more than Korean models, and that females smiled more than men no matter what their nationality.[20] Frith and Wesson used a combination of content analysis and semiotics to analyze advertisements in both American and British magazines, and they found significant differences in values involving individualism, egalitarianism, and direct speech.[21]

Magazine advertisements have been the focus of studies concerned with the financial and technical aspects of advertising. McGann, Russell, and Russell examined the advertising pricing structure of metro and regional editions of national magazines and found that they were not equivalently priced.[22] Reid, Rotfield, and Barnes evaluated attention-getting performance of nine layout designs based on the Nelson Classification system and related to attention-getting and discovered that copy-heavy and type specimen designs were less effective than seven other layout designs.[23] Wesson found that readability of magazine ads was curvilinearly related to copy recall.[24] In another study, Wesson found that the length of magazine ad headlines was not related to eliciting recall.[25] Stout, Wilcox, and Greer determined that the number of advertorials in eight magazines had increased between 1980-1986.[26]

Magazine Photo Coverage

Photo studies have evaluated magazine photo coverage in terms of news, magazine covers, presidential elections, and race. Tsang content-analyzed newsphotos in *Time* and *Newsweek* over three time periods and found that violent photos which were taken in international locations appeared more often.[27] Sherer compared battle zone photos taken during a single battle in both the Korean and Vietnam wars, and he concluded that Vietnam photos presented more combat views, while Korean War photos depicted a sense of desperation and discomfort.[28]

Christ and Johnson produced two studies which analyzed *Time* covers. In the first study, they found that the person most likely to be named Man-of-the-Year would be a U.S. born and raised white male, who averaged 54 years of age, and held a high ranking position in the government.[29] In the second study, they coded all *Time* covers between 1923 and 1987 for women and found that women appeared 14 percent of the time; the typical *Time* cover female was 39 years old, a U.S. citizen and probably an artist or an entertainer.[30]

Two studies have content analyzed all the 1984 and 1988 presidential campaign photos in three U.S. news magazines during the three-month period prior to Election Day. Moriarty and Garramone found that Republicans overall received more favorable coverage in the 1984 campaign, but they lost ground toward the end of the campaign when the Mondale and Ferraro effort spurted but fell short.[31] In the 1988 campaign, Moriarty and Popovich found that Vice President Bush received more favored treatment from the end of the party conventions right up to Election Day. Vice presidential coverage was practically nonexistent.[32]

Race was the focus in two photo studies. Ortizano found that the six magazines which he content analyzed underrepresented blacks in both advertising and editorial photos.[33] Lester and Smith, who selected photos from *Life*, *Newsweek*, and *Time* in five-year increments between 1937 and 1988, found that black photo coverage increased over time in all three magazines.[34]

Magazine Minority Coverage

Included here are studies which evaluate how magazines editorially have covered race and women's issues over the years. Sentman tabulated the number of pages devoted to blacks in *Life* in five-year increments from 1937 to 1972 and determined that black coverage failed to project a linear increase over time, which led her to conclude that *Life* had failed to expose whites to black everyday life.[35] Thibodeau found that blacks appeared infrequently in *New Yorker* cartoons, and that the percentage of blacks depicted as tokens rose over time.[36]

Loughlin replicated a 1969 study of short story heroines in three women's magazines and found that although some demographic changes had occurred, heroine portrayals had remained fairly conservative with the wife depicted as mother and housewife.[37] Andreasen and Stevens queried working women and found that more assertive women spent more time reading, and they chose progressive women's magazines and news magazines to read most often.[38] Ruggiero and Weston analyzed women's profiles presented in both established and new women's magazines and found similar occupations profiled in both groups; they concluded that working for pay was important to a woman's self-esteem, which is a core message in new magazines.[39] Johnson and Gross surveyed women in decision-making roles, and determined that decision makers make higher use of news and trade magazines for professional and work-related information.[40] Kessler found that articles about the health hazards of smoking were nonexistent in six women's magazines.[41] Pierce found some evidence that the feminist movement had affected article selection in *Seventeen* in 1972, but the changes were short-lived.[42]

Magazine Content Studies

Over the past ten years, magazine investigators have analyzed how magazines have dealt with social issues, news events, magazines and magazine journalists, and various personalities. In terms of social issues, Cardozo examined magazine coverage of the Nazi death camps.[43] Brenders and Robinson analyzed self-help articles in popular magazines.[44] Bonnstetter evaluated coverage of the mentally handicapped in popular magazines over a 20-year period.[45] Lieb was concerned with how black perceptions affected the redesign of the *Washington Post Magazine*.[46] Grube and Boehme-Duerr analyzed AIDS articles in international news magazines,[47] and Bramlett-Solomon and Wilson studied the elderly in ads carried by *Life* and *Ebony*.[48]

Research concerning the reporting function of magazines covers a wide spectrum of academic interests. Lemert and Ashman found that politically liberal news magazines carried more mobilizing information than politically conservative news magazines.[49] Patterson analyzed television and news magazine coverage of the Vietnam War over a five-year period. He found that television carried a higher percentage of war news, while magazines did not increase their photo coverage of the war over the same time period.[50] Burriss found that a majority of news sources used by the three major news magazines reported they were correctly quoted, even when taken out of context.[51] Kallan and Denton analyzed *People* profiles and determined that the subjects of those profiles were usually college-educated white males, living in eastern or western regions who were successful in business or entertainment.[52] Simmons and Lowry evaluated the use of the word "terrorist" in the three major news magazines during the 1980-1988 period and decided that the news magazines had not romanticized the concept, nor given undue legitimacy to it.[53] Martin found that science news magazines did not uniformly devote more editorial space to breaking science news than popular magazines.[54] Entman applied framing analysis to two news events involving U.S. interests, and found that television coverage of the events carried a higher percentage of negative coverage than did news magazines or newspapers. He concluded that the U.S. destruction of an Iranian plane was termed a technical problem, while the Russian destruction of a Korean jet was portrayed as a moral outrage.[55]

Studies involving magazines and magazine journalists were concerned with the accuracy of political forecasts in news magazines,[56] philosophical perspectives of trade magazines,[57] the "Darts and Laurels" column in the *Columbia Journalism Review*,[58] *Foreign Affairs*,[59] trade journal employment ads,[60] *TV Guide*,[61] research activity among magazine publishers,[62] southern magazine publishing,[63] media music critics,[64] and farm journalists.[65]

Magazine coverage of various personalities did not go unresearched. Dennis documented the climb and fall of Marshall McLuhan in popular magazines.[66] Fedler, Smith, and Meeske found that *Time* and *Newsweek* treated John F. Kennedy more favorably than either of his brothers.[67] Ogles and Howard used content and assertion analysis to evaluate popular magazine coverage of the Rev. Charles E. Coughlin, a controversial radio minister in the 1930s.[68] Yu and Riffe documented the shift in news magazine articles involving Chiang Kai-shek and Mao Tse-tung over a 27-year period.[69] Hart, Smith-Howell and Llewellyn conducted a rhetorical content analysis of presidential news reports in *Time* between 1945 and 1985. They concluded that *Time* had turned the presidency into theater; and by focusing on presidential personalities, *Time* was encouraging readers to forget the essence of politics.[70]

Two studies have dealt with news magazine coverage of the U.S. Supreme Court. Tarpley evaluated coverage of the Court between 1978 and 1981, and concluded that only major cases were being reported. He found a predominance of First Amendment stories and nonmedia legal stories.[71] Bowles and Bromley analyzed court coverage in the major news magazines between 1981 and 1989. They also found more story emphasis on First Amendment cases, but coverage of the court had decreased. News magazines were carrying more stories about the personalities of the nine justices.[72]

Magazine Effects

Magazine studies examined for this review could provide only two studies which focused exclusively on magazine effects on readers and subscribers. Towers, in applying a uses-and-gratifications strategy from previous research involving newspapers, radio, and television users, found that magazine readers scored highest on the diversion factor, which suggested that they use magazines to improve their lifestyles, to relax, or to help pass the time, among other similar activities.[73] Payne, Severn, and Dozier surveyed magazine readers to determine if uses and gratifications motivations could help predict use of various magazines. They found that diversion seeking was higher among consumer magazine readers than trade magazine readers. Trade-publication readers scored higher on interaction statements than general-interest magazine readers, as well as higher on surveillance statements than consumer-magazine readers. Also, reader demographic data appeared unrelated to uses and gratifications motives as predictors of magazine selection.[74]

Finally, a third study testing the agenda-setting phenomena was conducted by Eaton which involved the three major news magazines. Because of the way in which data was analyzed, Eaton could not evaluate the contribution of news magazines.[75] However, based on this and previous agenda-setting studies, it is probably safe to assume that magazines do play a role in helping the public to decide what to think about.

Conclusions

These research studies indicate that magazine researchers rely too heavily on content analysis techniques, remain fragmented in focus, and lack theoretical foundations from which to pose their research questions. Other media investigators have come to similar conclusions, as the following comment by Shoemaker and Reese illustrates:

> Although many content analyses have been carried out on newspapers, television, and magazines, these have been largely descriptive and are not often linked in any systematic way to either the forces that create the content or to its effects.[76]

Shoemaker and Reese suggest a way for magazine researchers to focus future studies. They call for an integration of media content studies with media effects studies. And there are many reasons why such a melding of strategies would be beneficial to communicators:

> There is ample evidence to show that the media do not mirror reality and that different media produce different content. These content differences are a function of a network of influences, ranging from communication workers' personal attitudes and role conceptions, routines of media work, media organizational structure and culture, the relationships between the media and other social institutions, and cultural and ideological forces.[77]

Media-effects researchers attempt to study those cultural and ideological forces which affect communication content. Agenda-setting, uses and gratifications, and media system dependency relations are a few of the strategies which present future directions to magazine researchers. These are directions which build on demographic data and content analysis techniques magazine researchers have embraced for the past three decades. Some of our colleagues have already accepted the challenge: Towers; Payne, Severn, and Dozier; Andreasen and Stevens; and Johnson and Gross. However, there have been few followup studies.

Agenda-setting proponents such as Shaw and Martin suggest that:

> Convergence of belief (and action) on the social agenda may be more important than demographic differences among audiences. More than ever we are what we read and view, not just the sum of attributes that we were born with.[78]

Based on what agenda-setters have learned from newspapers and television, it would be interesting, for example, for magazine researchers to examine the number and type of issues which magazine readers learn about from magazines. Are news magazine reporters more likely to watch those already in power, rather than those who challenge that power? Does increased news magazine readership mean more reader agreement with magazine agendas?

Researchers such as Loges and Ball-Rokeach, who have applied media system dependency relations to newspaper readership, provide another perspective:

> This argument does not contradict the observations of a generation of research studies which explains readership *per se* in terms of demographics; the theory of dependency relations enriches these explanations by identifying intervening variables which significantly influence the behavior of readers.[79]

They say that knowing if a newspaper reader wants social understanding, self-understanding, or action orientation provides more information about newspaper readership than just demographics alone. Does the same hold true for magazine readers? Loges and Ball-Rokeach determined that the highly educated do not seek social understanding from newspapers. Do these readers turn to magazines to fulfill those dependency relations?

Today, our understanding of magazine reader demographics gives us some insight into the type of readers who seek out magazines, and how long readers might pay attention to a particular magazine. But those same demographics do not give us any indication of the strength of the relationship readers may have with magazines or of what needs readers may seek to fulfill when turning to magazines to aid them in their own environments. Without that kind of information we have a poor perspective on the role which magazines play in our society today.

Notes

[1] Peter Gerlach, "Research About Magazines Appearing in Journalism Quarterly," Journalism Quarterly 64:1 (1987): 173-182.

[2] David Abrahamson, "The Rise of the Special-Interest Magazine in 'The Other 1960s': An Economic and Sociocultural History" (Ph.D. diss., New York University, 1992), 10.

[3] Bruce L. Stern, Dean M. Krugman, and Alan Resnik, "Magazine Advertising: An Analysis of its Information Content," Journal of Advertising Research 21:2 (1981): 39-44.

[4] Robert R. Harmon, Nabil Y. Razzouk, and Bruce L. Stern, "The Information Content of Comparative Magazine Advertisements," Journal of Advertising 12:4 (1983): 10-19.

[5] Linly Chou, George B. Franke, and Gary B. Wilcox, "The Information Content of Comparative Magazine Ads: A Longitudinal Analysis," Journalism Quarterly 64:1 (1987): 119-124, 250.

[6] Dan Sarel, "Trends in Factual Claims in Ads in magazines, 1858, 1968, and 1978," Journalism Quarterly 61:3 (1984): 650-654, 743.

[7] Lawrence Soley, "The Effects of Black Models on Magazine Ad Readership," Journalism Quarterly 60:4 (1983): 686-690.

[8] Ronald Humphrey and Howard Schuman, "The Portrayal of Blacks in Magazine Advertisements: 1950-1982," Public Opinion Quarterly 48 (Fall, 1984): 551-563.

[9] George M. Zinkhan, Keith K. Cox, and Jae W. Hong, "Changes in Stereotypes: Black and Whites in Magazine Advertisements," Journalism Quarterly 63:3 (1986): 568-572.

[10] George M. Zinkhan, William J. Qualls, and Abhijit Biswas, "The Use of Blacks in Magazine and Television Advertising: 1946 to 1986," Journalism Quarterly 67:3 (1990): 547-553.

[11] Leonard N. Reid and Lawrence C. Soley, "Decorative Models and the Readership of Magazine Ads," Journal of Advertising Research 23:2 (1983): 27-32.

[12] James W. Pokrywczynski, "Sex in Ads Targeted to Black and White Readers," Journalism Quarterly 65:3 (1988): 756-760.

[13] Lawrence C. Soley and Leonard N. Reid, "Taking It Off: Are Models in Magazine Ads Wearing Less?," Journalism Quarterly 65:4 (1988): 960-966.

[14] Gary B. Wilcox and Sandra E. Moriarty, "Humorous Advertising in the Post, 1920-1939," Journalism Quarterly 61:2 (1984): 436-439.

[15] Russell W. Belk and Richard W. Pollay, "Images of Ourselves: The Good Life in Twentieth Century Advertising," Journal of Consumer Research 11:4 (1985): 887-897.

[16] Barbara L. Gross and Jagdish N. Sheth, "Time-Oriented Advertising: A Content Analysis of United States Magazine Advertising, 1890-1988," Journal of Marketing 53:4 (1989): 76-83.

[17] Patricia A. Stout and Young Sook Moon, "Use of Endorsers in Magazine Advertisements," Journalism Quarterly 67:3 (1990): 536-546.

[18] Linda J. Busby and Greg Leichty, "Feminism and Advertising in Traditional and Nontraditional Women's Magazines, 1950s-1980s," Journalism Quarterly 70:2 (1993): 246-264.

[19] Oddina Pittatore, "The Image of Italy in Ads in Five U.S. Magazines," Journalism Quarterly 60:4 (1983): 728-731.

[20] Jae-Hyun Choe, Gary B. Wilcox, and Andrew P. Hardy, "Facial Expressions in Magazine Ads: A Cross-Cultural Comparison," Journalism Quarterly 63:1 (1986): 122-126, 166.

[21] Katherine Toland Frith and David Wesson, "A Comparison of Cultural Values in British and American Print Advertising: A Study of Magazines," Journalism Quarterly 68:1-2 (1991): 216-223.

[22] Anthony F. McGann, Judith F. Russell, and J. Thomas Russell, "Variable Pricing in Advertising Space for Regional and Metro Magazines," Journalism Quarterly 60:2 (1983): 269-274, 322.

[23] Leonard N. Reid, Hubert J. Rotfield, and James H. Barnes, "Attention to Magazine Ads as Function of Layout Design," Journalism Quarterly 61:2 (1984): 439-441.

[24] David A. Wesson, "Readability as a Factor in Magazine Ad Copy Recall," Journalism Quarterly 66:3 (1989): 715-718.

[25] David A. Wesson, "Headline Length as a Factor in Magazine Ad Readership," Journalism Quarterly 66:2 (1989): 446-468.

[26] Patricia A. Stout, Gary B. Wilcox and Lorrie S. Greer, "Trends in Magazine Advertorial Use," Journalism Quarterly 66:4 (1989): 960-964.

[27] Kuo-jen Tsang, "News Photos in Time and Newsweek," Journalism Quarterly 61:3 (1984): 578-584, 723.

[28] Michael Sherer, "Comparing Magazine Photos of Vietnam and Korean Wars," Journalism Quarterly 65:3 (1988): 752-756.

[29] William G. Christ and Sammye Johnson, "Images Through Time: Man of the Year Covers," Journalism Quarterly 62:4 (1985): 891-893.

[30] Sammye Johnson and William G. Christ, "Women Through Time: Who Gets Covered?," Journalism Quarterly 65:4 (1988): 889-897.

[31] Sandra E. Moriarty and Gina M. Garramone, "A Study of Newsmagazine Photographs of the 1984 Presidential Campaign," Journalism Quarterly 63:4 (1986): 728-734.

[32] Sandra E. Moriarty and Mark N. Popovich, "Newsmagazine Visuals and the 1988 Presidential Election," Journalism Quarterly 68:3 (1991): 371-380.

[33] Giacomo L. Ortizano, "Visibility of Blacks and Whites in Magazine Photographs," Journalism Quarterly 66:3 (1989): 718-721.

[34] Paul Lester and Ron Smith, "African-American Photo Coverage in Life, Newsweek and Time, 1937-1988," Journalism Quarterly 67:1 (1990): 128-136.

[35] Mary Alice Sentman, "Black and White: Disparity in Coverage by Life Magazine from 1937 to 1972," Journalism Quarterly 60:3 (1983): 501-508.

[36] Ruth Thibodeau, "From Racism to Tokenism: The Changing Face of Blacks in New Yorker Cartoons," Public Opinion Quarterly 53:4 (1989): 482-494.

[37] Beverly Loughlin, "The Women's Magazines Short-Story Heroine," Journalism Quarterly 60:1 (1983): 138-142.

[38] Margaret Andreasen and H. Leslie Stevens, "Employed Women's Assertiveness and Openness as Shown in Magazine Use," Journalism Quarterly 60:3 (1983): 449-457.

[39] Josephine A. Ruggiero and Louise C. Weston, "Work Options for Women in Women's Magazines: The Medium and the Message," Sex Roles 12:5-6 (1985): 535-547.

[40] Carolyn Johnson and Lynne Gross, "Mass Media Use by Women in Decision-Making Positions," Journalism Quarterly 62:4 (1985): 850-854, 950.

[41] Lauren Kessler, "Women's Magazines' Coverage of Smoking Related Health Hazards," Journalism Quarterly 66:2 (1989): 316-322, 445.

[42] Kate Pierce, "A Feminist Theoretical Perspective on the Socialization of Teenage Girls Through Seventeen Magazine," Sex Roles 23:9-10 (1990): 491-500.

[43] Arlene Rossen Cardozo, "American Magazine Coverage of the Nazi Death Camp Era," Journalism Quarterly 60:4 (1983): 717-718.

[44] David A. Brenders and James D. Robinson, "An Analysis of Self-Help Articles: 1972-1980," Mass Comm Review 11:3 (1985): 29-36.

[45] Cathy Meo Bonnstetter, "Magazine Coverage of Mentally Handicapped," Journalism Quarterly 63:3 (1986): 623-626.

[46] Thom Lieb, "Protest at the Post: Coverage of Blacks in the Washington Post Magazine, Mass Comm Review 15:2-3 (1988): 61-67.

[47] Anette Grube and Karin Boehme-Duerr, "AIDS in International News Magazines," Journalism Quarterly 65:3 (1988): 686-689.

[48] Sharon Bramlett-Solomon and Vanessa Wilson, "Images of the Elderly in Life and Ebony, 1978-1987," Journalism Quarterly 66:1 (1989): 185-188.

[49] James B. Lemert and Marguerite Gemson Ashman, "Extent of Mobilizing Information in Opinion and News Magazines," Journalism Quarterly 60:4 (1983): 657-662.

[50] Oscar Patterson III, "Television's Living Room War in Print: Vietnam in the News Magazines," Journalism Quarterly 61:1 (1984): 35-39, 136.

[51] Larry L. Burriss, "Accuracy of News Magazines as Perceived by News Sources," Journalism Quarterly 62:4 (1985): 824-827.

[52] Richard A. Kallan and J.D. Denton, "People's People: An Internal Demographic Analysis," Mass Comm Review 13:1-2-3 (1986): 40-43.

[53] Brian K. Simmons and David N. Lowry, "Terrorists in the News, as Reflected in Three News Magazines, 1980-1988," Journalism Quarterly 67:4 (1990): 692-696.

[54] Shannon E. Martin, "Using Expert Sources in Breaking Science Stories: A Comparison of Magazine Types," Journalism Quarterly 68:1-2 (1991): 179-187.

[55] Robert M. Entman, "Framing U.S. Coverage of International News: Contrasts in Narratives of the KAL and Iran Air Incidents, Journal of Communication 41:4 (1991): 6-27.

[56] Michael W. Singletary, Raymond Boland, William Izard, and Terry Rosser, "How Accurate Are News Magazines' Forecasts?," Journalism Quarterly 60:2 (1983): 342-344.

[57] Hugh M. Culbertson and Lujuan Thompson, "A Comparison of The Quill and Columbia Journalism Review Relative to Three Critical Perspectives," Mass Comm Review 11:1-2 (1984): 12-21.

[58] Lianne Fridiksson, "A Content Analysis of the Darts and Laurels Column in Columbia Journalism Review," Mass Comm Review 11:3 (1985): 2-7.

[59] Thomas J. Price, "The Changing Nature of Foreign Affairs: The Most Influential Periodical in Print," Journalism Quarterly 63:1 (1986): 155-160, 187.

[60] Susan Caudill, Ed Caudill, and Michael Singletary, "'Journalist Wanted': Trade-Journal Ads as Indicators of Professional Values," Journalism Quarterly 64:2-3 (1987): 576-580, 633.

[61] Jean E. Dye and Mark D. Harmon, "TV Guide: Images of the Status Quo, 1970-1979," Journalism Quarterly 64:2-3 (1987): 626-629.

[62] Thomas Jacobson, "Research Activity of Magazine Publishers," Journalism Quarterly 65:2 (1988): 511-514.

[63] Sam G. Riley and Gary Selnow, "Southern Magazine Publishing, 1764-1984," Journalism Quarterly 65:4 (1988): 898-901.

[64] Robert O Wyatt and Geoffrey P. Hull, "The Music Critic in the American Press: A Nationwide Survey of Newspapers and Magazines," Mass Comm Review 17:3 (1990): 38-43.

[65] Robert G. Hayes and Ann E. Reisner, "Farm Journalists and Advertiser Influence: Pressure on Ethical Standards," Journalism Quarterly 68:1-2 (1991): 172-178.

[66] Everette E. Dennis, "Post-Mortem on McLuhan: A Public Figure's Emergence and Decline as Seen in Popular Magazines," Mass Comm Review 1:2 (1974): 31-40.

[67] Fred Fedler, Ron Smith, and Mike Meeske, "Time and Newsweek Favor John F. Kennedy, Criticize Robert and Edward Kennedy," Journalism Quarterly 360:3 (1983): 489-496.

[68] Robert M. Ogles and Herbert H. Howard, "Father Coughlin in the Periodical Press, 1931-1942," Journalism Quarterly 61:2 (1984): 280-286, 363.

[69] Yang Chou Yu and Daniel Riffe, "Chiang and Mao in U.S. News Magazines," Journalism Quarterly 66:4 (1989): 913-919.

[70] Roderick P. Hart, Deborah Smith-Howell, and John Llewellyn, "The Mindscape of the Presidency: Time Magazine, 1945-1985," Journal of Communication 41:3 (1991): 6-25.

[71] J. Douglas Tarpley, "American Newsmagazine Coverage of the Supreme Court, 1978-81," Journalism Quarterly 61:4 (1984): 801-804, 826.

[72] Dorothy A. Bowles and Rebekah V. Bromley, "Newsmagazine Coverage of the Supreme Court during the Reagan Administration," Journalism Quarterly 69:4 (1992): 948-959.

[73] Wayne M. Towers, "Uses and Gratifications of Magazine Readers: A Cross-Media Comparison," Mass Comm Review 13:1-2-3 (1986): 44-51.

[74] Greg A. Payne, Jessica J.H. Severn, and David M. Dozier, "Uses and Gratifications Motives as Indicators of Magazine Readership," Journalism Quarterly 65:4 (1988): 909-913, 959.

[75] Howard Eaton, Jr., "Agenda-Setting with Bi-Weekly Data on Content of Three National Media," Journalism Quarterly 66:4 (1989): 942-948, 959.

[76] Pamela J. Shoemaker and Stephen D. Reese, "Exposure to What? Integrating Media Content and Effects Studies," Journalism Quarterly 67:4 (1990): 649.

[77] Shoemaker and Reese, 650.

[78] Donald L. Shaw and Shannon E. Martin, "The Function of Mass Media and Agenda Setting," Journalism Quarterly 69:4 (1992): 919.

[79] William E. Loges and Sandra J. Ball-Rokeach, "Dependency Relations and Newspaper Readership," Journalism Quarterly 70:3 (1993): 602.

Acknowledgements

The author would like to thank Lisa Gebken, graduate student in the Department of Journalism, Ball State University, for her investigative and math skills.

3

An Overview of
Political Content Analyses of Magazines

Lawrence J. Mullen

ABSTRACT

This article reviews the scholarly work that uses content analysis to study political substance in magazines. Following a brief history of this subarea of research, a modified version of Lasswell's communication model is used to classify the current literature. Problematic issues are discussed and possible solutions are offered.

Introduction

Krippendorff argued for the importance of content analysis as a tool, claiming that it was "potentially one of the most important research techniques in the social sciences."[1] It is also a very popular method for analyzing magazine political content. The purpose of this review is to describe the extant research in this "subarea" and define some of the problems and possible solutions. Starting with a brief history of magazine political content analysis, Lasswell's formula of communication is utilized to facilitate the review of current literature on magazine political content analysis.

History

Harold Lasswell did some of the earliest known political content analysis with magazines. He investigated themes of Nazism in U.S. publications for legal purposes during World War II. *Reader's Digest* and *Saturday Evening Post* were compared to publications allegedly guilty of Nazi propaganda.[2] It was not until after World War II, however, that traditional, formal, or conventional content analysis developed. The method stressed quantitative scientific methods for developing empirical indicators to make generalizations with the purpose of description and theory-building.[3] Magazine analyses were rare, but a few political content studies in the 1950s and 1960s analyzed such topics as American and Soviet themes and values in popular magazines [4] and biographical sketches of political figures in news magazines.[5] Biased portrayals of Truman, Eisenhower, and Kennedy were studied in *Time* magazine.[6] Another study analyzed the 1960 presidential candidates as they were depicted in *Time*, *Newsweek*, and *U.S. News and World Report*.[7] These early content studies are, at times, replicated to bring ideas up-to-date in light of changing social environments, changes in magazine editorial management and ownership, and to try modified content analysis techniques.[8]

In recent years, strict quantitative description has become less important. Instead, studies use magazine content to support rhetorical arguments,[9] show ideological manipulation in the news media,[10] or to support an argument about how the media portray individuals, for instance, how magazines depict politicians' wives,[11] or how media content and form are inseparable.[12] This raises the issue of whether content studies should be qualitative or quantitative.[13]

Should content be analyzed qualitatively rather than quantitatively? This question incorrectly assumes that the two are mutually exclusive. The suggestion that content analysis be qualitative rather than quantitative usually comes off the heels of criticism of a content study, but such a criticism may indicate the study's failure to be fully systematic. Stempel and Westley say that advocates of qualitative content analysis neglect the element of meaning that quantitative research adds to a study. "It is not," they say, "particularly meaningful to say that *Newsweek* had references to both Jimmy Carter and Gerald Ford during the 1976 presidential campaign."[14] The number of references is a significant fact. One might also find significant how favorable the references were, whether they were attributed or not, or whether issues were mentioned. It does not matter if the method is qualitative or quantitative; the researcher can analyze these elements of a text in either case.

Recent Studies

There are several ways to classify the political content studies done with magazines over the past 20 years or so: topically, by the system of enumeration, by purpose, or by the inferences made. Hofstetter says that content analysis of political information can be organized around several methodological and substantive areas: sampling units, recording units, or context units.[15]

Magazine analysts may find most relevant those studies that use the method to draw inferences about individuals, groups, and institutions which are generally inaccessible. The behavior of public officials, key political actors, historical figures, and others long since dead have been the objects of content study.

Another classification scheme could be oriented around the descriptive inferences about the media that content analysis attempts to do. Many of these studies examine the way some political actor, issue, event, institution, or process is portrayed. Some of these studies can have a substantial evaluational component. The media impact on electoral campaigns, public opinion in general, and just paying scholarly attention to media information is also a part of these studies. Thematic analysis is a mainstay unit of analysis of this type of research. Assessing accuracy, biased coverage, and influences on news coverage are familiar topics. Content analysis has also been combined with effects research in order to draw a more definite link between the content and its influence on public perceptions.[16] Because of its relevance to content analysis and simplicity as a categorizing scheme, a version of Lasswell's classic communication formula will be used as the basis for classifying magazine political content studies.

Who Says...

When content researchers study "who" sent the message they want to find evidence to make inferences about the message's sender. These studies often employ traditional content analysis methods, but also use interviews and other research methods requiring access to political newsmakers and reporters.[17] These studies investigate the relationship between the news media and the people making the news.

Manipulation is a topic that often comes up in these studies: manipulation of a political actor, such as the president, by the news media, and manipulation of the press by the president. Other studies have made compelling cases for media manipulation of public opinion,[18] political actors exploiting their celebrity status,[19] and the hows, whys, and whens of the president as a speechmaker.[20] Magazines are always one of two or three media analyzed in these studies.

The "who" aspect of political content study also lends itself to the study of the editorial nature of the magazine under analysis. In this sense, "who" might be the magazine's style of presentation as a reflection of the editorial policy, staff, or ownership. When the researcher considers who wrote what, or who decided what will be published, then "what" may become the focus of the study. The purpose of a study of this sort may be to make inferences about the sender or the gatekeeper of the message based on patterns the researcher finds in the messages themselves. This idea leads us into the next section on "what" is communicated.

...What...

Analyzing "what" is communicated is probably the most frequent application of content analysis. In these studies the researcher is concerned with the characteristics of the message sent. Probably the most frequently researched concept is "bias." Biased depictions of political actors and the events surrounding them are the objects of several studies.[21] To a lesser extent, bias concerning social issues has been the object of content analysis.[22] The study of magazine content has played a significant role in these areas.

Election periods are popular for bias studies. Biased content from the 1960 nominating conventions,[23] the 1972 campaign,[24] and photographs of the 1984 [25] and 1988 campaign [26] have been analyzed using magazines exclusively. Biased magazine coverage of third-party candidates was studied during the 1976 election.[27] A comprehensive content study of the 1976 election included magazines as one of two or three media analyzed.[28] Some researchers have looked at biased coverage of presidents beyond the campaign period.[29]

The study of political bias has been soundly criticized. One reason is that "bias" is an extremely slippery concept to get a handle on because, except in rare instances, "truth," or "what actually happened," is disputable. In addition, it ignores the fact that any account of an event is necessarily going to be different from the event. That does not necessarily make it "biased"; it simply makes it "different." One of the harsher criticisms states that evidence of media bias is scanty, that the more sophisticated studies tend to be overoperationalized and clumsy while others are so case-specific that they defy generalization.[30] In all, content research has failed to find political bias operating systematically in mass media reportage.

...To Whom in which Channel...

Magazine users and the magazine medium are unique. Magazines tend to highly target their audience. So, the magazine reader gets specially tailored information resulting in high-involvement media use. Readers are generally well-educated and more affluent than nonmagazine readers.[31] Since magazines usually come out in weekly or monthly intervals, the political information in them tends to summarize and reflect on longer trends than television or newspapers generally do. Although the differences between the media are interesting, the similarities may be more fascinating.

In his study of CBS, NBC, *Time*, and *Newsweek*, Gans found the similarities between the electronic media and print to be more compelling than the differences. Television news, he remarks, tends to favor news that produces dramatic, action-packed film, while news magazines emphasize stories that lend themselves to dramatic narrative, vivid quotes, and action-packed still photographs. Both types of news are selected and produced by journalists who look at America in much the same way.

Magazines are, nevertheless, important conduits of political information. In fact, presidential assistants prefer to go to the news magazines rather than the newspapers when they want their message to resonate throughout the country.[32] A cover story is always a coveted prize by a politician. Several studies have investigated magazine political information compared to newspapers and television news.[33] News magazines were found to have two distinct advantages over the other two media. First, magazines tend to give more space to individual issues and they give more in-depth coverage. Second, the media differ along structural syntax dimensions with magazines framing issues early with opinions, newspapers framing their stories with facts and television news framing news with basic, introductory material, which is usually descriptive. Magazine and television news never seem to present as much factual detail as do newspapers.[34]

...*How*...

How a political message is sent, how it is depicted in words and pictures, and how it changes are some of the topics covered by political content analysts who focus on "how" magazines transmit information. The research in this area considers topics ranging from the general structure, pattern, or form of the political message [35] to very specific studies about the way Senators and the Supreme Court are depicted.[36] Other topics include how the Kennedy brothers were depicted in each of their presidential campaigns,[37] how the Birmingham civil rights crisis was depicted,[38] and how issues of the 1960s were depicted.[39]

Content researchers who study how a message is depicted often also attempt to make inferences about why the message appears as it does. To make these assertions, the researchers will look for social patterns occurring in conjunction with media content. For instance, issues reported in magazines have been compared to Gallup Poll data to see if an agenda-setting effect exists.[40] Studies concerning foreign politics have included content analyses focusing on how foreign leaders' portrayals have changed in conjunction with changes in U.S. foreign policy,[41] how reportage of French and U.S. campaigns differ,[42] and how French presidential campaigns are depicted in French weeklies.[43] Comparing magazine issue reportage to trends in related statistics to see if the amount of coverage of an issue bears resemblance to the facts has been the object of at least one important study.[44] How presidential images change in conjunction with technological, political, and social events,[45] and how magazine images of war change with public opinion [46] are studies that look at magazine photographs. The problem with research in this area is that some of it tends to be speculative with no definite causal links between the content and the social indicators identified.

There is, however, a need to validate content analysis by comparing it to social, cultural, or audience indicators. Irving Janis pointed out that there is a "need for validating the results of content analysis of mass communications by relating them to audience perceptions or to behavioral effects."[47] Content should be analyzed to predict "something that is observable in principle, to aid decision making, or to help conceptualize that portion of reality that gave rise to the analyzed text."[48] To this end, content analysis must be done relative to and supported in terms of the context of the data. The context of the data is the environment in which the content was created and in which it exists. In other words, the data are interpreted through what is known.

Meaning is drawn in the connection between the data and their context. Data are the actual physical stimuli or sign vehicles like type on a page, images from a screen, or words spoken, but most concerns with meaning, Krippendorff says, start with higher level stimuli such as written documents, films, dialogue, paintings, and television shows. The context is their environment and, he says, "the analyst can choose the environment and its conceptualization."[49] The communication researcher, then, may focus attention on the sender's intentions, a receiver's cognitive and behavioral effects, the institution within which it is exchanged, or the culture within which it plays a role.

Analysis of Photographs. Analysis of magazine photographs forms its own subarea of research under this category. Studies have included the images of war [50] and the president's visual image.[51] Often the researcher is interested in "how" a political actor, or event is visually depicted in the media and a categorization scheme is used as an exploratory device.

Content analysis of photographs is different from the analysis of words because of the amount of time a researcher invests in this research. One reason for its tediousness is that photographs cannot be analyzed using computer techniques like words can. Each photograph must be analyzed manually, so to speak. Although researchers have been working on computerized methods for analyzing pictures,[52] others do not see it coming to fruition for quite some time.[53] Despite its laborious nature, many researchers find picture analysis an important area to study.

...With What Effects

There is a lack of content research that deals satisfactorily with the media account as a stimulus for readers' interpretations. To meaningfully examine the validity or utility of an account, one ought to explain not only what is on a page of text, but what meanings or messages it leads the bulk of the audience members to construct. To put this another way, it seems as if much content research of political discourse fails to adequately problematize the issue:

> We know a good deal about the media's impact on the social and political behavior of individuals. But although we know more and more about media effects we seem to know less about how individuals "take" the information they receive from other individuals and the mass media, how they *think* about it, change or accept it, and finally arrive at a conclusion that prompts their actions.[54]

Despite the lack of research on this problem, the theoretical underpinnings to conduct this type of investigation have been around for a number of years.[55] The major methodological issue is determining the optimum unit of analysis for the particular questions one is trying to answer or the theoretical ideas one is attempting to explore. A more subtle methodological issue is whether the unit of analysis ought to depend in whole or in part on how readers process political information from a particular medium. To put this in terms of a question, why should we analyze by words, for example, if people do not tend to process such information by words? In essence, the answer to this question is that the unit of analysis should match the unit of cognitive processing. The problem here, however, is that such a study is difficult to do and even harder to do right.

This problem is not new. The debate concerning analysis units and cognitive units is decades old now, yet not much has been done about it. In answer to attacks by humanists claiming that content analysis did not get at what was really meaningful, Holsti talks about different units of analysis, larger units of analysis, and even thematic analysis as a way to meet the challenge.[56]

The studies of Hart et al attempt just such a project.[57] Their specific purpose was to go beyond traditional content analysis and categorize news magazine content in a way that is meaningful to readers. They use a rhetorical approach in conjunction with a variety of content analytic approaches. Their study is unique in that it focuses on the human aspects of presidential portrayals with an eye to estimating how portrayals of the president might influence what citizens come to expect of the presidency. Hence, its concerns are phenomenological in nature (compared to the functionalistic emphasis of past studies dealing with agenda-setting, media economics, information processing, lobbying influences, etc.).

Another way to solve this problem is to use multiple methods. One study used content analysis, surveys, experiments, and depth interviews to understand how people learn about news.[58] Magazines, television, and newspapers formed their sampling frame from which a cross section of important issues were chosen. Their fourpronged research approach represents an effort to understand the link between news content and how people process it.

Discourse analysis is another approach that may help to solve the problem discussed here.[59] With this method, media content is seen as a particular type of language or text and as a specific kind of sociocultural practice. The media then are analyzed at several levels and not limited to grammatical structures like themes, sentences, words, phrases, and the like. Media discourse is also analyzed in terms of its relation to overall topics, other themes, sentences, and words, and along stylistic and rhetorical dimensions. So, discourse is not seen simply as an isolated text or dialogical structure, but as a complex communicative event that also embodies a social context that affects real people at psychological and social levels.

Conclusion

When categorizing content studies one realizes that the "who, what, how, to whom in what channel, with what effects" scheme of categorization is artificial. The categories are really inseparable. Who sends what to whom with what effect is simultaneously addressed to greater or lesser degrees in all content studies. When a researcher analyzes how content is sent, or how content has changed, she or he must also understand what was sent, which is determined by who sent it. What the message is and how the message is sent and presented are almost the same question. Finally, one should note that there is always some effect of the message itself, although many content researchers stop short of this step.

This article has cataloged magazine political content studies in terms of how they address Lasswell's model of communication. The inventory was based on each study's perceived goals. Others might disagree with the scheme and how the studies have been categorized, but as with any study of content, there are multiple ways of categorization and multiple meanings attached to the message.

Notes

[1] Klaus Krippendorff, "Content Analysis," in Erik Barnouw, ed., The International Encyclopedia of Communications (New York: Oxford University Press, 1989), 403-407.

[2] Richard C. Hofstetter, "Content Analysis," in Dan D. Nimmo and Keith R. Sanders, eds., Handbook of Political Communication (Beverly Hills, CA: Sage, 1981), 529-560.

[3] Hofstetter, "Content Analysis."

[4] Ivor Wayne, "American and Soviet Themes and Values: A Content Analysis of Pictures in Popular Magazines," Public Opinion Quarterly 20:1 (1956): 314-320.

[5] Lionel S. Lewis, "Political Heroes: 1936 and 1960," Public Opinion Quarterly 42 (Winter 1965): 116-118.

[6] John C. Merrill, "How Time Stereotyped Three U.S. Presidents," Journalism Quarterly 42 (1965): 563-570.

[7] Bruce H. Westley, Charles E. Higbie, Timothy Burke, David J. Lippert, Leonard Maurer, and Vernon A. Stone, "The News Magazines and the 1960 Conventions," Journalism Quarterly 40 (1963): 525-531, 647.

[8] Fred Fedler, Mike Meeske, and Joe Hall, "Time Magazine Revisited: Presidential Stereotypes Persist," Journalism Quarterly 56:2 (1979): 353-359; Mark A. Bailey, "Bias in Presidential Coverage by Time and Newsweek," (Master's thesis, Ball State University, Muncie, IN, 1986).

[9] Roderick P. Hart, Deborah Smith-Howell, and John Llewellyn, "The Mindscape of the Presidency: Time Magazine, 1945-1985," Journal of Communication 41:3 (1991): 6-25.

[10] Edward S. Herman and Noam Chomsky, Manufacturing Consent: The Political Economy of the Mass Media (New York: Pantheon Books, 1988).

[11] Dan Nimmo and James E. Combs, Mediated Political Realities (New York: Longman, 1983). See especially Chapter 4: "Political Celebrity in Popular Magazines," 92-104.

[12] David L. Altheide and Robert P. Snow, Media Logic: A Sage Library Research Book #89 (Beverly Hills, CA: Sage, 1979).

[13] This issue is discussed in detail in Ole R. Holsti, Content Analysis for the Social Sciences and Humanities (Reading, MA: Addison-Wesley, 1969). See also Guido H. Stempel and Bruce H. Westley, eds., Research Methods in Mass Communication (Englewood Cliffs, NJ: Prentice-Hall, 1981), 119-131.

[14] Stempel and Westley, Research Methods, 212.

[15] Hofstetter, "Content Analysis."

[16] Thomas E. Patterson, The Mass Media Election: How Americans Choose Their President (New York: Praeger, 1980).

[17] Herbert J. Gans, Deciding What's News: A Study of CBS Evening News, NBC Nightly News, Newsweek and Time (New York: Vintage Books, 1979); Michael B. Grossman and Martha J. Kumar, Portraying the President: The White House and the News Media (Baltimore: Johns Hopkins University Press, 1981); David L. Paletz and Robert M. Entman, Media Power Politics (New York: The Free Press, 1981).

[18] Herman and Chomsky, Manufacturing Consent.

[19] Nimmo and Combs, Mediated Political Realities.

[20] Roderick P. Hart, The Sound of Leadership: Presidential Communication in the Modern Age (Chicago: University of Chicago Press, 1987).

[21] E.F. Einsiedel and M. Jane Bibbee, "The News Magazines and Minority Candidates— Campaign '76," Journalism Quarterly 56 (1979): 102-105; Dru Evarts and Guido H. Stempel, "Coverage of the 1972 Campaign by TV, News Magazines and Major Newspapers," Journalism Quarterly 51 (1974): 645-648, 676; Sandra E. Moriarty and Gina M. Garramone, "A Study of Newsmagazine Photographs of the 1984 Presidential Campaign," Journalism Quarterly 63 (1986), 728-734; Sandra E. Moriarty and Mark N. Popovich, "Newsmagazine Visuals and the 1988 Presidential Election," Journalism Quarterly 68:3 (Fall 1991): 371-380; Patterson, Mass Media Election.

[22] Matilda Butler and William Paisley, "Equal Rights Coverage in Magazines," Journalism Quarterly 55:1 (Summer 1978): 157-160.

[23] Westley, Higbie, Burke, Lippert, Maurer, and Stone, "The News Magazines."

[24] Evarts and Stempel, "Coverage of the 1972 Campaign."

[25] Moriarty and Garramone, "A Study of Newsmagazine Photographs."

[26] Moriarty and Popovich, "Newsmagazine Visuals."

[27] Einsiedel and Bibbee, "Newsmagazines and Minority Candidates."

[28] Patterson, Mass Media Election.

[29] Bailey, "Bias in Presidential Coverage." [30] Hart, Smith-Howell, and Llewellyn, "Mindscape of the Presidency," 6.

[31] Kathleen H. Jamieson and Karlyn K. Campbell, The Interplay of Influence: Mass Media & Their Publics in News, Advertising, Politics (Belmont, CA: Wadsworth, 1983), 15.

[32] Grossman and Kumar, Portraying the President, 62.

[33] Evarts and Stempel, 1974; Gans, 1979; W. Russell Neuman, Marion R. Just, and Ann N. Crigler, Common Knowledge: News and the Construction of Political Meaning (Chicago: The University of Chicago Press, 1992); see also Paletz and Entman, Media Power Politics, and Patterson, Mass Media Election.

[34] Neuman, Just, and Crigler, Common Knowledge.

[35] Altheide and Snow, Media Logic.

[36] Dorothy Bowles and Rebecca Bromley, "Newsmagazine Coverage of the Supreme Court During the Reagan Administration," Journalism Quarterly 69:4 (Winter 1992): 948-959; Michael Solimine, "Newsmagazine Coverage of the Supreme Court," Journalism Quarterly 57 (1980): 661-663; J.D. Tarpley, "American Newsmagazine Coverage of the Supreme Court," Journalism Quarterly 61:4 (1984): 801-804, 826; David H. Weaver and G. Cleveland Wilhoit. "News Magazine Visibility of Senators," Journalism Quarterly 51:1 (1974): 67-72.

[37] Fred Fedler, Ron Smith, and Mike Meeske, "Time and Newsweek Favor John F. Kennedy, Criticize Robert and Edward Kennedy," Journalism Quarterly 60 (1983): 489-496.

[38] Richard Lentz, "The Prophet and the Citadel: News Magazine Coverage of the 1963 Birmingham Civil Rights Crisis," Communication, 10 (1987): 5-29.

[39] G. Ray Funkhouser, "Trends in Media Coverage of the Issues of the '60s," Journalism Quarterly 50 (1973): 533-538.

[40] Aileen Yagade and David M. Dozier, "The Media Agenda Setting Effect of Concrete Versus Abstract Issues,"- Journalism Quarterly 67 (Spring 1990): 3-10.

[41] Yang-Chou Yu and Daniel Riffe, "Chiang and Mao in U.S. Magazines," Journalism Quarterly 66:4 (Winter 1989): 913-919.

[42] Ann Marie Major and L. Erwin Atwood, "U.S. Newsmagazine Coverage of the U.S. and French Presidential Elections: Mediated Construction of the Candidates and Issues," in Lynda Lee Kaid, Jacques Gerstl, and Keith R. Sanders, eds., Mediated Politics in Two Cultures: Presidential Campaigning in the United States and France (New York: Praeger, 1991), 161-172.

[43] Jean-Claude Sergant and Yves Deloye, "Newsmagazine Coverage of the French Campaign," in Kaid, Gerstl, and Sanders, eds., Mediated Politics, 145-160.

[44] Funkhouser, "Trends in Media Coverage."

[45] Lawrence Mullen, "The President's Visual Image from 1945 to 1974: An Exploratory Analysis of the Pattern of Pictorial Variables Over Time" (Ph.D. diss., University of Iowa, Iowa City, IA, 1992).

[46] Michael D. Sherer, "Vietnam War Photos and Public Opinion," Journalism Quarterly 66 (1989): 391-395, 530.

[47] Klaus Krippendorff, Content Analysis: An Introduction to Its Methodology, (Beverly Hills, CA: Sage, 1980), 23.

[48] Krippendorff, Content Analysis, 23.

[49] Krippendorff, Content Analysis, 24.

[50] Michael D. Sherer, "Comparing Magazine Photos of Vietnam and Korean Wars," Journalism Quarterly 65 (1988): 752-756; see also Sherer, "Vietnam War Photos."

[51] Moriarty and Garramone, "A Study of Newsmagazine Photographs"; Moriarty and Popovich, "Newsmagazine Visuals"; Mullen, "The President's Visual Image."

[52] For example, Robert Tiemens at the University of Utah.

[53] For example, David Fan at the University of Minnesota.

[54] Sidney Kraus, "The Studies and the World Outside," in Sidney Kraus and Richard M. Perloff, eds., Mass Media and Political Thought, (Beverly Hills, CA: Sage, 1986), 293.

[55] For example, see Walter Lippmann, Public Opinion, (New York: The Free Press, 1922) and Wilbur Schramm, "Information Theory and Mass Communication," Journalism Quarterly 32 (1955): 131-146.

[56] Holsti, Content Analysis.

[57] Roderick Hart, Deborah Smith-Howell, and John Llewellyn, "Evolution of Presidential News Coverage," Communication and Persuasion 7 (October-December 1990): 213-230; see also Hart, Smith-Howell, and Llewellyn, "Mindscape of the Presidency."

[58] Neuman, Just, and Crigler, Common Knowledge.

[59] Teun A. Van Dijk, News Analysis: Case Studies of International and National News in the Press (Hillsdale, NJ: Lawrence Erlbaum, 1988).

Acknowledgements

The author would like to thank Eric W. Rothenbuhler and Samuel L. Becker, both at the University of Iowa, and David Fan at the University of Minnesota for their comments, suggestions, and guidance on this article.

II

Professional Issues in Magazine Publishing

4

Research Review:
Magazine Editors and Editing Practices

Lee Jolliffe

ABSTRACT

In spite of barriers to magazine editing research, a considerable literature has been created in this subfield. Chief areas of emphasis have been (a) biographical studies of individual editors and (b) various types of studies of editorial practices, including surveys, magazine content analyses, and close qualitative examinations of editors' relationships with others. After literature in these areas is reviewed and critiqued, suggestions for future study of magazine editing are offered.

Introduction

Magazine research in general has formed a very small part of the communication research accepted by scholarly journals,[1] and research into the subfield of magazine editing forms only a small fraction of that work. Indeed, with the dearth of magazine research accepted by academic journals, most works on magazine editing appear through the book industry as editors' biographies, autobiographies, and collected letters, with a wide range of scholarly quality displayed.

An additional research problem in the magazine editing subfield is the poor indexing of its research materials. Indexes to the academic journals on communication are spotty at best, with no one index or CD-ROM providing access to *all* the relevant studies. The best journalism bibliographies available may still mix magazine research irretrievably with works on newspapers[2] or with popular press articles that are by no means empirical.[3] And individual library holdings cannot offer the complete array of book-length works on magazines that have been produced. Thus, to date, research on magazine editing and editors has not been viewed as a body, its parts having been published at wide intervals in a disparate range of publications and made relatively inaccessible due to poor cataloging and indexing.

It is the purpose of this article to survey and organize the existing scholarship and available sources on magazine editors and editing, and to suggest directions and possible frameworks for future research that may help to unify this branch of media study. The end result sought is an improved rigor in this scholarly field, along with development of stronger general editorial principles that can be of practical use to the magazine industry.

The two primary forms of magazine editing research have been biographies of individual magazine editors and examinations of editorial practices. Studies of editorial practices have usually taken one of three forms: surveys and interviews with editors, a plethora of raw empiricism on magazine editorial contents, and a few close examinations of editorial activities. A bibliographic analysis of the two broad areas, along with their main branches, is presented in upcoming sections, with a concluding section suggesting future directions and frameworks for this research stream.

The Biographical Emphasis

The earliest works on magazine editors and editing in the U.S. were biographies and autobiographies of editors, which began appearing in the 19th century[4] and have been published regularly since then.[5] Such books have been a popular choice on the "lists" of trade book editors in recent decades, and the latest selections are readily available.[6]

These books are rarely scholarly in nature, more often taking the form of chatty reminiscences of magazine editors who became public figures during their careers. Nonetheless, they form the earliest and most recurring chronicles of individual magazine editors. They offer a potential research source to current scholars, provided that additional sources can be found to verify contentions made in these largely anecdotal biographies and autobiographies.

These works also, perhaps unfortunately, have set magazine scholars on a biographical path. From the earliest magazine histories to the most recent studies of magazine editors appearing in *Journalism Quarterly* and *Journalism History*, by far the greatest number have taken the biographical form.[7]

The hazards of a scholarship built on biography are threefold: First, an unplanned series of individual biographies will almost certainly give a field a lack of continuity. Second, a few editors will achieve popularity among researchers, sometimes through a gradual celebrity based on the number of previous biographers' attentions and sometimes because those editors present the most accessible records and "paper trail." So the lives and works of a few editors are overemphasized, giving a false impression of the field as a whole. Finally, such biographically based histories as our current history of magazines have been criticized, especially since the 1960s, as taking an unwarranted "great man" approach—making the Romantic era assumption that individual genius, outside of political or cultural milieu, created the circumstances by which these editors rose to prominence.

This is not to say that many excellent biographical studies of magazine editors have not been offered, because they have. But an overall weakness in magazine editing research as a field stems from the biographical emphasis. Let us explore first the overall effects of this tendency toward biography, before examining the best research of this kind.

Effects of the Biographical Form on Magazine Editing Research

Lack of Continuity. The sporadic nature of magazine editing research is clear to anyone attempting to build a literature review in this field, and almost goes without saying. Comprehensive studies of magazine editing processes are few, and even descriptive synthesis is difficult to achieve, as one can see at the moments when Mott attempts it.[8]

A Popularity Factor. Whether because researchers become intrigued with a particular editor through previous biographies or because certain editors left more accessible records, magazine editing research gives great popularity to a very few editors, whose names have appeared again and again, while others are ignored who have perhaps an equal claim to history's notice.

E.L. Godkin, for instance, in spite of the comparatively small circulation of *The Nation* under his editorship and the existence of other news magazines in his era, has attracted numerous scholars and taken up a preponderance of magazine research's small space in the refereed journals. Ogden offered a biography and collected letters in 1907, and J. Murray built a 1954 dissertation on Godkin's life.[9] In 1974, Armstrong presented another collection of Godkin's letters.[10] Nevins' laudatory 1950 article on Godkin was echoed by McWilliams in 1965.[11] That same year, Miller's great-man biography of Godkin traced his life in great detail—birth, parentage, collegiate course of study, etc.[12] In 1968, Beisner profiled Godkin's "prejudices" against U.S. expansionism.[13] And in 1974, R. Murray rehashed Godkin's views on most everything.[14] Greater contributions to scholarship are made by Kaplan's 1963 examination of Godkin's influence on the Harvard- groomed U.S. power elite,[15] by Caudill's 1989 exploration of Godkin's influence on the developing social sciences,[16] and by Armstrong's 1954 dissertation on Godkin's relation to American foreign policy.[17]

Another editor who has captured many writers' imaginations is Sarah Josepha Hale, editor of the widely circulated and imitated 19th century magazine *Godey's Lady's Book*. Profiled by muckraker Ida Tarbell in 1910, [18] Hale has remained popular in successive decades, garnering no fewer than 15 biographies.[19] Horace Greeley, founding editor of the *New York Tribune*, has been another common biographical subject.[20] Edward Bok of *Ladies' Home Journal* and the muckraking editor Samuel McClure follow closely in popularity.[21] Thus, these four editors are overemphasized, while hundreds of others who were equally pathbreaking or influential have received little or no attention.

The "Great Man" Fallacy. Many, though assuredly not all, magazine editors' biographies are great man or great woman histories, presenting individuals as achieving fame chiefly through inherent genius. This approach tends to isolate these individuals conceptually from their circumstances, except perhaps when a biographer elects to show success obtained through the editor's personal conflict against circumstances, in the classic American "triumph over adversity" or "rags to riches" narrative. The Romanticism of this approach is no longer acceptable to most scholars not just because of its philosophical weakness, but because individual lives presented in isolation do not teach us enough about the broader subject, in this case, magazine editing.

Biography When Broadened

Fortunately, some scholars have worked from biographical forms to present research that shows editors in the editing role or in relationship to other elements of magazine editing as a process. Such elements have included editors' writings, the views expressed in their magazines, the influence of cultural milieu on their works, or conversely, the influence of their works on their cultural milieu and their audiences. It is from these researches that we can begin to discern some general principles of magazine editing for further exploration.

Editors in the Editing Role

Too few treatments of magazine editors' lives have focused on their performance of the tasks of an editor: negotiations with publisher and stock-holders, relationships with writers and other contributors, handling of texts, imprint of the editor's personal style upon the magazine.

Frank Luther Mott, in his seminal work of historical magazine research, the five-volume *History of American Magazines*, is among the few to offer commentary on editors at work.[22] His treatment is a mix of the biography with other forms (chiefly the case study). What Mott offers, though, tend to be unsupported evaluative comments appearing at intervals throughout his ency-clopedic work. These appear in three types of text: (a) within the "biogra-phies" of individual magazines, (b) in occasional two- to four-page summaries of general editing practices in an era, and (c) in brief summaries describing the "great" editors of an era.

In the context of his case histories of individual magazines, Mott often includes brief biographies of their editors. For example, in Volume 2 he de-scribes Rufus Porter, the peripatetic founder of *Scientific American* magazine (then named *New York Mechanic*), through his various incarnations as a cob-bler, housepainter, gunboat painter, drummer, sleigh painter, country school-master, inventor, and itinerant portrait painter, between which jobs he stopped in to edit the magazine. Porter sold the magazine shortly after starting it, to concentrate on obtaining patents for his washing machine, horsepowered boat, corn sheller, steam carriage, portable house, rotary plow, and so forth (pp. 316-317). Mott's intention in including personality sketches like this one seems to be to explain how the character of the editor led to the establishment and character of each magazine.

Mott also summarizes the editorial practices of an era in separate sections in all but the uncompleted final volume, usually taking only a few pages. In Volume 3, for instance, he quotes W.C. Brownell (of *The Nation*), describing how "we all three proof-read the entire paper and 'corrected' on occasion the editorial as well as the contributed material" (p. 19). In general, these summa-ries are too brief to offer much insight into editing processes. Finally, Mott presents sections on "great editors" of an era, chiefly offering the reader his unsupported judgments; for instance:

> William Dean Howells was perhaps a better editor than Holland [Dr. Josiah
> G. Holland of *Scribner's Monthly*]....In some respects Howells was a greater
> editor than Lowell had been; he had wider geographical sympathies, and he
> was a better worker. His delightful personality and his ability as a reviewer
> were helpful in his task. Henry Ward Beecher, of the *Christian Union*, was a
> great contributing editor, but not an office worker; and Henry C. Bowen, of
> the *Independent*, was a great publisher-editor. Atwater, Whedon, Bellows,
> and Bledsoe were able editors in the limited field of the religious review....
> (Volume 3, pp. 22-24).

Thus while Mott's volumes laid the groundwork for future researchers, there is not enough information on the editorial role to consider this work an adequate exploration.

Work initiated by Riley in 1988 and 1989, however, catalogs and depicts magazine editors with the depth Mott reserved for the magazines themselves.[23] Riley's *American Magazine Journalists* series, to which many current magazine scholars contributed, does show magazine editors at work. Using a biographical form, entries detail both the editor's biography *and* performance in the editing role. Each entry also includes the editor's positions, major writings, scholarly works about the editor, and location of library holdings of personal papers. The volumes are well edited and Riley directed the project so that each entry offers information on editorial performance.

The Riley volumes suggest ways of handling editorial biographies for future researchers planning longer treatments than were possible in the "dictionary" format that confined Riley's project. In general, the entries in Riley's work describe how the editor was drawn into this vocation, relationships of the editor to others at the magazine, influence of the editor, working style, major moments of decision or contention during the magazine editing career, remuneration and lifestyle, and themes of the editor's work.

Editors as Authors

A few researchers have examined editors' writings, both personal and published, and shown the relationships between these writings and performance in the editorial role. This research stream will eventually allow development of theories about magazine editors. We can learn, in particular, the relationships between various types of early writings and people's later development in the editorial role.

Journalism History has taken the lead in publishing these studies. Among them are Sullivan's work depicting G.D. Crain, Jr., in the role of 41-year publisher and editor of *Advertising Age*.[24] Also in the pages of *Journalism History*, Garrison showed how prolific writer Robert Walsh, who authored most of the text of his *American Review*, would persevere through several magazine business failures before reviving his *Review* and writing it successfully for the rest of his professional life.[25] Dickerson described William Cowper Brann's feisty *Iconoclast*, in which he attacked everything from the Baptists to the Hearsts in scathing terms Joseph Pulitzer would have shuddered to publish.[26] Dickerson didn't tell readers (but Rivers[27] did) the ultimate end of this kind of editorial performance. Brann was killed by a lawyer from Waco, Texas. Whitfield, also in the pages of *Journalism History*, showed how Dwight Macdonald's writings in his *Politics* magazine were reflective of his personal attitudes and his extraordinarily broad editorial judgments. And while these judgments did not result in financial success, Whitfield credits Macdonald's magazine with providing a critical bridge between the old Left and the new radicals of the 1960s.[28]

These articles are too few to provide an understanding of the relationships between editors' writings and their editorial success rate or their contributions to history. However, a continued effort to explore this area, particularly in broader studies, will help us to ascertain whether or not editors' writings can be used to predict editorial success.

Editorship as a "Platform"

Magazine editors often express strong views in their magazines; this is one general principle of magazine editing that has been well-researched at the individual case level. It has been amply demonstrated that editors' strong personal opinions lead to well-defined, closely targeted magazine contents. Whether these magazines are typically successful or not in the marketplace remains to be tested.

Gould showed that Josephine Turck Baker used her editorship of *Correct English* magazine to promulgate a usage-based English grammar.[29] Her views are still common among language teachers. Leverette and Shi examined Herbert Agar's use of his magazine *Free America* to promote a decentralized American government as "a Jeffersonian alternative to the New Deal."[30] Barrett Wendell is shown to have used the *Harvard Monthly* to provide a literary outlet for the New England school of writers,[31] while Noah Webster set out to create a showcase for American writers and to defend them from British critics with his *American Magazine*.[32] Mead described how Henry Cowells used *New Music Quarterly* to promote and offer an outlet for "ultra-modern" music,[33] while Servos explored Wilder Bancroft's editorial use of the *Journal of Physical Chemistry* to promote his views about the study of chemistry.[34]

Women's rights were championed by many 19th century magazine editors, as reported by Stearns,[35] Tinling,[36] Gaylor,[37] and Jolliffe,[38] perhaps because women were a major target audience for magazines in that century, giving women's rights a clear audience appeal.

Broad liberal reform platforms have been common among magazine editors since the 1820s, according to researchers. Joseph Bristow published *Irrigation Farmer* to crusade for liberal farm reform,[39] and Freda Kirchwey used her editorship at *The Nation* to campaign for birth control freedom, social welfare, and political liberalism.[40] Editor Max Aesoli promoted liberal views on civil liberties, nuclear testing, and American foreign policy from the platform of *The Reporter Magazine* in the 1950s and the 1960s.[41] Dorothy Day advocated broad employment reform measures in the *Catholic Worker*,[42] and Philip Rav espoused a wider range of radical views in the *Partisan Review*.[43]

A key area for future exploration will be broader tests of the success rates of magazines when editors use them as platforms for the expression of decided opinions. Are these editors as attractive to their own readers as they have been to scholarly researchers? Is strength of purpose indeed an attribute that will predict editorial success? Or are these particular editors simply more attractive to historians because they offer so much contentious material or appeal to modern liberal social values?

Editors and Societal Influences

While most biographies and autobiographies of editors do not relate the life stories of their main subjects without *any* reference to society, culture, and politics, most use world events as a backdrop against which their character acts. However, a few very fine studies show the constant interplay between the magazine editor and society with an engaging conceptual depth.

Chief among these is James Baughman's biography of Henry Luce, subtitled *And the Rise of the American News Media*.[44] Baughman avoids the "great man" history style often seen in biographical treatments of Luce.[45] Instead, he offers close descriptions of Luce's activities and the actions and reactions of his colleagues, competitors, and audience to the contents of Luce's news media—and then Luce's actions and reactions to these events. Baughman's use of this action-reaction pattern helps offer a richer view of Luce than is obtained from other biographical treatments that center chiefly on the actions initiated by the protagonist. (Moreover, the book, despite its conceptual complexity, is eminently readable.)

Another such work is Rusnak's intriguing look at Walter Hines Page's early 20th century editorship of *World's Work*.[46] While it comes to no resounding conclusion, the monograph offers a model of editorial biography, in that Rusnak moves from Page's private thoughts (in diaries and letters) to his public thoughts (in his novels and in his magazine, *World's Work*) to an audience reaction so strong that Page began to hide his identity behind pseudonymous writing. Rusnak also judges Page, who wrote a great deal on race and labor issues, using the standards of Page's own era; where Page appears racist today, his ideas were moderate to progressive early in the century, according to Rusnak. Like Baughman, Rusnak offers a biographical treatment with great depth that explores the interconnectedness of the editor, era, and audience.

Several shorter works explore editors' magazine work in relation to audiences and audience reaction. McDonald describes the editors of two late 19th-century women's magazines that attempted to start free correspondence universities for their readers.[47] The strengths of McDonald's approach are that she shows how these two editors were capitalizing on ideas from larger, more expensive magazines in the same market and that she shows how their audiences responded—first by enrolling in the People's University in great numbers (50,000 joined) and then by abandoning the project when rumors of financial malfeasance began to circulate.

Socolofsky's examination of Arthur Capper's agricultural magazines is another study that shows the interrelatedness of editor, magazine, audience, and environment,[48] as does Hoover's 1948 biography of *New England* magazine editor Park Benjamin, who influenced and was influenced by developments in American literature in his day.[49]

Another important study in this vein is Gillespie's 1991 article on children's magazine editor and publisher Samuel Griswold Goodrich.[50] Gillespie shows the exchanges of influence between Goodrich and the progressive educational theoreticians of his lifetime. He used the vehicle of children's periodicals to influence the style of children's education available in the 19th century, making learning more entertaining. But he was by no means the architect of this new learning style, which was developed by many teachers both in America and in Europe. Like Baughman and Rusnak, Gillespie draws upon the public and private writings of the magazine editor, while also exploring competing publications and using the pedagogical journals of the day to establish the tenor of 19th century educational theory.

Of all the biographical approaches to the study of magazine editors and editing, these six are the most sophisticated and the most worthy of imitation. They stand back far enough from their subject editor to treat that editor as an individual among other individuals. Working style, personal writings, social and political influence, and relationships and interactions become the foci of the research. The reader gains insight, then, into more than the cradle-to-grave narrative of a single life.

Editorial Practices

In the 1980s, a new way of looking at magazine editors began to develop in the literature. Scholars became interested in the interpersonal relations that occurred as magazines were edited. Four methods of testing editorial practices have been used thus far: surveys, content analyses, close studies of a few editor-writer or editor-publisher relationships, and, most recently, quantitative studies of editorial interactions.

Surveys and Interviews

Surveys and interviews that explore magazine editing practices are largely a product of the late 1970s and early 1980s, when Ranly's study of Sunday newspaper magazine editors' attitudes was published,[51] as well as Hayes' look at newspaper magazines' relations with freelancers,[52] and Smith and Fowler's 1979 questionnaire on in-office socialization of underlings by magazine editors.[53]

The chief difficulty with using surveys or interviews to study editorial practices is that the researcher can find that empiricism has been essentially delegated to the nonresearcher answering the survey questions. Respondents are generally honest, but they may provide answers that they perceive as "ideal"—or include falsehoods that they perceive as true. In either case, direct observation might prove the respondents' perceptions to be inaccurate. Thus, the safest use of surveying is to test respondents' perceptions and attitudes. In a few cases, survey-based studies of magazine editing have indeed sought to clarify editors' attitudes.

Ranly, for instance, studied Sunday magazine editors.[54] The Ranly study remains one of the most sophisticated magazine editing surveys, because the editors were asked to respond more to attitude questions and less to factual questions about their activities. Statistical techniques were used to cluster editors' agreement or disagreement with various attitude statements, showing when one attitude was likely to be related to another. Ranly was able to identify four main types of Sunday newspaper magazine editors, in two larger groups: 1) committed intellectuals writing for real "readers," 2) contented and rather unambitious editors; and two smaller groups, 3) editors who felt Sunday magazines were undervalued and understaffed, and 4) light-minded, leisure-oriented editors. If the Ranly study has a flaw, it is the small population studied, but since Ranly sent the survey to the entire population (of 51) and obtained a 67% response rate, he can hardly be faulted for that.

A second intriguing approach is offered by Jeffers, who developed survey results on editors' perceptions of their readers' involvement, problem identification skills, and constraints, versus the editors' perceptions of their roles in helping readers solve their problems through the magazine.[55] The editors he surveyed perceived their readers as being most concerned about issues that were both proximate and "personally manageable". The chief difficulty of relying on Jeffers' findings is that this survey went to only 29 editors of "single-breed livestock magazines in the U.S." Researchers now have an opportunity to broaden the sample Jeffers used, to learn whether consumer magazines or less specialized magazines—or other equally specialized magazines—would yield similar results. Further exploration should also include a test of the audiences. Do they indeed rely on their magazines for problem-solving advice on proximate and controllable problems, as these editors believe?

Other surveys, while interesting, do not offer this depth of analysis. Smith and Fowler's 1979 survey of magazine editors, meant to test relationships between editor demographics and certain office management styles, does not offer the solid findings hoped for because the authors rely on their respondent editors for assessments of their own assertiveness, decision-making style, involvement with staff, willingness to compromise, etc.[56] These self-assessments are not likely to be reliable.

Hesterman's two survey-based studies of the ethics practices and policies of magazines are stronger because her questions are chiefly questions of fact: Do you have policies and what are they? These represent a useful development of baseline information about broad editorial practices current in the magazine industry. However, unlike Ranly, Hesterman does not report more complex analysis of these findings to provide some sense of how presence of one policy might influence or preclude presence of another.[57]

Hayes offers the most simplistic of editorial practices surveys, asking editors whether interest in their magazine had increased in the past five years, whether the magazine accepted free-lanced articles, what formats were preferred for submissions, and what payments might be expected. Simple percentages of responses were offered, though results were inconclusive on the final two items.[58]

Clearly, the survey method has not been adequately explored by magazine editing researchers. Several roadblocks to survey research exist in this field. First, the expense of surveying may not be justified, since magazine research often does not find an outlet in the journals. (Note that only two of the surveys cited above appeared in the academic journals, and those were published 15 years ago.) Also, response rates are typically low, even after three mailings,[59] and, as Prior-Miller notes, no standard typology of magazines exists, so that categorization and sampling are chronically open to challenge.[60] Nonetheless, surveys and interviews remain a largely open opportunity for researching magazine editors' attitudes and perceptions.

Content Analyses: Ethical Tests
versus Relationship Tests

Not covered in depth here is the enormous literature on magazine editors' editorial choices—that is, the hundreds of content analyses of magazines. Researchers have perused magazines for coverage of everything from motorcycles[61] to the elderly[62] and from insects[63] to architectural modernism.[64]

Ethical Tests. Most such studies are built on the unstated assumption that magazines bear a Hutchins' Commission-type "social responsibility" to the public. There are two problems with this.

First, the social responsibility of magazines to present a broad, unbiased, whole-world view is an arguable premise, even for those who would hold newspapers to such a standard. From their inception in the U.S., magazines have generally been created to serve specific audiences and particular advertiser categories.[65] (See, for instance, any *Simmons Market Research Bureau* volume on magazines.)

Second, if the researcher has an expectation of social responsibility from magazines, let it be a stated assumption from a clearly defined ethical standard, and let the research project be developed openly from that theoretical base. Lambeth's *Committed Journalism* describes a current ethic of social responsibility as "'otherdirectedness' in attitude and a willingness to consider the effects of individual actions and institutional practices upon others, upon the public." (p. 8) However, Lambeth also notes that social responsibility theory is not useful in many cases; researchers must carefully explore the ethical premises under which they will operate, and the ramifications of these, before beginning to count up favorable, unfavorable, and neutral magazine articles.[66]

Relationship Tests. A few content analysis researchers *have* offered more analytical examinations of magazine editorial choices, however. What differentiates these studies from social-responsibility-based content analyses is that the magazine contents are shown *in relation to* some other factor, for example, a prevailing social condition, the editor's philosophy, or the structure or organization of the magazine.

Kessler examined the relationship of cigarette advertising income on the smoking-related warnings in women's magazine editorial contents, after first documenting the growing cancer risk to American women from cigarettes.[67] Bradley uses hegemony theory to compare the daily life of magazine editor Margaret Cousins to the life Cousins prescribed for her women readers.[68] While Cousins preached the nuclear family and stay-at-home "mom" to *Good Housekeeping* readers, she lived with a woman friend in a home kept clean by their maid—and had all her parties catered. Bradley's work suggests that Cousins' career can be interpreted using hegemony theory because Cousins participated in a shared societal value system that benefited an elite, but not herself. Not only did she promulgate instructions on a lifestyle she didn't embrace, but her career was eventually stifled by hegemonic controls on women; women rarely moved into controlling positions in the elite in Cousins' era, which eventually stopped her upward promotion at the magazine.

Finally, Jolliffe and Catlett test the common assumption that adding more women to a medium's reporting and editing staff will decrease stereotyping of women.[69] Using the "seven sisters" magazines over a 20-year period, they look for correlations in gender role stereotyping and the presence and/or dominance of women on the editorial and executive staffs at those magazines. Their findings suggest that women magazine editors may be no more or less likely to stereotype or talk down to their audiences than men editors are; instead, women "go with the flow," editing in response to society's general attitudes toward women.

Content analysis is a greatly overworked method of examining magazine editing, most likely because it is inexpensive and provides large sample sizes easily. The large sample sizes give an appearance of statistical importance to the findings, increasing the likelihood of publication.

Also helping boost these studies' "publishability" is often the appeal of the subject matters studied. Content analyses of magazine coverage of disadvantaged groups or women, for instance, appeal to this generation of scholars' liberal social values (or political correctness). Content analyses of political coverage appeals to the many reporters-turned-academicians to whom the political power of the press is more important than its actual internal workings.

Future studies should be openly developed as social responsibility or ethical performance tests or, better, should tie content findings with the magazine's societal environment, the editor's life, background, or attitudes, or the magazine's staffing, as illustrated above—or set out to test relationships between the magazine contents and some other aspect of the magazine organization.

Qualitative Studies

A few editorial process studies have been offered that delve closely into a single relationship between an editor and a specific writer or publisher. Bradshaw briefly describes Horace Greeley's relationships with his correspondents,[70] and Robinson explores the working relationship between editor S.S. McClure and writer Willa Cather.[71] Most charming is Leary's 1985 article describing how *New Yorker* editor Katherine White served as both mentor and matchmaker for writer Jean Stafford.[72] And Graybar details, with perhaps less charm but equal erudition, the strained relationship between editor Albert Shaw, founder of the *Review of Reviews*, and his financier-publisher William Stead.[73]

Finally, Cyganowski, in her book *Magazine Editors and Professional Authors in Nineteenth-Century America*, provides the finest model of qualitative research on editorial practices.[74] Describing first the magazine industry in the 19th century and its cultural and social settings, Cyganowski then explores in detail how such editors as James Russell Lowell, William Dean Howells, and Richard Watson Gilder conducted their relationships with contributing writers. She shows these editors balancing their need for profit against their desire to improve American literature and yet to appeal to broad audiences. These editors also coached a generation of writers to make their artistic output more palatable to the newly literate mass audience of the day.

Such studies of editors "at work" are no doubt more difficult to perform than studies of single individuals, but have the potential to offer more insight into the techniques, processes, and thinking of successful editors.

Quantitative Studies

Only two quantitative studies of the magazine editing process were discovered for this review, both by this article's author.[75] In 1993, I reported a multiple case study in which I observed the activities of editors at six major magazines during the editorial selection process. The editors' activities were compared with those of over 400 managers in other industries, using Luthans' typology of managers' activities. Successful and effective magazine editors' activities were found to closely parallel the activities of managers in other industries.

Again using a multiple-case-study approach, I tested the sequential interactions among senior editors, editors, and writers during editorial meetings at four highly successful consumer magazines.[76] I determined that the exertion of power and influence by senior editors over their staff members was minimal in these meetings, with most conversational exchanges conducted at the "simple exchange" level. Very little aggression or contention occurred during the meetings except among equally-ranked staff members, and ideas were rarely greeted with negative responses by superiors.

Clearly, quantitative analysis is a wide-open frontier for the magazine editing researcher. Tests of magazine editing processes are a largely unexplored territory.

New Directions

Magazine editing research has had a long-time focus on the individual editor as a person, rather than as an editor. Biographies of magazine editors in the model established by Riley will remain an important portion of magazine research in the future. Many major contributors to the magazine industry have yet to be examined in substantial biographies. In addition to a greater range of subjects, future biographical studies should investigate the editorial role and should seek an intellectual depth that steps back from individual personalities to show the exchange of influences between the editor, the magazine text, the audience, and the society.

Additional studies of editorial practices are also needed. Surveys of editors' attitudes and perceptions, built on those by Ranly[77] and Jeffers,[78] would give us much greater insights into commonalties in how editors think. A whole new fabric of content analyses can be developed, either building an ethical framework from which to measure magazine performance[79] or tying contents to other measures (as in Kessler,[80] Bradley,[81] or Jolliffe and Catlett[82]).

In addition to these types of studies that build on the past, future magazine researchers will have a whole range of possibilities for exploration, opened up by the current generation of magazine researchers and their attempts to build a platform of magazine theories to test and expand. This "platform of theories" can provide a springboard to greater insights and new directions of attention.

Future researchers in the magazine editing subfield will explore relationships among various players in the making of magazines. They will closely examine influence exchanges—influences of editors and influences on editors. They will examine the effects of organizational structures and flow of communication on magazine texts. And they will step outside the magazine to explore deliberate access attempts, as outside interest groups work to influence editors and thus magazine contents.

Future researchers may eschew biography and "plain vanilla" content analyses in favor of other methods, such as ethnography, semantic or rhetorical analysis, tests of information flow patterns, Q-analysis, sequential communication charting, attitude surveys, and a myriad of experimental tests of editing processes.

Greater sophistication and stronger theoretical frames will undoubtedly increase the magazine researchers' access to academic journals as the research itself offers greater insights.

Notes

[1] Marcia Prior-Miller and Kellie L. Esch, "A Census and Analysis of Journals Publishing Research About Magazines, 1977-1987," Paper presented at the Association for Education in Journalism and Mass Communication (AEJMC) annual meeting, Minneapolis, August, 1990; Peter Gerlach, "Research about Magazines Appearing in Journalism Quarterly," Journalism Quarterly 54:1 (Spring 1987): 179-182.

[2] See, for example, Wm. David Sloan, compiler, American Journalism History: An Annotated Bibliography (Greenwood Press: New York, 1989).

[3] See, for example, Fred K. Paine and Nancy E. Payne, Magazines: A Bibliography for Their Analysis, with Annotations and Study Guide (Metuchen, NJ: Scarecrow, 1987).

[4] Horace Greeley, Recollections of a Busy Life (New York: J.B. Ford, 1858).

[5] See, for example, Edward Bok, The Americanization of Edward Bok (New York: Scribner's, 1920); Edna Woolman Chase and Ilka Chase, Always in Vogue (Garden City, NY: Doubleday, 1954); Bruce Gould and Beatrice Blackmar Gould, American Story (New York: Harper and Row, 1968); Arthur J. Larsen, ed., Crusader and Feminist: Letters of Jane Grey Swisshelm, 1858-1865 (St. Paul: Minnesota Historical Society, 1934); S.S. McClure, My Autobiography (New York: Stokes, 1914); Roy Newquist, Conversations (Chicago: Rand McNally, 1967), 384-397; Rollo Ogden, ed., Life and Letters of Edwin Lawrence Godkin, 2 vols. (New York: Macmillan, 1907); Whitelaw Reid, Horace Greeley (New York, 1879); Lucy E. Sanford, "Mrs. Sarah J. Hale," Granite Monthly 3 (March 1880): 208-211.

[6] Douglass Cater, "Max Ascoli, of the Reporter," Encounter 50 (April 1978): 49-52; Gardner Cowles, Mike Looks Back: The Memoirs of Gardner Cowles (New York: Gardner Cowles, 1985); Osborn Elliott, The World of Oz (New York: Viking Press, 1980); Martha Foley, The

Story of Story Magazine (New York: Norton, 1980); Lenore Hershey, Between the Covers: The Lady's Own Journal (New York: CowardMcCann, 1983); Elizabeth Moulton, "Remembering George Davis," Virginia Quarterly Review 55 (Spring 1979): 284-295.

[7] E. Caudill, "Godkin and the Science of Society," Journalism Quarterly 66:1 (Spring 1989): 57-64; Gary Coll, "Noah Webster, Magazine Editor and Publisher," Journalism History 11:1-2 (Spring/Summer 1984): 26-31; Donona Dickerson, "William Cowper Brann: Nineteenth Century Press Critic," Journalism History 5:2 (Summer 1978): 42-45; Bruce Garrison, "Robert Walsh's American Review: America's First Quarterly," Journalism History 8:1 (Spring 1981): 14-17; Frank Luther Mott, History of American Magazines, in 5 vols. (Cambridge, MA: Harvard University Press, 1938-1968); Randall Murray, "Edwin Lawrence Godkin: Unbending Editor in Times of Change," Journalism History 1:3 (Autumn 1974): 77-81, 89; Nora C. Quebrad, "Wilmer Atkinson and the Early Farm Journal," Journalism Quarterly 47 (Spring 1970): 65-70, 80; Paul W. Sullivan, "G.D. Crain Jr. and the Founding of Advertising Age," Journalism History 1:3 (Autumn 1973/74): 94-95; Stephen J. Whitfield, "Dwight MacDonald's Politics Magazine," Journalism Quarterly 25 (Spring 1948): 212-217.

[8] Mott, History of American Magazines.

[9] James G. Murray, "Edwin Lawrence Godkin and The Nation: A Study in Political, Economic and Social Morality" (Ph.D. diss., New York University, 1954); Ogden, Life of Godkin.

[10] William M. Armstrong, ed., The Gilded Age Letters of E.L. Godkin (Albany, NY: State University of New York Press, 1974).

[11] Carey McWilliams, "One Hundred Years of The Nation," Journalism Quarterly 42 (1965): 189-197; Allan Nevins, "E.L. Godkin, Victorian Liberal," Nation, 22 July 1950, 76-79.

[12] Aaron Miller, "The Paradoxical Godkin, Founder of the Nation," Journalism Quarterly 42 (Spring 1965): 198-202.

[13] Robert L. Beisner, Twelve Against Empire: The Anti-Imperialists, 1898-1900 (New York: McGraw-Hill, 1968).

[14] R. Murray, "Godkin: Unbending Editor."

[15] Sidney Kaplan, "Harvard and the Influence of Godkin's Nation," Journalism Quarterly 40 (Autumn 1963): 599-602.

[16] Caudill, "Godkin and the Science of Society."

[17] William M. Armstrong, "E.L. Godkin and American Foreign Policy, 1865-1900" (Ph.D. diss., Stanford University, 1954).

[18] Ida M. Tarbell, "Sarah Josepha Hale," American 69 (March 1910): 666-669.

[19] Walter Davenport and James C. Derieux, Ladies, Gentlemen and Editors (New York: Doubleday, 1960); Isabelle Webb Entrikin, Sarah Josepha Hale and Godey's Lady's Book, (Lancaster, PA: Lancaster Press/Entrikin, 1946); Ruth E. Finley, The Lady of "Godey's": Sarah Josepha Hale, (Philadelphia: Lippincott, 1931); Karol Gyman, "The 'Woman's Sphere': A Study of the Life and Work of Sarah Josepha Hale" (Master's thesis, Bowling Green State University, 1973); Ralph Nading Hill, "Mr. Godey's Lady," American Heritage, October 1958, 20-27; Merle M. Hoover, Park Benjamin: Poet and Editor (New York: Columbia University Press, 1948); Lawrence Martin, "The Genesis of Godey's Lady's Book," New England Quarterly 1 (1928): 41-70; Patricia Ann Okker, "Feminizing the Voice of Literary Authority: Sarah J. Hale's Editorship of the Ladies' Magazine and Godey's Lady's Book" (Ph.D. diss., Dissertation Abstracts International, Vol. 51:4, October 1990), 1230A-1231A; Glenda Gates Riley, "The Subtle Subversion: Changes in the Traditional Image of the American Woman," The Historian 32 (1970): 210-227; Sherbrooke Rogers, Sarah Josepha Hale: A New England Pioneer, 1788-1879 (Grantham, NH: Tompson & Rutter, 1985); Richard F. Warner, "Godey's Lady's Book," American Mercury 2 (July 1924), 399-405; Helen Beal Woodward, "The Oblique Editor: Sarah Josepha Hale," in The Bold Women (Freeport, NY: Books for Libraries Press, 1953), 181-200; Richardson Wright, "The Madonna in Bustles," in Forgotten Ladies: Nine Portraits from the American Family Al-

bum (Philadelphia: J.B. Lippincott, 1928), 187-217; Angela Marie Howard Zophy, "For the Improvement of My Sex: Sarah Josepha Hale's Editorship of Godey's Lady's Book, 1837-1877" (Ph.D. diss., Ohio State University, 1978).

[20] Greeley, Recollections; William Harlan Hale, Horace Greeley, Voice of the People (New York: Harper, 1950); Lurton D. Ingersoll, The Life of Horace Greeley, Founder of the New York Tribune (Chicago: Union, 1873); Jeter Allen Isley, Horace Greeley and the Republican Party, 1853-1861: A Study of the New York Tribune (Princeton, NJ: Princeton University Press, 1947); James Parton, Life of Horace Greeley (New York: Mason Brothers, 1855); Reid, Greeley; R.M. Robbins, "Horace Greeley: Land Reform and Unemployment," Agriculture History 7 (1933); Earle D. Ross, "Horace Greeley and the South, 1865-1872," SA Quarterly 16 (1917): 324-338; Earle D. Ross, "Horace Greeley and the West," Mississippi Valley Historical Review 20 (1933): 63-74; Glyndon Garlock Van Deusen, Horace Greeley: Nineteenth Century Crusader (New York: Hill and Wang, 1953); Osward Garrison Villard, Fighting Years: Memoirs of a Liberal Editor (New York: Harcourt, Brace, 1939); Francis N. Zabriskie, Horace Greeley, the Editor (New York: Funk & Wagnalls, 1890).

[21] See Bok, Americanization; Ernest Schell, "Edward Bok and the Ladies' Home Journal," American History Illustrated, February 1982, 16-23; David Ski, "Edward Bok and the Simple Life," American Heritage, December 1984, 100-109; Sarah Stage, Female Complaints: Lydia Pinkham and the Business of Women's Medicine (New York: W.W. Norton, 1979); Salme Harju Steinberg, Reformer in the Marketplace, (Baton Rouge, LA: Louisiana State University Press, 1979); James P. Wood, The Curtis Magazines (New York: Ronald Press, 1971), for studies of Bok; and McClure, Autobiography; Peter Lyon, Success Story: The Life and Times of S.S. McClure (New York: Scribner's, 1963); Robert Stinson, "S.S. McClure's My Autobiography: The Progressive as Self-made Man," American Quarterly 22 (1970): 203-212; Robert William Stinson, "McClure's Road to McClure's: How Revolutionary Were 1890s Magazines?" Journalism Quarterly 47 (1970): 256-262; Robert William Stinson, "S.S. McClure and His Magazine: A Study in the Editing of McClure's, 1983-1913" (Ph.D. diss., Indiana University, 1971).

[22] Mott, History of American Magazines.

[23] Riley, Sam G., ed., Dictionary of Literary Biography: American Magazine Journalists, 1741-1850 and 1850-1900 (Ann Arbor: Gale Research, 1988, 1989).

[24] Sullivan, "G.D. Crain, Jr."

[25] Bruce Garrison, "Robert Walsh's American Review: America's First Quarterly," Journalism History 8:1 (Spring 1981): 14-17.

[26] Donona Dickerson, "William Cowper Brann: Nineteenth Century Press Critic," Journalism History 5:2 (Summer 1978): 42-45.

[27] William L. Rivers, "William Cowper Brann and his Iconoclast," Journalism Quarterly 35 (1958): 433-438.

[28] Whitfield, "Dwight MacDonald's Politics Magazine."

[29] Christopher Gould, "Correct English Magazine and the 'Science' of Language Study," Paper presented at the Conference on College Composition and Communication annual meeting, Atlanta, GA, 19-21 March 1987.

[30] William E. Leverette, Jr., and David E. Shi, "Herbert Agar and Free America: A Jeffersonian Alternative to the New Deal," Journal of American Studies 16 (April 1982): 189-206.

[31] Paul E. Cohen, "Barrett Wendell and the Harvard Literary Revival," New England Quarterly 52 (December 1979): 483-499.

[32] Coll, "Noah Webster, Editor and Publisher."

[33] Rita H. Mead, "Cowell, Ives and New Music," Music Quarterly 66 (October 1980): 538-559.

[34] John W. Servos, "Disciplinary Program that Failed: Wilder D. Bancroft and the Journal of Physical Chemistry, 1896-1933," Isis 73 (June 1982): 207-232.

[35] Bertha Monica Stearns, "A Speculation Concerning Charles Brockden Brown," Pennsylvania Magazine of History and Biography 59 (1935): 99-105.

[36] Marion Tinling, "Hermione Day and The Hesperian," California History 94 (Winter 1980): 282-289.

[37] Annie Laurie Gaylor, "Jane Grey Swisshelm: A Notorious Editor," Feminist Connection (January 1985): 3.

[38] Lee Jolliffe, "Lucy Stone," in Sam Riley, ed., American Magazine Journalists, 1850-1990 (Detroit: Gale/Bruccoli Clark Layman, 1989), 283-285; Jolliffe, "Liberal Feminism: The Strategies of an Activist Audience," Paper presented at the AEJMC annual meeting, Minneapolis, MN, 14 August 1990; Jolliffe, "Women's Magazines in the 19th Century, Part I: A Popular Medium Gives Women Power as a Cultural Force" and "Part II: Lucy Stone's Journal Popularizes Women's Suffrage," Journal of Popular Culture 27:4 (Winter 1994): 125-140.

[39] A. Bower Sageser, Joseph L. Bristow: Kansas Progressive (Lawrence: University Press of Kansas, 1968).

[40] Sara Alpern, Freda Kirchwey: A Woman of The Nation (Cambridge, MA: Harvard University Press, 1987).

[41] Martin K. Doudna, Concern About the Planet: The Reporter Magazine and American Liberalism, 1949-1968, (Westport, CN: Greenwood, 1977).

[42] Nancy L. Roberts, Dorothy Day, and The Catholic Worker (Albany: State University of New York, 1984); Nancy L. Roberts, "Journalism for Justice: Dorothy Day and the Catholic Worker," Journalism History 10 (Spring/Summer, 1983): 2-9.

[43] William Barrett, "Portrait of the Radical as an Aging Man," Commentary, May 1979, 40-47.

[44] James L. Baughman, Henry R. Luce and the Rise of the American News Media (Boston, MA: Twayne, 1987).

[45] See, for example, David Halberstam, The Powers That Be (New York: Knopf, 1979).

[46] Robert J. Rusnak, Walter Hines Page and The World's Work, 1900-1913 (Washington, DC: University Press of America, 1982).

[47] S.W. McDonald, "Two Popular Editors of the Gilded Age: Mass Culture, Magazines and Correspondence," Journal of Popular Culture 15:2 (Fall 1981): 50-61.

[48] Homer E. Socolofsky, "The Capper Farm Press Experience in Western Agricultural Journalism," Journal of the West 19 (April 1980): 22-29.

[49] Hoover, "Park Benjamin: Poet and Editor."

[50] Erin Claire Gillespie, "The Children's Periodicals of Samuel Griswold Goodrich: Insight into an Era of Educational Evolution," Paper presented at the AEJMC annual meeting (Boston, MA, 7-10 August 1991).

[51] Don Ranly, "A Look at Editors, Content, and Future of the Sunday Newspaper Magazine," Journalism Quarterly 58 (Summer 1981): 279-285.

[52] John P. Hayes, "Newspaper-sponsored Magazines as a Market for Freelancers," Journalism Quarterly 56:3 (Autumn 1979): 586-589.

[53] Edward J. Smith and Gilbert L. Fowler, Jr., "A Preliminary Report on Five Questions Concerning Magazine Editors and Magazine Operations," Paper presented at the AEJMC annual meeting, Houston, August, 1979.

[54] Ranly, "A Look at Editors."

[55] Dennis W. Jeffers, "A 'Situational' and 'Coorientational' Measure of Specialized Magazine Editors' Perceptions of Readers," Paper presented at the AEJMC annual meeting, Gainesville, August 1984.

[56] Smith and Fowler, "A Preliminary Report on Five Questions."

[57] Vicki Hesterman, "Consumer Magazines and Ethical Standards: A Preliminary Study of 100 American Magazines," Paper presented at the AEJMC annual meeting, Norman, OK, August 1986; Vicki Hesterman, "The Practices and Policies of City and Regional Magazines: A Survey of Media Managers," Paper presented at the AEJMC annual meeting, Portland, OR, July 1988.

[58] Hayes, "Newspaper-sponsored Magazines."

[59] See, for example, Hayes, "Newspaper-sponsored Magazines."

[60] Marcia Prior-Miller, "Toward a Typology of Magazines," Paper presented at the AEJMC annual meeting, Montreal, August, 1992.

[61] Richard B. Christensen, Motorcycles in Magazines, 1895-1985 (Metuchen, NJ: Scarecrow Press, 1985).

[62] S. Bramlett-Solomon and V. Wilson, "Images of the Elderly in Life and Ebony," Journalism Quarterly 66:1 (Spring 1989): 185-188; Catherine Lucille Wells, "The Portrayal of the Elderly in General Circulation Magazines: 1960-1980" (Ph.D. diss., Wayne State University, 1989).

[63] Wayne S. Moore, David R. Bowers, and Theodore A. Granovsky, "What Are Magazines Telling Us About Insects?", Journalism Quarterly 59:3 (Fall 1982): 353-359.

[64] Daniel Platt Gregory, "Magazine Modern: A Study of the American Architectural Press, 1919-1930" (Ph.D. diss., University of California, Berkeley, 1982).

[65] Jolliffe, "Women's Magazines in the 19th Century."

[66] Edmund Lambeth, Committed Journalism, (Bloomington: University of Indiana Press, 1986).

[67] Lauren Kessler, "Women's Magazines' Coverage of Smoking Related Health Hazards," Journalism Quarterly 66:2 (Summer 1989): 316-322.

[68] Patricia Bradley, "Maintaining Separate Spheres: The Career of Margaret Cousins," Paper presented at the AEJMC annual meeting, Memphis, TN, 3-6 August 1985.

[69] Lee Jolliffe and Terri Catlett, "Seven Sister's Women's Magazines, 1965-1985: The Effects of Women Editors on Contents," Journalism Quarterly (Winter 1994), in press.

[70] James Stanford Bradshaw, "'To Correspondents'— Horace Greeley," Journalism Quarterly 58 (1981): 644-646, 673.

[71] Phyllis C. Robinson, "Mr. McClure and Willa," American Heritage, October 1983, 26-31.

[72] William Leary, "Jean Stafford, Katharine White, and the New Yorker," Sewanee Review 93 (Fall 1985): 584596.

[73] Lloyd J. Graybar, "Albert Shaw and the Founding of the Review of Reviews, 1891-97," Journalism Quarterly 49 (Winter 1972): 692-7; 716.

[74] Carol Klimick Cyganowski, Magazine Editors and Professional Authors in Nineteenth-Century America (New York & London: Garland, 1988).

[75] Lee Jolliffe, "Power and Influence in the Magazine Editorial Meeting: A Sequential Analysis," Paper presented at the AEJMC annual meeting, August 1994, Atlanta, GA.

[76] Lee Jolliffe, "Magazine Editors — 'Personalities', Copyeditors, or Managers?" Paper presented at the AEJMC annual meeting, August 1993, Kansas City; Jolliffe, "Power and Influence."

[77] Ranly, "A Look at Editors."

[78] Jeffers, "Situational and Coorientational Measure."

[79] Lambeth, Committed Journalism.

[80] Kessler, "Women's Magazines' Coverage of Smoking."

[81] Bradley, "Maintaining Separate Spheres." [82] Jolliffe and Catlett, "Seven Sister's Women's Magazines."

Additional Sources Examined

Martin S. Ackerman, The Curtis Affair (New York: A. Nash Publishing Co., 1970).

P. Benson, "No 'Murmured Thanks'; Women and Johnson Brigham's Midland Monthly," American Studies 21:1 (Spring 1980): 57-72.

Noel F. Busch, Briton Hadden: A Biography of the Co-founder of Time (New York: Farrar Straus, 1949).

H.F. Cline, "Benjamin Orange Flower and the Arena, 1889-1909," Journalism Quarterly 17 (June 1940): 139-50.

Mathew J. Culligan, The Curtis Culligan Story (New York: Crown, 1970).

John Eldridge Drewery, Some Magazines and Magazine Makers (Boston, MA: The Stratford Co, 1924).

W.E.B. DuBois, "Editing 'The Crisis'," Crisis 58 (1951): 147-151, 213.

Michael Emery and Edwin Emery, The Press and America: An Interpretive History of the Mass Media, 7th ed., (Englewood Cliffs: Simon & Schuster, 1992).

Jean Folkerts and Dwight Teeter, Voices of a Nation: A History of Mass Media in America, 2nd ed. (Columbus, OH: Macmillan, 1993).

Joseph C. Goulden, The Curtis Caper (New York, G.P. Putnam's Sons, 1965).

Billy Joe Hill, Jr., "Controversy over Free Expression Viewed as Social Drama: A Case Study of Larry Flynt and Huster Magazine" (Ph.D. diss., Florida State University, 1982).

M.A. DeWolfe Howe, The Atlantic Monthly and Its Makers, (Boston: Atlantic Monthly Press, 1919).

Dale Kramer, Ross and The New Yorker (Garden City, NY: Doubleday, 1951).

Benjamin Morgan Lewis, A Register of Editors, Printers, and Publishers of American Magazines, 1741-1810 (New York: New York Public Library, 1957).

Beverly J. G. Loftus, "Ezra and Bollingren Prize: The Controversy in Periodicals," Journalism Quarterly 39 (Summer 1962): 347-354.

Jayne E. Marek, "I know Why I say What I Do Say: Women Editors and Critics in the 'Little' Magazines, 1912-1933" (Ph.D. diss., University of Wisconsin-Madison, 1991).

August Meier, "Booker T. Washington and the Negro Press: With Special Reference to the Colored American Magazine," Journal of Negro History 38 (1953): 67-90.

Seiji Noma, Noma of Japan: The Nine Magazines of Kodansha, Being the Autobiography of a Japanese Publisher, (New York: Vanguard Press, 1934).

Hank Nuwer, "An Appreciation of Ezra Pound, Editor," Rendezvous: Journal of Arts and Letters 22:1 (Fall 1986): 74-80.

Ann Parry, "The [Sir George] Grove Years 1868-1883: A 'New Look' for Macmillan's Magazine," Victorian Periodicals Review 19:4 (Winter 1986): 149-157.

Sam Ragan, "Macleod as Editor," Pembroke Magazine 12 (1980): 92-93.

Carol Reuss, "Better Homes and Gardens and Its Editors: An Historical Study from the Magazine's Founding to 1970" (Ph.D. diss., University of Iowa, 1971).

Sam G. Riley, American Magazine Journalists, 1741-1850, (Detroit: Gale, 1988).

Sam G. Riley, American Magazine Journalists, 1850-1900, (Detroit: Gale, 1988).

Mary Jane Roggenbuck, "St. Nicholas Magazine: A Study of the Impact and Historical Influence of the Editorship of Mary Mapes Dodge" (Ph.D. diss., University of Michigan, 1976).

Elliott M. Rudwick, "W.E.B. Du Bois in the Role of Crisis Editor," Journal of Negro History 48 (1963): 206-16.

George Streator, "Working on the Crisis," Crisis 58 (1951): 159-163.

John W. Tebbel, George Horace Lorimer and The Saturday Evening Post (Garden City, N.Y. 1948).

William David Washington, "The Penny Magazine: A Study of the Genesis and Utilitarian Application of the Popular Miscellany" (Ph.D. diss., Ohio State University, 1967).

Roy Wilkins, "The Crisis, 1934-49," Crisis 58 (1951): 154-156.

Guy R. Woodall, "The Connection of Robert Walsh Jr. as an Editor and Reviewer with The American Register and The Analectic Magazine (1817-1819)," Journal of Newspaper and Periodical History 4:1 (Winter 1987-1988): 12-28.

Acknowledgments

The author wishes to acknowledge support of this research by a $9,000 grant from the University of Missouri Research Council and additional support from the Missouri School of Journalism's Research and Faculty Development Fund. Able research assistance has been supplied by Pam Jordan and Kewen Zhang.

5

Research Review:
The Specialized Business Press

Kathleen L. Endres

ABSTRACT

This article reviews the scholarly research dealing with the specialized business press. It focuses on research produced journalism and communication departments, as well as that of business schools and humanities programs. The author notes the lack of theory building and ties across disciplines, and anticipates that new advances in CD-ROM technology may increase research into the field as well as strengthen ties across disciplines.

Introduction

The business press in this country predates the American Revolution.[1] Nonetheless this branch of journalism continues to confound the nation's researchers. Perhaps the problem emanates from nomenclature. Researchers have never been quite sure what to call this branch of journalism. Julien Elfenbein, who wrote a book on the topic, preferred the term "businesspaper."[2] That term, however, never quite stuck. Nor did the related term "business press"[3] or "industry magazine."[4] The more common term in academic circles is "trade press,"[5] a name at which the industry bristles.[6] Publications within this field, as well as the associations which represent them, prefer the term "specialized business press."[7] That term is designed to describe the industry while differentiating it from the general business books such as *Forbes*, *Fortune*, and *Business Week*.

Researchers also are never quite sure how to categorize this branch of journalism. Traditionally, it is grouped within the magazine category. Yet many of the articles and books on magazines fail to incorporate this segment of the field.[8] Even in their indices, some academic journals fail to include articles on the business press under the magazine category.[9]

One other problem continues to plague the specialized business press: the charge that this branch of journalism somehow lacks the same integrity and high editorial standards of other fields. It is an old charge that is often cited.[10] In part, this stems from a distribution method that differs from other branches of print journalism. Controlled circulation, sending the periodical free to individuals qualified by occupation, remains the distribution system of choice for the largest number of specialized business publications.[11] This means that the largest amount of revenue comes from advertising.

Research Review

Research into this branch of journalism must be seen against this backdrop. Few fields of journalism have had to deal with such confusion with regard to name, categorization, integrity, or the roles they play within the industries they cover. The confusion had been so widespread that Harold McGraw, a publisher of specialized business periodicals, created an editorial foundation to explain the industry to professors in journalism/communication programs. The Business Press Educational Foundation has since come under the umbrella of the trade association for the industry, the American Business Press (ABP). The organization continues to focus its efforts on journalism and communication programs across the nation. These programs, however, are not always responsible for generating scholarly research about the field. Indeed, research into the specialized business press is just as likely to come from business schools and humanities programs as journalism/communication departments.

Business academics often do research that has direct, pragmatic impact. Researchers with this orientation tend to view the specialized business press as a medium for marketing and advertising and design their studies accordingly. A number of studies have attempted to gauge the effectiveness of the specialized business press as an advertising medium. John E. Morrill's study in the *Harvard Business Review* is a case in point.[12] Morrill attempted to measure the effectiveness of advertising campaigns placed in a number of business periodicals, covering a variety of industries. Morrill then interviewed buyers, those who had been exposed to the campaigns and those who had not, and found that the advertising in these specialized publications brought about a change in attitude and opinion. However, in order to achieve success, advertising had to appear frequently—at least six pages of advertising in a 12-month period.

Alicia Donovan came to similar conclusions in her study of one McGraw-Hill periodical, *Modern Plastics*.[13] In this experiment, one corporation introduced a new product in an advertising campaign published solely in *Modern Plastics*. The researcher performed pre- and post-tests on readers and found that the product enjoyed a substantial increase in "share of mind" awareness after the campaign.

Of course, the most recent and most widely reported study was the Advertising Research Foundation/ABP investigation of advertising effectiveness. This research covered 12-month advertising campaigns for four products and found that advertising in the specialized business press "will increase sales and profits; that increased frequency can increase qualified sales leads; that results can be seen within four to six months; that color enhances an ad's effect on business; and that an ad campaign's effectiveness can outlast the campaign itself."[14] This study was widely reported in publications covering the advertising and publishing industries. However, no report appeared in the scholarly periodicals. This points to a difficulty. Unless researchers include specialized business periodicals in their search of the literature, they are likely to overlook important and salient industry reports.

Advertising effectiveness was behind Lynette S. McCullough and Ronald K. Taylor's cross-cultural study of humor of advertising appearing in specialized business magazines.[15] Drawing on a substantial body of literature in psychology and business that points to humor's potential in conveying persuasive communication, the two researchers looked at advertising in American, British, and German specialized business periodicals and found that humor was used extensively. There were no differences among the three nationalities. However, there were differences among industries. Advertising in the marketing/advertising, business, dental, travel, and toy publications had the highest average humor ratings; advertising in the paper/pulp, mining, safety, fur, and security industry magazines had the lowest.

Most scholarly business research on the business press focuses on the advertising/marketing side of publishing. J. Ronald Milavsky's study was one of the few looking at the editorial side.[16] His research question revolved around how magazines reported on marketing and social effects from an international perspective. Milavsky found that the publications he studied dealt with this subject primarily in straight news reports or consultative studies of uneven quality. Like other forms of journalism,[17] these magazines underrepresented countries outside of Europe; even Asia, Central and South America and Africa received little attention, although much industrial production has shifted to these areas.

Business researchers tend to leave the historical development of the specialized business press to others. One exception was Ronald B. Smith's look at the beginnings of business publishing in the United States.[18] This study, however, has only limited usefulness because much of the research is based on secondary sources.

Historical analysis is best left to the humanities. Researchers from many disciplines—from history to theatre, from American studies to art—have examined the specialized business press, primarily from an historical perspective. This variety of disciplines and their differing points of view have brought a rich diversity to the research into the history of the specialized business press. Unfortunately, because this research covers so many different disciplines and such a range of scholarly periodicals not always consulted by journalism/communication scholars, this material is not always found or used. The benefits of the research from these differing disciplines are too often lost.

Historians have long tilled the specialized business press as an important area of research. The verb is especially appropriate because the agricultural business press has captured the imagination—and the research questions—of a number of historians. While many of these studies can, at best, be called case studies of one publication or one editor, others place the journalism of the agricultural business press into a broader historical framework.

Homer E. Socolofsky's study of the Capper farm press offered an interpretation of how the westward movement explained the continuing specialization within the agricultural business press.[19] Soil and weather conditions changed with each new frontier, requiring different, more specialized publications to serve a farm audience in each new frontier. Joseph Cote saw the editor of the *Progressive Farmer* as a product of both the Populist and Progressive movements.[20] However, his editorial campaigns in favor of mechanization and modernization only worked against the yeoman farmer. In the end, the yeoman farmer declined in numbers and importance, a development inconsistent with Populist and Progressive ideals. And Donald Marti transformed agricultural journalism into a question of the diffusion of knowledge and the democratization of America.[21] These publications went from voices of small, private, elite agricultural societies in the eighteenth century to independent journals with much larger circulations in the pre-Civil War period. The shift also brought changes to the publications themselves, as editors began to rely for information primarily on university-trained scientists.

The changing nature of agricultural publications was also the topic that interested Karl B. Raitz and Stanley D. Brunn.[22] However, because their discipline of geography differed from Cote's—history—the two brought a different perspective to their work. Raitz and Brunn tied the development of farm journals to geographical variations and the growing dominance agriculturally of those regions.

Other branches of the specialized business press have not received as much attention. The publications of the printing trade have drawn their share of scholarly examination from a wide range of disciplines in the humanities. Patricia

Frantz Kery, who has a degree in journalism but works in the fine arts, combined both interests in her magnificent book on magazine front covers. Here, she includes the art of many specialized business periodicals and pays special attention to the *Inland Printer* for its role in developing the changing front cover.[23] John Bidwell built on Ray Nash's work, *Printing as an Art*. Bidwell studied *The Engraver and Printer*, a case study of the rise and demise of a periodical covering the printing trade.[24]

Other studies have used the specialized business press to examine topics and issues of historical importance. For example, historian Thomas DiBacco used a wide range of periodicals covering the industrial and financial fields, marketing and transportation industries to chart business response to the Vietnam War.[25] James Hilgenberg Jr. focused on business response to the occupation of Japan following World War II and the early Cold War.[26] Hilgenberg, though, drew more heavily from the general business press than the specialized business periodicals in his book. What marks both works is that the specialized business press does not speak with a single voice. It cannot be interpreted as a monolithic body. The humanities, then, have added a rich literature to the study of the specialized business press, a literature that should not be ignored by journalism/communication scholars.

Frank Luther Mott represented a bridge between humanities scholarship and journalism/communication research. In his five-volume study of American magazine journalism history,[27] he incorporated the specialized business press into each time period, offering perspectives on the field as it followed— or differed from—patterns on the consumer side. Likewise, he fit the specialized business press into an economic framework that helped explain how this branch of journalism developed.

Mott differed from many of the important early writers on the specialized business press in several key respects. First, Mott looked at the business press as part of the magazine industry. Both business and consumer periodicals were studied. Most of the earlier writers on the business press preferred to isolate this branch of journalism from its consumer cousins. Second, Mott's professional background does not appear to be in the business press. Most of the early writers on this topic had worked for a time in the field. Jesse H. Neal, who wrote a brief history on the field in the 1920s, was executive secretary of the Association of Business Papers in New York, after a career at United Publishers Corp., a forerunner of the Chilton Co. Horace M. Swetland, who offered a book-length examination of "industrial publishing" in 1923,[28] was president of Class Journal Co. and United Publishers. Julien Elfenbein, who provided a 1945 examination of the "business press" as well as a 1960 update,[29] had been an editor for eight national business magazines. Edgar A. Grunwald, who wrote a 1980s text on the industry,[30] had edited one specialized business publication and worked for another. Sal Marino, who offered a business side appraisal,[31] remains chief executive officer of Penton, a large publisher of specialized business periodicals. David P. Forsyth, who has written the only book on the history of the industry to date,[32] was manager of communication research for Chilton and later a consultant for a variety of specialized business publications.

The Swetland, Elfenbein, Grunwald, and Marino books complement each other. Each provides an overview at a pivotal moment in the development of the specialized business press. Swetland offered a look at the 1920s as the specialized business press adjusted to the unbridled growth after the first world war. In his first edition, Elfenbein charted how the field was about to explode after the second world war. His update explained the phenomenal growth of the 1940s and 1950s. Grunwald wrote his book as a text, introducing students in journalism/communication programs to a field that had grown large in the 1960s, 1970s, and 1980s. Grunwald's work focused on the editorial side; Marino's the business side. Based on about 50 years of professional experience on the business side, Marino's book offered practical advice for would-be publishers and CEOs.

David P. Forsyth's book looked at the roots of the industry. The author offered an industry-by-industry breakdown of specialized business periodicals published prior to the Civil War. Unfortunately, in the almost 30 years since this book was published, no one has analyzed the second half of the nineteenth century, when economic, industrial and technological changes revolutionized the nation and its business press. The only thing close to that is a volume scheduled for publication in 1994.[33] This book, edited by Kathleen Endres, offers histories of important periodicals in the specialized business press.

Heretofore, histories of the specialized business publications have been left to the periodicals themselves. Most are done to commemorate anniversaries. *American Banker* issued a large, special edition in 1986 to celebrate its 150th anniversary; *American Salon* its 50th in 1927; *American Machinist* its 75th in 1952; *Editor & Publisher* its 100th in 1984; *Publishers Weekly* its 100th in 1972; and *Travel Weekly* its 25th in 1983. Even the ABP published its own history, "Adventure...in cooperative progress."[34]

Historical studies that have appeared in scholarly journals in the journalism/communication field have been rare, too. These have covered media or academic journals, the publications that many journalism/communication instructors read. Paul Sullivan, for example, looked at the launch of *Advertising Age*; Bruce Currie studied the evolution of the *Chronicle of Higher Education*.[35] These historical treatments of individual publications are typical of much of the historical research of the business press done by journalism/communication researchers. Unlike the historians who often link the business periodicals to broader themes or developments, journalism/communication researchers often lack that richness of interpretation.

Of course, there are exceptions. Pama A. Mitchell's work illustrated how the business press can be used as a primary source to explain historical developments. In a paper delivered to the national convention of the Association for Education in Journalism and Mass Communication,[36] Mitchell looked at the periodicals covering the broadcasting and advertising industries and found that these publications were caught up in the anti-Communist fervor that swept the nation in the first half of the 1950s. The editors of these periodicals felt that Communist infiltration of television represented a legitimate threat to national security.

These studies add much to the understanding of the periodicals that cover the mass communication and academic fields. However, these two fields represent only a small segment of the specialized business press. Examining only these types of periodicals may actually lead to a misrepresentation of the business press. Historical research also needs to be done on periodicals covering the industrial, retail, transportation, construction, science/medical, and other areas, the periodicals not typically read or written about by journalism/communication researchers.

Research that draws upon the breadth of the business press has been left to another group of journalism/communication scholars. These researchers concentrate on the current state of the specialized business press. Endres, for example, worked with a cross section of specialized business publications in her examination of ownership and employment patterns within the industry.[37] She found that most specialized business publications were magazines (usually monthlies), tend to rely on small editorial staffs (although sold publications typically had larger editorial departments), and were owned by corporations that issued other periodicals (often specialized business publications). However, she failed to include newsletters, a shortcoming of most researchers in the field.

Dennis Jeffers looked into opportunities for women in one field, livestock industry magazines, and found that opportunities were improving, although discrepancies in promotion and salaries between the genders continue. That does not appear to be peculiar to the periodicals covering the livestock industry. Discrepancies between the genders in salary and job were also reported in Endres's study of the business press journalists in a variety of industries. While women outnumbered men in periodicals covering certain industries, women tended to be relegated to lower editorial positions and were paid substantially less than the men.[38]

One of the consistent criticisms of the business press deals with advertising pressure. Robert G. Hays and Ann E. Reisner looked at that question in their survey of journalists working for farm magazines.[39] The researchers reported that the majority of the respondents reported pressure from advertisers; about half reported that advertising had, indeed, been withdrawn; and more than a third thought advertiser pressure was harming agricultural journalism.

The studies on the specialized business press done by journalism/communication researchers, however informative their content, often lack a theoretical base. The study by Greg A. Payne, Jessica J.H. Severn and David Dozier illustrated that the uses and gratifications model works well with the specialized business press.[40] This study is particularly enlightening because it pointed out differences between how readers use consumer and business magazines. Theoretical weakness is not peculiar to the scholarship covering the specialized business press, however. In general, theoretical foundations to the research into the magazine industry have not been strong, as Marcia Prior-Miller pointed out in her work.[41]

Journalism/communication researchers in the specialized business press have also failed to build links across disciplinary lines. A notable exception is the article by Susan Caudill, Ed Caudill, and Michael Singletary on professional values in newspaper journalism.[42] Building on the research on professionalization done in sociology, the three researchers used the classified advertising in one business publication, *Editor & Publisher*, to chart changes over time (or, in this case, the lack of changes over time). Professionalization research, especially, lends itself to the use of the business press from a wide variety of industries as a primary source.

The shortcomings in research in the specialized business press should be, perhaps, forgiven because of the rudimentary state of the field. However, it is unclear why the business press has not been studied as extensively as newspapers, broadcasting, advertising, public relations, or consumer magazines. It is older than many of these areas. It remains a lucrative branch of American journalism. It performs a service to the industries it covers.

Several explanations have been offered. First, a lack of awareness of the specialized business press in journalism/communication programs. The industry itself may be known, but research opportunities in the field may not be recognized. Part of this may be related to the professional backgrounds of those teaching. Few have received their professional training in the specialized business field, and this appears to be an important factor for researchers examining this field and possibly others as well. Certainly, this merits examination.[43]

Second, the age-old shortages of time and resources. Unlike other branches of research where grants are available, there are few foundations ready to fund research into the specialized business press. Moreover, the magazine instructors, the natural group to do such research, lack the time to do so. As Peter Gerlach pointed out in his study of magazine research in *Journalism Quar-*

terly,[44] those who publish on magazines often lack the time, interest, resources, and expertise to do a considerable amount of research into the field.

Third, the lack of primary sources. This especially affects historical research into the field. Until recently, libraries did not retain long runs of specialized business publications. The holdings for periodicals covering transportation, retail, service, construction, and industrial fields have been especially neglected. Lack of sources means that even if resarchers wanted to do historical research in these periodicals, they would find it difficult. Moreover, publishing companies and individual editors from the specialized business press have seldom contributed corporate and/or personal files to libraries. Nor have archivists made much of a point to solicit such contributions. Yet again, this hinders extensive research into the field.

Future Possibilities

In spite of all these shortcomings, there are some positive developments that might help trigger additional research. During the past 10 years, a number of dissertations have been written on the specialized business press. Anthony D. Hill has written on J.A. Jackson's page in *Billboard* and noted how he covered the Harlem Renaissance. Jean Russel Moss has used the nursing journals to retell the history of nursing, plugging in a cultural interpretation of changing expectations of women. Mary Norman Woods studied the *American Architect and Building News* as the first successful architectural magazine and as part of a larger communication revolution in the late nineteenth century. Unfortunately, none of these has come out of journalism/communication programs. Hill is a product of a theatre program; Moss comes from American Studies; and Woods has a fine arts background. Nonetheless, these dissertations[45] represent interesting interpretations of specialized business publications covering a variety of fields.

Advances in computer technology, likewise, may be a boon to studying the specialized business press. Because research is done in a number of different disciplines, it has been difficult to locate these studies, papers, and dissertations. With advances in CD-ROM technology, however, it has become easier to locate such materials and, thereby, build upon the research and interpretations in other disciplines. This should bring a new richness to the journalism/ communication research into this field. Advances in computer technology should also trigger new research into the business press. The ABI/Inform reference group, alone, represents an easy access point to some 800 business-related publications, including professional, academic and trade journals. For academics already lacking time, this tool represents an easy, fast way to search vast amounts of periodicals quickly by topic, event, issue, or individual. Its usefulness was already demonstrated by Milavsky's study on journal and trade publication treatment of globalization.

Thus these new developments may lead to new and better research into the business press. New studies may not necessarily be generated within journalism/communication programs. Departments of humanities and schools of business are likely to continue their work on the business press. However, advances in computer technology should allow each area—business, humanities, and journalism/communication— to build on the work of the other. This access should lead to better research, research that benefits from different interpretations, new theoretical approaches and methodologies. And that can only lead to a fuller understanding of a branch of American journalism that will soon celebrate its 220th birthday.

Notes

[1] The South-Carolina Price-Current dates to 1774 and has generally been credited as one of the first business publications in what became the continental United States. David P. Forsyth, The Business Press in America, 1750-1865 (Philadelphia: Chilton Books, 1964), 20.

[2] Julien Elfenbein, Business Journalism, 2d ed. (New York: Greenwood Press, 1960), 1.

[3] Thomas V. DiBacco, "The Business Press and Vietnam: Ecstacy or Agony?" Journalism Quarterly 45 (Autumn 1968): 426-435; Derry Eynon, "U.S.-Based Business Periodicals for Overseas Readers," Journalism Quarterly 48 (Autumn 1971): 547-550.

[4] Dennis Jeffers, "A Descriptive Study of Perceived Impact of Gender in Working Environment and Job Satisfaction in Livestock Industry Magazines," Paper presented at the annual meeting of the Association of Education in Journalism and Mass Communication, San Antonio, TX, 1 August 1987.

[5] Susan Caudill, Ed Caudill, and Michael Singletary, "'Journalist Wanted': Trade Journal Ads as Indicators of Professional Values," Journalism Quarterly 64 (Summer/Autumn 1987): 576-580, 633; Greg A. Payne, Jessica J.H. Severn, and David Dozier, "Uses and Gratifications Motives as Indicators of Magazine Readership," Journalism Quarterly 65 (Winter 1988): 909-913, 959; J. Ronald Milavsky, "Journal and Trade Publication Treatments of Globalization in Mass Media Marketing and Social Change," International Journal of Advertising 12 (February 1993): 45-56.

[6] Paul W. Sullivan, "G.D. Crain Jr. and The Founding of 'Advertising Age'," Journalism History 1 (Autumn 1974): 94-95.

[7] See, for example, how the term is used in the material issued by the trade association for these periodicals. "Call for Editorial Interns," Business Press Education Foundation, n.d. "The Jesse H. Neal Awards," American Business Press, 1993.

[8] Edward J. Smith and Gilbert L. Fowler Jr., "The Status of Magazine Group Ownership," Journalism Quarterly 56 (Autumn 1979): 572-576; Benjamin M. Compaine, "The Magazine Industry: Developing the Special Interest Audience," Journal of Communication 30 (Spring 1980): 98-103.

[9] See Journalism Quarterly index, 1988.

[10] Sullivan, "G.D. Crain and The Founding of 'Advertising Age'," 94; Chris Welles, "The Bleak Wasteland of Financial Journalism," Columbia Journalism Review (July/August 1973): 42-43, 436.

[11] Kathleen L. Endres, "Re-examining the American Magazine Industry: A 1990s Look at Changing Realities in Periodical Publishing," Paper presented to the annual meeting of the Association for Education in Journalism and Mass Communication, Kansas City, MO, 14 August 1993.

[12] John E. Morrill, "Industrial Advertising Pays Off," Harvard Business Review 48 (March/April 1970): 4-14, 159-169.

[13] Alicia Donovan was research manager for Modern Plastics at this time this study was done. Alicia Donovan, "Awareness of Trade-Press Advertising," Journal of Advertising Research 19 (April 1979): 33-35.

[14] Amy Alson, "The ARF/ABP Study: Facing Facts," Marketing & Media Decisions 23 (May 1988): 79-82.

[15] Lynette S. McCullough and Ronald K. Taylor, "Humor in American, British, and German Ads," Industrial Marketing Management 22 (February 1993): 17-28.

[16] Milavsky, "Journal and Trade Publication Treatments of Globalization in Mass Media Marketing and Social Change," 45-56.

[17] W. J. Potter, "News from Three Worlds in Prestige U.S. Newspapers," Journalism Quarterly 64 (Spring 1987): 73-77; D.K. Perry, "The Image Gap: How International News Affects Perceptions of Nations," Journalism Quarterly 64 (Summer/Autumn 1987): 416-421.

[18] Ronald B. Smith, "The Genesis of the Business Press in the United States," Journal of Marketing 19 (October 1954): 146-151.

[19] Homer E. Socolofsky, "The Capper Farm Press Experience in Western Agricultural Journalism," Journal of the West 19 (April 1980): 22-29.

[20] Joseph Cote, "Clarence Hamilton Poe: The Farmer's Voice, 1899-1964," Agricultural History 53 (January 1979): 30-41.

[21] Donald B. Marti, "Agricultural Journalism and the Diffusion of Knowledge: The First Half-Century in America," Agricultural History 54 (January 1980): 28-37.

[22] Karl B. Raitz and Stanley D. Brunn, "Geographical Patterns in the Historical Development of Farm Publications," Journalism History 6 (Spring 1979): 14-15, 31-32.

[23] Patricia Frantz Kery, Great Magazine Covers of the World (New York: Abbeville Press, 1982).

[24] John Bidwell, "The Engraver and Printer, a Boston Trade Journal of the Eighteen Nineties," The Papers of the Bibliographical Society of America 71 (January/March 1977): 29-48; Ray Nash, Printing as an Art: History of the Society of Printers, Boston (Cambridge, MA: Harvard University Press, 1955).

[25] Thomas DiBacco, "The Business Press and Vietnam: Ectasy or Agony?" 426-435.

[26] James F. Hilgenberg Jr., From Enemy to Ally: Japan, The American Business Press & The Early Cold War (Lanham, MD: University Press of America, 1993).

[27] Frank Luther Mott, A History of American Magazines, vol. 1: 1741-1850 (New York: D. Appleton, 1930); vol. 2: 1850-1865 (Cambridge, MA: Harvard University Press 1938); vol. 3: 1865-1885 (Cambridge, MA: Harvard University Press, 1938); vol. 4: 1885-1905 (Cambridge, MA: Belknap Press of Harvard University Press, 1957); vol. 5: 1905-1930 (Cambridge, MA: Belknap Press of Harvard University Press, 1968).

[28] Jesse H. Neal, "A Review of Business Paper History," N.W. Ayer & Son Annual and Directory (Philadelphia: N.W. Ayer & Son, 1922), 12-45.; Horace M. Swetland, Industrial Publishing: The Foundations, Principles, Functions and General Practice (New York: New York Business Publishers Assn., 1923).

[29] Julien Elfenbein, Business Journalism (New York: Harper & Bros., 1945); 2d ed. (New York: Greenwood Press, 1960).

[30] Edgar A. Grunwald, The Business Press Editor (New York: New York University Press, 1988).

[31] Sal Marino, Business Magazine Publishing (Lincolnwood, IL: NTC Business Books, 1992).

[32] Forsyth, The Business Press in America, 1750-1865.

[33] Kathleen L. Endres (ed.), The Trade, Industrial and Professional Periodicals of the United States (Westport, CT: Greenwood Publishing, forthcoming).

[34] American Banker. 150th Anniversary Edition 1836-1986 (New York: American Banker Inc., 1986); American Hairdresser, January 1927; American Machinist, November 1952; Editor and Publisher, March 31, 1984; Publishers Weekly, January 17, 1972; Travel Weekly, May 31, 1983; Associated Business Publishers, "Adventure...in cooperative progress," internal history, n.d.

[35] Paul Sullivan, "G.D. Crain Jr. and The Founding of 'Advertising Age'"; Bruce F. Currie, "The Emergence of a Specialized Newspaper: The Chronicle of Higher Education from 1966 to Date," Journalism Quarterly 52 (Summer 1975): 321-325.

[36] Pama A. Mitchell, "The Response of the Broadcasting and Advertising Trade Press to Television Blacklisting Practices, 1950-1956," Paper presented to the annual meeting of the Association for Education in Journalism and Mass Communication, Washington, DC, 10 August 1989.

[37] Kathleen L. Endres, "Ownership and Employment in the Specialized Business Press," Journalism Quarterly 65 (Winter 1988): 996-998.

[38] K. Jeffers, "A Descriptive Study of Perceived Impact of Gender on Working Environment and Job Satisfaction in Livestock Industry Magazines"; Kathleen L. Endres, "Business Press Journalists: Who They Are, What They Do, and How They View Their Craft," Gallatin Review 8 (Winter 1988-1989): 23-45.

[39] Robert G. Hays and Ann E. Reisner, "Farm Journalists and Advertiser Interference: Pressures on Ethical Standards," Journalism Quarterly 68 (Spring/Summer 1991): 172-178.

[40] Greg A. Payne, Jessica J.H. Severn, and David Dozier, "Uses and Gratifications Motives as Indicators of Magazine Readership," Journalism Quarterly 65 (Winter 1988): 909-913, 959.

[41] Marcia Prior-Miller, "An Analysis of 'Magazine Type': Toward an Empirically Based Typology of Magazines and Non-Newspaper Periodicals," Paper presented at the annual meeting of the Association for Education in Journalism and Mass Communication, Montreal, Canada, 5 August 1992.

[42] Caudill, Caudill, and Singletary, "'Journalist Wanted': Trade Journal Ads as Indicators of Professional Values," 576-580, 633.

[43] The link between the professional experience of a researcher and the scholarly work done by that individual needs to be explored.

[44] Peter Gerlach, "Research About Magazines Appearing in Journalism Quarterly," Journalism Quarterly 64 (Spring 1987): 178-182.

[45] Anthony Duane Hill, "J.A. Jackson's Page in Billboard: A Voice for Black Performance during the Harlem Renaissance between 1920-1925" (Ph.D. diss., New York University, 1988); Jean Russel Moss, "Walking the Tightrope: The Study of Nursing as Told by Nineteenth-Century Nursing Journals" (Ph.D. diss., University of Iowa, 1987); Mary Norman Woods, "The American Architect and Building News, 1876-1907" (Ph.D. diss., Columbia University, 1983).

6

Research Review:
Magazine Management and Economics

Robert Worthington

ABSTRACT

Magazines are different than other print media because: the delivery system is more leisurely; they better reflect changing tastes and interests of our society; and magazines offer advertisers a viable advertising vehicle. While magazines are different, they have not been able to avoid the decline in circulation and advertising revenues experienced by other print media. To survive, the magazine publishing industry is attempting to maintain editorial quality; expand in ways other than increasing ad pages; charge readers more; look toward international expansion; and take advantage of emerging technology. Against this backdrop a review of research on magazine management has been conducted. The findings are: little has been published on the topic in academic journals; most citations in published research are from business and trade publications; research in the area is being conducted and presented at conferences but not published; most management research covers industry trends rather than specific industry topics; case histories are published but most outside of academic journals; and there is not a solid base of conceptual and theoretical magazine management research available in the literature.

Introduction

Some in the magazine publishing business view the term magazine management as an oxymoron.[1] This may explain why little magazine research is published in the more widely circulated mass communications academic journals. Media management research articles abound in the professions of television and newspapers, but scant information is available for the field of magazine management. Research on theories, concepts, or the practice of managing magazines in most communications academic journals is limited. On the other hand the topic is found in media management textbooks [2], the business and trade press[3], and other books on the profession.[4] The most prevalent source of magazine management studies are unpublished research papers presented at various academic mass communications conferences.

This paper discusses the current status of management concerns in the magazine publishing industry and then reviews pertinent research that has been conducted and presented or published. Conclusions will be offered with suggestions for further research.

Background

Magazines are seen as different from other print media because of three unique characteristics: (a) Since magazines are not published as often as newspapers, the delivery system can be more leisurely; (b) Magazines reflect changing tastes and interests of different segments of United States society; and (c) national and regional magazines still offer advertisers a viable advertising vehicle in spite of television.[5]

In recent years the business of magazine publishing has become a financial minefield. Circulation and advertising revenues remain sluggish with no major improvements visible on the horizon. But by mid-1992 magazine editors and publishers, gathering in Bermuda for the annual American Magazine Conference, thought an upturn was forthcoming. Ad revenues for the first half of 1992 had risen 8 percent over the same period in 1991; better than newspapers' 3 percent. Magazines' shares of ad revenues had gone up 17 percent. Optimism was high.

A 1993 study by David Sumner examining circulation revenues and advertising revenues from 1985-1991 reported ad rates and ad income increasing at a much greater rate than circulation revenues. A special report in the October 11, 1993 issue of *Advertising Age* reveals that expectations for a continued escalation of magazine industry earnings are not materializing. While that is the bad news, the good news is that the market has apparently bottomed out. The soft TV and newspaper markets leave magazines up-beat by comparison. The future is expected to be flat at its worse, possibly with a slight increase at its best.[6]

American Society of Magazine Editors president Steve Shepard (also editor-in-chief of *Business Week*) stated the industry's solution to the problem is "to maintain editorial quality and to get expansion in ways other than from additional ad pages. That is, to charge the reader more...to look for other areas of expansion such as international; and to take advantage of emerging technologies to develop new products."[7]

Shepard's comment on technology is seen by some in the industry as a major driving force for magazines of the future. Computer and satellite technology, for example, allows *Sports Illustrated* to accept ads on Monday for an issue which is distributed on Wednesday.[8] This same technology allows publishers to locate and target narrowly defined audiences and design specific interest magazines for small but loyal follower groups. In fact this trend has even led marketeers to launch their own publications designed to promote their own products. In the trade this is known as "custom publishing."[9]

Changing magazine tastes are chronicled on a regular basis by the head of the University of Mississippi's Magazine Journalism program, Samir Husni, who writes and publishes the annual *Guide to New Magazines*. In spite of economic downturns magazines will continue to be an important method of mass communications. Each year new magazines come and both new and old magazines disappear. It is the best medium designed to present detailed information covering a diverse range of topics in a timely and easily portable fashion. Additionally, in today's world of electronic computerization utilizing desktop publishing technology and direct mail consumer lists, a print entrepreneur with a minimum of capital and maximum of creative ideas can readily become a magazine publisher; most fail, but some do live on.[10]

The Magazine Publishing Process

While specific duties may vary from magazine to magazine, basically the process of publishing a magazine is split into two major divisions: the business side of the house and the editorial side.

The person in charge of running the magazine as a business entity is the publisher; responsible for the magazine managerial functions of finance, marketing, personnel, operations, and production. Essentially those functional departments under the publisher are charged with the fiscal management of the magazine; the business aspects of running the magazine (payroll, invoices, billings, accounting, etc.); advertising sales; promoting the magazine; circulation and subscriptions; and physically producing the magazine.[11]

The other side of the publishing company contains the editorial functions of creating the magazine. This area includes editors, staff writers, artists, photographers, layout people, and designers. While not part of the staff, a crucial adjunct to the regular editorial personnel are contributing editors and writers and free-lancers. The functions of the editorial staff are to plan the issues (usually up to a year in advance), create the editorial content, put together the pages, and prepare the entire magazine for publication.[12]

With today's computer technology magazines are able to reduce full-time editorial staff significantly. Many slick-looking, 80-to-100-page magazines can be put together and a graphic design artist experienced in magazine layout can put out a 100-page magazine on a monthly basis. Most of the writing will be done by free-lancers. One editor assigns the work and monitors progress. The assistant editor prepares the stories for publication and the artist arranges the pages. The free-lance work comes in by modem, is transmitted to the editor's computer for editing. Next, via an internal computer system, articles go to the graphic artist who creates the page layout using various type styles, sizes and colors. Photographs are electronically scanned and put on the appropriate page in the computer. Quickly an entire magazine can be created this way. Advertising copy is handled by the advertising sales people, again using the computer process. The completed computer-generated issue is sent by modem to a computer operated printing plant which may be across the continent. Modern technology makes possible the immediate assemblage of a magazine with almost no staff. As previously mentioned, most advances within the magazine publishing industry can be attributed to changing technologies more than any other factors.

Magazine Management Research

Most published research involving the magazine publishing industry involves output issues rather than input issues. This means that research about magazines examines the product itself instead of the process needed to produce the magazine. Many research articles involving magazines seem to be comparative studies such as advertising trends over time or how similar magazines report on the same topic. Published research articles on the management process inherent in magazine publishing are missing. On the other hand, research articles on management in the newspaper and television industries appear frequently in academic communications journals.

In 1990 Caroline Dow reported on the progress of magazine research.[13] She believed not enough scholarly research about magazines was being done. A previous study by Peter Gerlach in 1987 reported that from 1963 through 1983 only 116 magazine research articles were published in *Journalism Quarterly* representing six percent of the total research articles published.[14] Of these articles, 11 percent or 13 articles addressed magazine economic (business) issues. Marcia Prior-Miller though, in a ten-year study from 1977-1987, found that there were more magazine research studies published than was commonly perceived.[15]

Does this mean research on magazines, especially management, is not being conducted? No, research in this area is being conducted, but much of it is not being published. The main reason for this may be attributed to a lack of an appropriate outlet. Mainstream communications academic journals publishing research often will not accept narrowly focused research manuscripts simply because the topic has little appeal to the majority of the journals' readers. There is no academic journal, at this time, devoted to media management studies, although the AEJMC Media Management and Economics division is exploring this possibility. There is the *Journal of Media Economics* published by Lawrence Earlbaum Associates which publishes articles on the economic aspects of mass media as well as economic policy issues affecting the media industry. In the past three issues no articles on magazine research were noted.

An outlet for research in areas of magazines is the numerous books published by Greenwood Press of Westport, CT. These references cover a variety of magazine topics such as *American Mass-Market Magazines, Trade Publications in the U.S.*, or *Sources on the History of Women's Magazines*. Usually they contain compilations of research on magazines which fall within certain categories and, as each magazine is described, information on the management of that magazine is also presented. These books are not published in great quantities and can be expensive.

An examination of research presentations at the annual AEJMC meetings for the first four years of the 1990s reveals the following papers were presented in areas of magazine management.[16] In 1990 the magazine division presented 14 papers with only one on management, a study of distribution channels for magazines. The media management division presented eight papers with none on magazine management. In 1991 the magazine division presented 16 papers with two on management: the impact of microcomputers on magazine design and an examination of magazine staff salaries. Media management had 13 papers with none on magazine management. In 1992 the magazine division presented 10 papers with three related to management; one examined the repositioning of a trade publication, another discussed classifying magazines into types, and the third paper studied why magazines flourished or died in the last half of the 1980s. Media management presented 17 papers with none on magazine management. Last year, 1993, revealed a record high of 20 papers presented by the magazine division with six papers on management topics. These were: an examination of the American magazine publishing industry; writer/editor relationships; roles of city magazines; magazine editors: personalities or managers; editors and the writing process; and who pays for a magazine: consumers or advertisers? Media management presented 19 papers with none on magazine management. Within the magazine division the recent trend has been an increase in both magazine research and magazine management research.

Most information on management within the magazine publishing industry will be found in business and trade periodicals such as *Folio, Advertising*

Age, *The Wall Street Journal*, *Time*, *Business Week*, *Fortune*, and others. Current industry trends as well as in-depth, highly researched articles, such as case studies, are often found in these publications.

A Review of Research in Magazine Management

Most research in magazine management can be categorized as fitting into one of three areas: trend studies, case studies, or specific topic studies. Trend studies focus on overall trends in the magazine publishing industry or specific trends such as circulation or advertising. Case studies typically are in-depth research projects which concentrate on a particular magazine or magazine publishing company. These studies examine the business from an historical perspective describing what the magazine or company did over time to explain why the magazine is doing so well or how its demise came about. Specific topic studies tend to examine a distinct issue related to the management process of a magazine. It might analyze the pay of magazine staff, or editorial-advertising relationships, or how computers and desk top technology are impacting on putting out a magazine. Each type of study, in its own way, contributes to the overall knowledge of magazine management.

Trend Studies

A market report prepared in 1979 by Benjamin Compaine documented how the then century-old publishing form had evolved from the primary mass medium in American society to special interest or limited audience publications.[17] Magazines, as Compaine pointed out, had been replaced by television. He described how, before TV, magazines could rely on more leisurely delivery systems and offer advertisers national coverage. The number of new titles since 1950 had increased by 38 percent but for many magazines circulation had not grown and for some it had even gone down. The changing face of the country with an increased desire for more recreational time and material things, job specialization, new freedoms and tastes, a better educated public, and a consumer-oriented citizenry have created different challenges for magazine managers.

What this means is different for editors than for publishers. Editors see this as an opportunity to present new and different information; a task fulfilled by preparing more articles by different writers. For publishers, this translates into the magazine being a delivery system to tap into a specific audience, a target market attractive to advertisers. Compaine's study presented data dividing magazines into groups according to circulation size (type of audience) and editorial content (active or passive). Using his category placement system magazine publishers could better understand how to create a special interest publication that would better meet the needs and demands of special interest groups. This understanding would be crucial for magazine survival into the 1980s.

Kathleen Endres in 1988 examined the impact of the external environment (recession, inflation, unemployment, deregulation, and technology) on the publishing business.[18] She found that survival in the business world relied on knowledge and information that leaders and executives need to make the right decisions. A new market was born, specialized business publications. Again magazine management must be in a position to recognize and act on changes in the market place in order to continue to produce a product that is in demand.

Mayo and Pasadeos, in a 1991 study, reported on changes in editorial content of business magazines related to international stories from 1964 to 1988.[19] While the relative amount of international news stories did not change in the three decades, more stories were published at the end of the period but the stories were shorter. The findings again demonstrated a shifting story focus over time which implies management must constantly be aware of changing consumer demands regarding editorial content.

Worthington, in 1991, examined the external environment and reported on what issues and concerns would affect magazine managers in the 1990s.[20] This study presented data describing the battered status of the magazine industry and how changing financial, personnel, legal, and technological environments affect the industry. Suggestions were presented recommending ways publishers could prepare to successfully withstand the rigors of adverse changes. One problem noted by Worthington was the lack of published research on problems media managers face.

A 1992 study by Marcia Prior-Miller, a major effort which began in 1987, described a reconciliation of the five approaches commonly used to classify magazines in communications literature.[21] This in-depth study presented an excellent historical review of magazine industry research conducted since the 1960s. She also offered a well developed discussion that argued that a problem with current magazine research is a lack of sufficient past research upon which to create and develop a strong theoretical base. Part of the problem, as Prior-Miller saw it, was a lack of congruence in classifying magazines. How, she asked, can research on magazines be conducted if magazines cannot be uniformly categorized across studies? Her list of end notes is similarly impressive in breadth and depth.

A trend study done by Endres in 1993 looked at publishing in the consumer, specialized business, health, and agricultural categories in the 1990s.[22] Endres found that there has been a shift in types of periodicals published. The health and agriculture fields have become more specialized and in business and consumer areas certain publications are enjoying increased popularity. Publishing is becoming geographically decentralized, moving away from the East Coast, especially for books launched since 1980. Frequency cycles are decreasing with fewer issues per year gaining popularity. Overall circulation of most types of magazines is down except for business areas. Magazine topics are constantly shifting.

Another area of trend studies concerns advertising and reader audiences. Vincent Norris in 1982 found that the old belief that magazines are made possible only through advertising revenues was not supported by current data.[23] His research presented a good overview of the economic realities of magazine publishing (as does numerous sections of Robert Picard's *Media Economics*). Another study examining advertising by Stout, Wilcox, and Greer in 1989 found an interesting trend in the increased use of advertorials.[24] The authors studied the emerging field of advertorials and found that usage between 1980 and 1986 increased while overall ad pages were decreasing. In 1986 revenues from advertorials were $116 million with some magazines earning 14 percent of ad revenue from advertorials. Their paper also provided a brief but interesting background on the history of advertorials.

The spending of advertising dollars on magazine space is obviously related to the readership of the magazines. David Abrahamson conducted a 1991 study of gender analysis of readers for U.S. consumer magazines.[25] Abrahamson defined consumer magazines and discussed advertising changes as related to the number of readers, type of ads, and the type of audience. He found that over two-thirds of consumer magazines are gender specific (i.e., 60 percent or more of readers of one gender), with more publications created specifically for males but having smaller circulation than do women's magazines. This information can be important determinants for advertisers in deciding how much money to spend and what type of ads to run.

Case Studies

Case studies provide excellent ways to learn how to and how not to run a business. Definitive examples of successful and unsuccessful publishing companies can be found in academic journals, business publications, newspapers, or unpublished research papers. The cases typically showcase the publishing company as a business organization, such as Roger Hall's research in 1976 on the rise and fall of the old *Saturday Evening Post*.[26] Other cases focus on a key player in a publishing company[27], or a comparative study is done on several similar magazines or publishers to highlight how successful people or businesses are able to appropriately manage their talents and resources to succeed in enterprises where others have failed.[28]

Case studies utilize a similar approach whether the focus is on the business or the person. They present an historical perspective to set the stage and establish a base of understanding to better see how managerial decision-making evolved to lead the entity into success or failure. As a management training tool, case studies are seen as one of the best methods to allow readers to work through the process of organizing and analyzing data in order to select a course of action to correct problems or move forward into the future.

While business schools have used this concept (pioneered at Harvard Business School) for decades, it has been recently gaining more acceptance in media management courses.[29]

Specific Topic Studies

As previously explained these studies tend to focus on a specific topic of managerial concern or interest. This type of research is the least prevalent in areas of magazine management. There are not necessarily relationships between the various studies published. Many examine issues or concerns facing the editorial side of magazines. Some researchers may argue these studies reflect the editorial or education process of writing technicalities. Others can justifiably point out that these also are a part of an editor's managerial prerogative requiring leadership decisions be made regarding proper allocation of editorial resources or meeting reader needs with editorial content.

This same question was posed by Lee Jolliffe when she asked if editors of a magazine are concerned primarily with espousing their personalities (grammar, layout, design, content, etc.) on a magazine or are they concerned with controlling the process dedicated to producing a magazine.[30] She cited a variety of other research to support both viewpoints and then presented her findings after observing six magazine editors for a one-day period. Her results suggest editors function less as personalities or copy editors and more as successful and effective managers. The paper also has an extensive list of management functions and behaviors with observations of which ones the editors performed and how they were performed.

Editorial functions have also been examined by Endres and Schierhorn.[31] One study by these researchers looked at the process of how editors work with writers on professional magazines. The results are particularly interesting because they tend to report on the managerial process used to accomplish the creative aspects of publishing a magazine. The editing methods used in working with writers varied, usually depending on the writer the editors worked with. A second study by this pair examined the impact computer technology has had on producing a magazine. The study presented several interesting aspects of editorial management from equipment used to technological competency to how technological advances have affected editor-writer relationships.

The results clearly pointed out that technology is changing the way magazines are created and produced. This also impacts on writer-editor relationships, especially for free-lancers who may be unable to afford the latest technology and therefore not able to properly interact or connect with a magazine's technology.

Another area of specific topic interest involves gender and/or compensation. Considerable research in this area has been done by Sammye Johnson.[32] She has presented data showing that salary surveys are inconsistent, incomplete, and inconclusive. Like most of the research cited in this paper the value of Johnson's article resides not so much in the results but in the detailed data presented to yield the results, supported by 70 endnotes.

The study by Hall previously cited [See Note 26] on the old *Saturday Evening Post* examined the relationship of circulation and advertising dollars as each contributed to the overall financial health of a magazine. This pioneer study concluded that magazine publishing is a very complex interaction of circulation and advertising dynamics. Hall's findings have encouraged other researchers to use his model to further explore circulation-advertising interrelationships.

Krishman and Soley in 1987 published a paper on their research to determine if Hall's findings on circulation and advertising rates were applicable to a cross-section of current magazines. Their conclusions were yes; many of Hall's results were still valid. Additional research in these areas have been conducted by David Sumner, who continued to examine the relationships between ad revenues and circulation revenues.[33]

Discussion

A review of research conducted in areas of magazine management reveals the following:

a. Very little on the topic is published in academic journals.

b. An examination of the references cited in the research shows that many sources used are newspapers, business, and trade periodicals rather than academic journals.

c. Much of the research conducted in magazine management is not published but presented at academic conferences.

d. Most of the research that is conducted on magazine management falls in the area of overall management or industry trends rather than on specific industry topics.

e. Considerable research resulting in case histories of publications, editors, or publishers is published but more often than not in publications other than academic journals.

f. This lack of published research in areas of magazine management becomes evident when so many endnotes and reference citations are not from academic journals. This in turn perpetuates the paucity of academic research because the literature reviews cite so many sources other than academic journals.

g. Another problem this generates is magazine researchers lack a conceptual and theoretical base to build on.

Suggestions for the Future

The first question to attempt to answer is: why the lack of published magazine research, especially in areas of magazine management? Is this subspecialty too narrow, too limited to have an audience interested in the subject? Research is a process utilized to answer questions. Perhaps we are asking the wrong questions. On the other hand there may be no interest in the answers. Then again it may be that magazine researchers are competing for limited publication space against other journalism researchers whose findings are in demand by a larger audience than magazine academicians have. After all, how many journalism programs do not offer degree tracks in newspaper journalism? Then, how many journalism programs offer sequences in magazine journalism? It should be obvious that a small academic field naturally yields a limited share of academic research.

The next question is, can anything be done to increase interest in and publication of magazine management research? Yes. Media management is a professional area within journalism and mass communication which is gaining in interest and stature. Perhaps magazine management researchers should consider this area of journalism education as a potential outlet for presenting and publishing magazine management research. It might be that magazine management research is more suited to the area of media management than to the general topic of magazines. Recently more papers on magazine management are being presented; the apparent problem is a lack of suitable vehicles for publication. Hopefully as more studies are conducted, increased interest in the topic will lead to better opportunities for publication. One other area to consider for publication might be business journals; after all, magazine publication is a business.

Notes

[1] Editors of Folio Magazine, Magazine Publishing Management, Magazine Publishing Is Not a Management-Intensive Business, by James B. Kobak (New Canaan, CT: Folio Publishing Corporation, 1976), 45.

[2] See John M. Lavine and Daniel Wackman, Managing Media Organizations: Effective Leadership of the Media (White Plains, NY: Longman, 1988); Stephen Lacy, Ardyth B. Sohn, Jan Le Blanc Wicks, George Sylvie, Angela Powers, and Nora J. Rifon, Media Management A Casebook Approach (Hillsdale, NJ: Lawrence Ealbaum Associates, Incorporated, 1993); and Jim Willis and Diane B. Willis, New Directions in Media Management (Boston, MA: Allyn and Bacon, 1993).

[3] See Folio: The Magazine for Magazine Management; MagazineWeek: The Newsweekly of Magazine Publishing (defunct as of mid-1993); and Advertising Age.

[4] See Leonard Mogel, The Magazine, Second Edition (Chester, CT: Globe Pequot Press, 1988); Robert G. Picard, Media Economics: Concepts and Issues (Newbury Park, CA: Sage Publications, Incorporated, 1989); Stephen Lacy, Ardyth B. Sohn, and Robert H. Giles, editors, Readings in Media Management (Columbia, SC: Media Management and Economics Division of the Association for Education in Journalism and Mass Communication, 1992).

[5] Willis and Willis, New Directions in Media Management, 72.

[6] See E. R. Worthington, "Crucial Issues Facing Battered Magazine Publishers in the 1990's," Paper presented at the Association of Educators in Journalism and Mass Communication Magazine Division mid-year meeting, Oxford, MS, 9 November 1991; Magazine Buying and Planning, a special section in Advertising Age, 11 October 1993; Marc Boisclair, "Finally, A Little Sunshine," Magazine Week, 2 November 1992, 24, 26-27; David Sumner, "Who Pays the Piper—Consumers or Advertisers?", Paper presented at the Association of Educators in Journalism and Mass Communication annual meeting, Kansas City, MO, August 1993; and Scott Donaton, "Magazines Counting on Future Growth in Trouble," Advertising Age, 11 October 1993, S-4, S-22.

[7] Scott Donaton, "Shepard Offers Hits to Cope in '90s Era of Cost-Cutting," Advertising Age, 11 October 1993, S-10, S-18.

[8] Junu Bryan Kim, "Plan For a Year, But Execute Month to Month," Advertising Age, 11 October 1993, S-14.

[9] Julie Steenhuysen, "Custom Publishing is Catching On," Advertising Age, 11 October 1993, S-24, S-25.

[10] See Melvin L. Defleur and Everette E. Dennis, Chapter 4, Magazines: Voices for Many Interests, Understanding Mass Communication, Fourth Edition (Boston, MA: Houghton Mifflin Company, 1991), 110-137; Ray Eldon Hiebert, Donald F. Ungurait, and Thomas W. Bohn, Chapter 12—Magazines and Periodicals, Mass Media VI (White Plains, NY: Longman, 1991), 304-326; and Raymond Sokolov, "Musical Chairs in the Magazine Industry," The Wall Street Journal, 5 August 1992, A16.

[11] Leonard Mogel, The Magazine, Chapter Two: The Function and Responsibilities of the Publisher and the Business Staff, 13-21.

[12] Leonard Mogel, The Magazine, Chapter Three: The Role of the Editor, 23-45.

[13] Caroline Dow, "Togetherness in Magazine Research," Magazine Forum 1 (1990): 26-27.

[14] Peter Gerlach, "Research About Magazines Appearing in Journalism Quarterly," Journalism Quarterly 64 (1987): 182.

[15] Marcia R. Prior-Miller, "A Consensus and Analysis of Journals Publishing Research About Magazines, 1977-1987," Paper presented at the AEJMC annual meeting, Minneapolis, MN, 9 August 1990.

[16] For 1990 see the July issue of AEJMC News, pages 15-16 and 18-19; for 1991 see the July issue of AEJMC News, pages 14-15 and 18-19; for 1992 see the AEJMC News, pages 17-18 and 21-22; and for 1993 see the July issue of AEJMC News, pages 16-18 and 20-21.

[17] Benjamin M. Compaine, "The Magazine Industry: Developing the Special Interest Audience," Journal of Communication 30 (Spring 1980): 98-103.

[18] Kathleen Endres, "Ownership and Employment in Specialized Business Press," Journalism Quarterly 65 (Winter 1988): 996-998.

[19] Charles Mayo and Yorgo Pasadeos, "Changes in the International Focus of U.S. Business Magazines, 1964-1988," Journalism Quarterly 68 (Autumn 1991): 509-514.

[20] Worthington, "Crucial Management Issues Facing Battered Magazine Publishers in the 1990's."

[21] Marcia R. Prior-Miller, "An Analysis of 'Magazine Type': Toward an Empirically Based Typalogy of Magazines and Non-Newspaper Periodicals," Paper presented at the AEJMC annual meeting, Montreal, Canada, 5 August 1992.

[22] Kathleen L. Endres, "Re-Examining the American Magazine Industry: A Look at Changing Realities in Periodical Publishing," Paper presented at the AEJMC annual meeting, Kansas City, MO, 11 August 1993.

[23] Vincent P. Norris, "Consumer Magazine Prices and the Mythical Advertising Subsidy," Journalism Quarterly 59 (Summer 1982): 205-211, 239.

[24] Patricia A. Strout, Gary B. Wilcox, and Lorrie Greer, "Trends in Magazine Advertorial Use," Journalism Quarterly 66 (Winter 1989): 960-964.

[25] David Abrahamson, "A Quantitative Analysis of U.S. Consumer Magazines: Baseline Study and Gender Determinants," Paper presented at the AEJMC Magazine Division mid-year meeting, Oxford, MS, 8 November 1991.

[26] Roger I. Hall, "A Systematic Fall of the Old Saturday Evening Post," Administrative Science Quarterly 21 (June 1976): 185-211 and A Systems Model of a Magazine Publishing Firm (Seattle: Unpublished doctoral dissertation, University of Washington: 1973). For other examples see Carol Reuss, "Better Homes and Gardens: Consistent Concern Key to Long Life," Journalism Quarterly 51 (Summer 1974): 292-296; Patricia Prijatel and Marcia Prior-Miller, "An Analysis of the Failure of Flair Magazine," paper presented at the AEJMC annual meeting, Boston, MA, 7 August 1991; or Veronique Vienne, "Make It Right...Then Toss It Away," Columbia Journalism Review (July/August 1991): 28-29, 32-34.

[27] As examples see Paula Renfro and Yorgo Pasadeos, "TV Guide Under Murdoch: Less Serious Analysis, More Entertainment," Southwestern Mass Communication Journal 7 (2, 1992): 119-131; or Eric Utne, "Tina's New Yorker," Columbia Journalism Review (March/April 1993): 31-37.

[28] An example is Patrick M. Reilly, "Three Small Magazine Firms Make It Big," The Wall Street Journal, 19 October 1992, B1, B4.

[29] Examples of this trend are seen in the two 1993 media management texts by Willis and Willis (New Directions in Media Management) and Media Management, A Casebook Approach by Lacy et al. The Willis book has an appendix containing 21 short cases, and the Lacy book contains 48 short cases and three extended cases.

[30] Lee Jolliffe, "Magazine Editors: Personalities, Copy Editors—or Managers?" Paper presented at the AEJMC annual meeting, Kansas City, MO, 11 August 1993.

[31] See Ann B. Schierhorn and Kathleen L. Endres, "Magazine Editors and the Writing Process: An Analysis of How Editors Work with Staff and Free-Lance Writers," Paper presented at the AEJMC annual meeting, Kansas City, MO, 11 August 1993; and Endres and Schierhorn, "New Technology and the Writer/Editor Relationship: Shifting Electronic Realities," Paper also presented at the 1993 AEJMC annual meeting.

[32] See Sammye Johnson, Women's Employment and Status in the Magazine Industry, Chapter 10 in P. J. Creedon, editor, Women in Mass Communication: Challenging Gender Values, Sage Focus Editions, No. 106 (Newbury Park, CA: Sage Publications, 1989), 193-213; and Sammye Johnson, "Magazine Industry Salary Status Surveys: Limitations and Difficulties as a Mass Communications Research Area," Southwestern Mass Communication Journal 6 (2, 1990-91): 1-14.

[33] See R. Krishnan and Lawrence Soley, "Controlling Magazine Circulation." Advertising Research 27 (August/September 1987): 17-23; and David Sumner's two paper presentations, "Winners and Losers: Making it in the Magazine Marketplace, 1969-90," AEJMC annual meeting, Montreal, Canada, 5 August 1992 and "Who Pays the Magazine Piper—Consumers or Advertisers?" AEJMC annual meeting, Kansas City, MO, 11 August 1993.

7

Ms.ing the Free Press:
The Advertising and Editorial Content
of Ms. Magazine, 1972-1992

Lori Melton McKinnon

ABSTRACT

In 1972, publishers introduced *Ms.* as a forum for feminist debate. However, conflicts occurred between editors' ideology and advertisers' wishes. In 1990, it was reintroduced: ad-free. A content analysis showed that although *Ms.* sometimes compromised its promise to be a mass-mediated forum, its current format has allowed *Ms.* to present a renewed vision of feminism.

Introduction

It has been charged that advertisers limit the diversity of news and entertainment American women receive. Although advertisers may influence both print and electronic content, the most obvious relationship between advertisers and their control of editorial content appears to be found in women's magazines. Historically, editors have made the final decisions about what to publish. However, these decisions may have been influenced more by advertisers' pressures than by readers' wishes. With few exceptions, advertising dollars continue to support today's magazines. Leading one to ask, "Who actually sets the agenda in women's periodicals? Readers, editors, or advertisers?"

When *Ms.* began publication in July 1972, its editors hoped that it would serve as a "laboratory," useful to both advertisers and readers. Editors encouraged readers to write letters to *Ms.* and to its advertisers if the readers disapproved of any ads, and they adopted the policy, "Obviously, *Ms.* won't solicit or accept ads whatever the product they're presenting, that are down-right insulting to women...Nor will we accept product categories that might be harmful."[1]

Ms. vowed to be unlike traditional women's magazines. When *Ms.* began, it didn't consider not accepting ads. According to Steinem, *Ms.* established two goals: (a) to obtain ads for products used by both men and women but advertised mostly to men; (b) to attract ads for traditional female products (clothes, cosmetics, etc.) that surveys showed readers used. In both cases, *Ms.* would ask advertisers to "come in without the usual quid pro quo of complementary copy."[2]

Unfortunately, the advertisers that *Ms.* managed to obtain were quick to cancel their ads when something upset them. For example, after years of trying to avoid harmful ads, *Ms.* decided to accept ads for Virginia Slims cigarettes. Editors explained that readers wouldn't appreciate the "You've come a long way, baby," slogan, but Phillip Morris was convinced it would work. When a test ad didn't succeed, Philip Morris took away ads for all their brands. This cost *Ms.* about $250,000 the first year.[3]

As ad revenue began to decrease, *Ms.* began to ignore its original policy. Ferguson, Kreshel, and Tinkham showed that *Ms.*'s ads became more sexist and more harmful as the years progressed.[4] McCracken explained that *Ms.* tried to be a feminist forum and a business venture. In fact, of *Ms.*'s 1983 revenues totalling $9.3 million, ad revenue accounted for $5.1 million.[5] Faludi wrote, "The magazine that had once investigated sexual harassment, domestic violence, the prescription-drug industry, and the treatment of women in third world countries now dashed off gushing tributes to Hollywood stars, launched a fashion column, and delivered the really big news—pearls are back."[6]

Hovey explained that changes in *Ms.*'s content accompanied changes in its ownership. In 1987, the magazine changed hands from *Ms.* Foundation for Education and Communication, a non-profit organization, to Fairfax Ltd. The new firm installed Anne Summers as editor after Gloria Steinem moved to a consulting role. After only one year, Matilda Publications took over as the new owner. Then in the fall of 1989 Dale Lang signed on as majority owner. Lang suspended *Ms.* in December 1989. In hopes of saving *Ms.*, he relaunched it as a subscriber-supported bimonthly. The ad-free *Ms.* debuted in July/August 1990.[7]

The newly launched *Ms.* sold for $4.50 an issue and $40 for the bimonthly issues. Lang knew that for readers to pay the high price, he had to give them what they wanted: a new forum for feminist ideology. Fortunately, the revamped *Ms.* is succeeding. Denworth said, "The success of *Ms.* defies not only publishing wisdom but also the frequent pronouncements that the women's movement is over."[8]

Literature

From the beginning of the modern feminist movement in the 1960s, the media have been objects of criticism. The two most frequently cited founding events of feminism, the publication of Friedan's *Feminine Mystique* in 1963 and the creation of NOW in 1966 contained critiques of the media.[9] According to Rakow, "In the early 1970s, research on media portrayals of women and their effects on audiences began to appear in academic journals, signaling that the topic was becoming a legitimate one within the existing frameworks of media research."[10]

Analyses of magazine ads have provided insight to media images of women. Courtney and Lockeretz's study of ads in eight magazines found that ads showed more men employed than women and presented men in higher status occupations.[11] Studies by Wagner and Banos [12] and by Culley and Bennett[13] produced similar results. Likewise, Warren found that ads portrayed women in stereotypical roles.[14]

Rossi and Rossi studied the appeal of magazine advertising to college students and how these students perceived sexism in ads. They concluded that both males and females found the target ads to be much more sexist than control ads.[15] In addition, Ferguson, Kreshel, and Tinkham studied the changes in the portrayal of women in ads appearing in *Ms.* between 1973 and 1987. Based on *Ms.*'s advertising policy, the authors felt that if the ads in *Ms.* were found to be sexist, then it could be assumed that ads in other magazines were equally pervasive. Unfortunately, the researchers found that nearly one-third of all ads in the sample promoted "harmful" products.[16]

Studies of articles and short stories have examined themes, images, norms, occupations, and attitudes found in women's magazines. Early examples appeared in several sections of the Spring 1974 *Journal of Communication*. Included was Franzwa's content analysis of heroines appearing in women's magazine fiction. She found that women were portrayed in four ways: single, but looking for a man; housewife/mother; spinster; widowed/divorced.[17] Other examples are found in *Hearth and Home*, edited by Tuchman, Daniels, and Benet. Included were three chapters on women's magazines which conclude that women's magazines project a similar image: women strive to please.[18]

In addition, the Winter 1978 *Journal of Communication* featured nine articles on women's issues. Included were several studies on the ERA. Butler and Paisley analyzed magazine coverage from 1922 to 1976 and found that more articles were devoted to women's rights from 1922-1926 than in any subsequent five-year period until the late 1960s.[19] Farley analyzed the content of 39 women's magazines that participated in an effort to increase ERA awareness. She concluded, "Editorial policy, circulation, and class of readership was linked to amount of magazine coverage, but not necessarily advocacy, of ERA."[20] In a later study, Spieczny examined 13 women's publications to determine how they covered the ERA between 1970 and 1979. Results showed that *Ms.* published the most articles on the ERA, 45. *Ms.* was followed by *Redbook* with 14 articles.[21]

Farrell explained that when *Ms.* changed from its non-profit status, editors claimed that only *Ms.*'s skin (cover, size, and format) would change. In an attempt to determine how readers "construct" meanings from covers, subjects examined old *Ms.* covers, new *Ms.* covers, and the November 1987 covers of *Self, Mademoiselle*, and *New Woman*. Respondents felt that *Ms.*'s new covers resembled typical women's magazines. However, when comparing *Ms.*'s covers to the others, readers felt that *Ms.* portrayed women more positively. Farrell observed, "Both the changes in 'skin' and the changes in 'heart' affect the way readers make meaning from texts."[22] In a subsequent study, Farrell, drew from a textual analysis of *Ms.*, interviews with its editors and writers, and an analysis of readers' letters, to show how "*Ms.* worked as a powerful, yet contradictory, channel for the women's movement, torn between articulating a bold vision while at the same time mediating, controlling, and sometimes undermining its initial promise to be a mass media resource for women around the country."[23]

Some studies indicate that publications feel pressured to run advertising-related stories. In Hays and Reisner's survey of 190 farm-journalists, about two-thirds said that advertisers have threatened their journals on occasion, and about one-half said that ads have been withdrawn.[24] Similarly, Hesterman examined the top 100 consumer magazines from 1972 to 1979 and found that despite the care given by the journalism industry to maintain the separation of editorial and ad interests, 49 percent of editors at the magazines studied felt some pressure from advertisers, and 2 percent said they felt considerable pressure.[25]

Other studies suggest that due to pressures from advertisers, women's magazines are less likely to cover controversial topics. Ballenger analyzed the 12 largest women's magazines' coverage of abortion from 1972 to 1991. These women's magazines, with combined circulations of 45 million, published only 137 articles on abortion during the last two decades.[26] Moreover, although more than 40,000 women die of lung cancer each year, many magazines that accept cigarette ads often fail to cover this issue. Hesterman found that *Good Housekeeping*, which does not accept cigarette ads and published an average of 11.2 health-related articles annually, presented the most coverage with an average of 2.1 articles per year. Although *Ms.* published an average of 5.7 health articles a year, it published no features related to smoking.[27] Likewise, Kessler found that although there were 1,300 articles on the dangers of smoking published in medical journals between 1983 and 1987, not one of the six magazines studied published any full-length article on the health hazards of smoking.[28] Sampling 99 magazines, Warner, Goldenhar, and McLaughlin analyzed the probability that magazines would publish articles on the risks of smoking in relation to whether they carried tobacco ads and to the proportion of revenues derived. Results indicated that the probability of a woman's magazine publishing an article for a given year was 11.7 percent for magazines that did not carry tobacco ads and 5.0 percent for those that did.[29]

In two studies Norris reported that magazines do not need advertisers to survive. In his 1982 study, he analyzed the prices of 45 magazines and the number of ads in each. He found that price per page is not related to the amount of advertising.[30] In 1984, Norris conducted an economic analysis of *Mad*. He found that *Mad* defied conventional wisdom that magazines without ads cannot be profitable.[31]

Research Hypotheses

Primary Study. Based on previous research on *Ms.* magazine, the following null hypotheses were formulated:

H1: There were no changes in advertising content over time for all three magazines considered together.

H2: There were no changes in the advertising content over time of each magazine considered individually.

H3: There were no changes in editorial content over time for all three magazines considered together.

H4: There were no changes in the editorial content over time of each magazine considered individually.

H5: There was no relationship between ad and editorial content over time for all three magazines considered together.

H6: There was no relationship between ad and editorial content over time of each magazine considered individually.

Secondary Study. The following null hypotheses were formulated:

H1: There were no changes in the ad content of *Ms.* during times of ownership change (Times 5-7).

H2: There were no changes in the ad content of *Ms.* during all times considered together (Times 1-3 and Times 5-7).

H3: There were no changes in the editorial content of *Ms.* during times of ownership change (Times 5-7).

H4: There were no changes in the editorial content of *Ms.* during all times considered together (Times 1-7).

Methodology

A content analysis of *Ms.* was performed to determine if a relationship existed between the ad and editorial content of the magazine. For comparison, this study examined selected issues of *Ms.*, *Mademoiselle*, and *Ladies Home Journal* published between July 1972 and July 1992. By examining these publications, it could be determined if similar changes had occurred in all three magazines. By sampling different types of women's publications, a greater diversity of sampled articles and ads could be analyzed.

The 20-year span studied was broken down into four periods to allow for a more equal representation of *Ms.*'s historical changes. To insure that an equal number of issues was studied in each period, the issues were not selected randomly. Beginning with July 1972 and selecting every sixth year, four periods were established: July 1972-May 1973 (Time 1), July 1978-May 1979 (Time 2), July 1984-May 1985 (Time 3), and July 1990-May 1991 (Time 4).

To avoid seasonal variations in ad and editorial content, every other month was selected. Entire issues of each magazine were studied. In addition, a secondary study was conducted to determine if changes in the ownership of *Ms.* magazine were related to changes in the publication's ad and editorial content. Therefore, the following three periods were also analyzed: September 1987-July 1988 (Time 5), September 1988-July 1989 (Time 6), and September 1989-December 1990 (Time 7).

In the primary study, seventy-two magazines which appeared between July 1972 and July 1992 were analyzed. This totaled six issues per year of each magazine for all four periods. To be selected for analysis, all magazine ads and articles had to be at least one-half page in length. Items greater than one full-page were considered only once. Ads were classified by product type, and articles were classified by feature type. The total sample yielded 4,601 ads and 1,940 articles. The proportions equaled: *Ms.*, 539 ads/554 articles; *Mademoiselle*, 1,939 ads/846 articles; and *Ladies Home Journal*, 2,123 ads/540 articles.

For the secondary study, fourteen issues of *Ms.* which appeared between September 1987 and December 1989 were analyzed. Magazine ads and articles were studied based on the criteria set in the primary study. The total sample yielded 440 ads and 276 magazine articles.

Three research coders, one male and two female, analyzed the selected magazine issues. Overall, inter-coder reliability equaled 94.4 percent. Coding was completed by following established guidelines. Coders classified both articles and ads based on category type. Category type was based on the most dominant theme and on previous research.

Ferguson, Kreshel, and Tinkham found that ads in *Ms.* could be classified as: (1) personal appearance; (2) business, travel, and transportation; and (3) home products.[32] For further clarification, the following categories were added: (4) entertainment (including cigarettes and alcohol); and (5) other. In addition, Land explained that most popular magazines offer their readers articles based on 21 subjects: (1) diets; (2) health; (3) sports; (4) money; (5) celebrities; (6) how-to; (7) self help; (8) first-person experiences; (9) human behavior; (10) marriage; (11) children; (12) travel; (13) fashion; (14) home furnishing; (15) cooking; (16) trends; (17) sex; (18) hobbies/art; (19) animals; (20) foreign news; and (21) national problems/politics.[33] The following were also added: (22) fiction; (23) history; and (24) beauty.

In the primary study each ad or article was coded according to the above categories. Next, raw scores for all of the ad and article subcategories were totalled. The scores for each subcategory were also combined for each period and for each of the three magazines. Simple Chi Square tests were used to see if there were any differences between the ad and article categories for each of the three magazines in each period studied. In addition, complex Chi Square tests were used to examine the relationships between the ad and the editorial content of the magazines together, over time, and individually.

As in the primary study, ads and articles in the secondary study were coded according to type, raw scores for subcategories were totalled, and scores for each subcategory were combined for each period of ownership change. Simple Chi Square tests were also used to see if there were any differences between the ad and article categories of *Ms.* in each time studied. In addition, a complex Chi Square test was used to examine the relationships between the ad and the editorial content of *Ms.* and between all of *Ms.*'s periods of ownership change considered over time.

Summary of Findings

Analyzing the ad and editorial content of *Ms.* from its beginning as a feminist forum to its current status as an ad-free medium helped to determine if relationships existed between topics depicted in advertising content and the types of articles printed. All of the null hypotheses were rejected based on Chi Square analyses performed at the .05 probability level.

Results from the primary study indicated that changes in the frequency of ads occurred in all magazines considered together during Times 1-4. For all magazines, the greatest percent (46.7%) of ads promoted "Personal Appearance." It also appears that over time changes occurred in the ad content of each magazine considered individually. During this time, most ads in *Ms.* promoted "Entertainment" (41.7%). The largest percent of ads in *Mademoiselle* (75.5%) and in *Ladies Home Journal* (51.4%) promoted "Personal Appearance" and "Home Products" respectively. In addition, results indicated that changes in article type occurred in all magazines considered together during Times 1-4.

For all magazines, most articles featured "Fashion" (11.3%). Results also indicated that significant differences occurred over time in the article content of each magazine. In *Ms.* the largest percent of articles focused on "National Problems/Politics" (20.8%). The majority of articles in *Mademoiselle* (29.9%) and *Ladies Home Journal* (12.6%) focused on "Fashion" and "Cooking" respectively.

The secondary study found that during periods of ownership change (Times 5-7), changes in *Ms.*'s ads occurred. The largest percent of ads promoted "Personal Appearance" (40.7%). Results also indicated that changes in *Ms.*'s ads occurred during all periods considered together (Times 1-3 and 5-7). During all periods, the largest percent of ads promoted "Entertainment" (32.6%). In addition, the results indicated that changes in article type occurred in *Ms.* during time periods of ownership change (Times 5-7). During these times, most articles focused on "First-person Experiences" (13.6%) and on "Celebrities" (13.1%). Moreover, results indicated that changes in article type occurred in *Ms.* during all times considered together (Times 1-7). During all times, most articles focused on "National Problems/Politics" (14.9%).

This study also speculated that as *Ms.*'s advertising policies gave way to the demands of advertisers, the ads and articles appearing in *Ms.* would begin to resemble those appearing in traditional women's publications. Although this relationship was not proven statistically, evidence exists to suggest that the theory may have merit. By comparing the percentages of *Ms.*'s ads in all seven periods, it seems that ads did become more like those in traditional women's periodicals. Ads for "Personal Appearance" increased over time. Moreover, until July of 1990 (Time 4), when *Ms.* contained no ads, articles increased on "Celebrities," "Fashion," and "Cooking."

Discussion

The findings of this study indicated that although *Ms.* sometimes compromised its original promise, its current ad-free format has once again allowed *Ms.* to present a renewed vision of feminism. *Ms.*'s status as a popular magazine with a feminist slant gave it the power to reach a mass audience of women. However, it also created conflict. Farrell wrote, "Both a 'marketing opportunity' for advertisers and a resource within the women's movement, *Ms.* magazine was an inherently contradictory text."[34]

Over time, *Ms.*'s ad content changed considerably. Originally, *Ms.* attracted ads for traditional male products (cars, travel, etc.). However, as *Ms.* strived to survive and changes in ownership occurred, the editors began accepting more ads for typical female products (fashion, cosmetics, etc.). In *Ms.*'s early days, editors encouraged readers to send in distasteful or sexist ads that they found in periodicals, and included them in their "No Comment" section. This section reappeared in the first ad-free *Ms.* However, this time the ads were not found in other publications but were *Ms.*'s own.[35]

Likewise, the early *Ms.* published articles which broke most of the conventions of women's magazines. However by the 1980s, editors disguised "feminist" articles behind more traditional topics, providing set-ups for products. For example, a 1973 article in *Ms.*, "Alice in Cosmeticsland," ridiculed the use of makeup to please a man and detailed the harms of many cosmetics.[36] On the other hand, a 1988 article, "Ode to Makeup," focused on the joys of Maybelline and other cosmetics.[37] In contrast, "Faith Healers, Holy Oil," appeared in 1991. Through this article, *Ms.* once again uncovered the myths of the multi-million dollar beauty industry.[38]

Throughout the years, the editors of *Ms.* found themselves caught between two worlds: the world of the women's movement and the world of the magazine industry. Eventually, *Ms.* became the only representative of feminism on commercial newsstands. This allowed *Ms.* to reach women who would not necessarily have read *Ms.* for its political stance. However, its mass-mediated popularity also forced the magazine to ignore its original advertising policy.

In July of 1990, *Ms.* re-emerged ad-free and subscriber-supported. Although *Ms.*'s absence from the commercial arena may prevent it from reaching a mass audience, it is once again free to communicate feminist ideology. *Ms.*'s content can now assume a feminist perspective, rather than strive to construct one.

Notes

[1] "Personal Report from Ms.," Ms., July 1972, 7.

[2] G. Steinem, "Sex, Lies, and Advertising," Ms., July/Aug 1990, 19.

[3] Ibid., 20-22.

[4] J. H. Ferguson, P. J. Kreshel, and S. F. Tinkham, "In the pages of Ms.: Sex Role Portrayals of Women in Advertising," Journal of Advertising 19 (1990): 40-51.

[5] E. McCracken, Decoding Women's Magazines (New York: St. Martin's Press, 1993), 279-280.

[6] S. Faludi, Backlash (New York: Crown, 1991), 108.

[7] S. Hovey, "A Radical Vow to Take Ms. Back to Its Roots," Folio, March 1990, 41-42.

[8] L. Denworth, "Sisterhood is Profitable," Newsweek, 26 August 1991, 60.

[9] B. Friedan, The Feminine Mystique (New York: Laurel, 1963).

[10] L. F. Rakow, "Women and the Communications Media," Women and Language (Spring 1985): 1-15.

[11] A. Courtney and S. Lockeretz, "A Woman's Place," Journal of Marketing Research 8 (1971): 92-95.

[12] L. Warner and J. Banos, "A Woman's Place," Journal of Marketing Research 10 (1973): 213-214.

[13] J. Culley and R. Bennett, The Status of Women in Mass Media Advertising (Newark, NJ: U. of Delaware, 1974).

[14] D. Warren, "Commercial Liberation," Journal of Communication (Winter 1975): 169-173.

[15] S. R. Rossi and J. S. Rossi, "Gender Differences in the Perception of Women in Magazine Advertising," Sex Roles 12 (1985): 1033-1039.

[16] Ferguson, Kreshel, and Tinkham, 40-51.

[17] H. H. Franzwa, "Working Women in Fact and Fiction," Journal of Communication (Spring 1974): 104-109.

[18] G. Tuchman, A. K. Daniels, and J. Benet, eds., Hearth and Home (New York: Oxford University Press, 1978).

[19] M. Butler and W. Paisley, "Magazine Coverage of Women's Rights," Journal of Communication (Winter 1987): 183-186.

[20] J. Farley, "Women's Magazines and the Equal Rights Amendment: Friend or Foe?" Journal of Communication (Winter 1978): 187-193.

[21] S. Spieczny, "Dancing Backwards," Paper presented at the annual meeting of the Association of Education in Journalism and Mass Communication, 1987.

[22] A. E. Farrell, "Ms. in Transition," Paper presented at the annual meeting of the Association of Education in Journalism and Mass Communication, 1988.

[23] A. E. Farrell, Feminism in the Mass Media: Ms. Magazine (Ph.D. diss., University of Minnesota, 1991): 2.

[24] R. G. Hays and A. E. Reisner, "Feeling the Heat From Advertisers: Farm Magazine Writers and Ethical Pressures," Journalism Quarterly (Winter 1990): 936-943.

[25] V. L. Hesterman, "Consumer Magazines and Ethical Standards," Paper presented at the annual meeting of the Association for Education in Journalism and Mass Communication, 1986.

[26] J. Ballenger, "Uncovering Abortion," Columbia Journalism Review (March/April 1992): 16.

[27] V. L. Hesterman, You've Come a Long Way Baby, Or Have You," Paper presented at the annual meeting of the Association for Education in Journalism and Mass Communication, 1987.

[28] L. Kessler, "Women's Magazines Coverage of Smoking Related Health Hazards," Journalism Quarterly (Summer 1989): 316-322, 445.

[29] K. E. Warner, L. M. Goldenhar, and C. G. McLaughlin, "Cigarette Advertising and Magazine Coverage of the Hazards of Smoking," The New England Journal of Medicine (30 January 1992): 305-309.

[30] V. P. Norris, "Consumer Magazine Prices and the Mythical Advertising Subsidy," Journalism Quarterly (Summer 1982): 205-211, 239.

[31] V. P. Norris, "Mad Economics," Journal of Communication (Winter 1984): 44-60.

[32] Ferguson, Kreshel, and Tinkham, 45.

[33] M. E. Land, Writing for Magazines (Englewood Cliffs, NJ: Prentice-Hall, 1987).

[34] Farrell, Feminism in the Mass Media, 15.

[35] "No Comment," Ms., July/August 1990, 1.

[36] L. Stewart, "Alice in Cosmeticsland," Ms., January 1973, 68-71, 106-110.

[37] I. Egan, "Ode to Makeup." Ms., January 1988, 14-15.

[38] N. Wolf, "Faith Healers, Holy Oil: Inside the Cosmetics Industry," Ms., May/June 1991, 64-67.

Acknowledgments

This article was the winner of the 1993 Top Graduate Paper Prize awarded by the Magazine Division of the Association for Education in Journalism and Mass Communication at the annual meeting held in Kansas City, MO in August 1993.

III

Pedagogical
and
Curricular Perspectives

8

Research Review:
Laboratory Student Magazine Programs

Tom Wheeler

ABSTRACT

This literature review seeks to analyze research devoted to student-produced magazines at journalism schools. It explores the publications themselves as well as the nature of various programs and curricular structures, with particular attention to ethical considerations and the role of faculty advisers. Because so few studies have focused on journalism school magazines, this review also addresses collateral sources that help provide practical and philosophical foundations for the establishment and conduct of magazine production programs; such sources include studies of, and articles about, student publications in general. The first section covers parameters of journalism school magazines (circulation, frequency, contents, etc.); curricular structure; First Amendment issues; funding; ethics; and the role of faculty advisers. The second briefly critiques the foremost studies and suggests topics for further research. The review finds that despite some useful preliminary research, the nature, curricular structure, and special problems of student publications at journalism schools remain largely unquantified.

Introduction

At most of the journalism schools offering magazine sequences, students are encouraged or required to pursue opportunities for hands-on work such as internships. For some, producing a laboratory magazine is one "real-world" experience that entails substantial motivation and satisfaction as well as the application of principles and skills acquired in class. A few books and many articles suggest what students and advisers *should* do, but with the exception of Click's *Governing College Student Publications* [1] and a few brief articles

111

in *College Media Review*, very little research prior to 1993 has documented the actual performance of students and faculty or the structure and goals of their programs, especially with respect to schools of journalism.

This article reviews the scant research examining journalism school laboratory magazines, as well as several mostly nonquantitative books and articles devoted to school publications in general. The relevance of some of the latter sources is limited because they are in part outdated or address literary magazines or even high school publications; regarding some topics, however, such articles comprise most of the literature extant. In several cases this review notes which of their sections may be extrapolated to journalism programs and which are outmoded or otherwise irrelevant. Generally, the usefulness of these collateral sources is inversely proportional to the publishing experience of the reader. Faculty recently charged with advising magazines, particularly new ones, will likely benefit from introductions to the challenges and goals of school periodicals, including those produced by, say, English majors or in a few cases even high school students.[2]

The question explored here is the extent to which the literature meets the needs of journalism faculty (and students) who publish laboratory magazines. For scholars, the topic is important because publication projects are often the most fully realized components of curricula intended to prepare graduates for professional work. The review is organized by subtopic rather than by chronology or other method. Section I discusses research examining general parameters of journalism school magazines (circulation, frequency, contents, etc.); curricular structure; First Amendment issues; funding; and particularly ethics and the role of faculty advisers. Section II critiques the foremost studies and suggests topics for further research.

General Parameters

Most of the studies discussed in this section are primarily descriptive in nature. Although 16 years old, *Ethics and Responsibilities of Advising College Student Publications* by Kopenhaver and Click remains a useful introduction.[3] The authors discussed several topics aside from those in the title, most in commentaries of about a page in length: editing, design, libel, obscenity, information sources,[4] business considerations, recruiting staff and more. These sketches are too brief and too old to suffice as comprehensive references, and insofar as they relate to journalism in general their subject matters are covered more completely and more recently in numerous books and articles; still, a significant benefit of *Ethics and Responsibilities* is that it casts these subjects in terms of college publications.

In "Survey Reveals Few Common Policies in Student Magazines," Lanan (1987) investigated college media advisers' roles, how magazines were delivered on campus, composition of advisory boards, and frequency of the publications (69 percent published either annually, biannually, or once/term, 31 percent more frequently). About a third of the three-page article was devoted to financial matters—revenues, funding, and compensation.[5]

The most significant studies of recent years are Frangoulis's "How We Teach Magazine Journalism: An Analysis of Today's Magazine Curricula" (1993)[6] and my own "Student Magazines at Journalism Schools" (1993).[7] Although his study concentrates on aspects of magazine instruction other than laboratory publications, Frangoulis found that 48 percent of responding professors required students to develop a magazine prospectus, and 45 percent required students to create a dummy issue. At 63 schools (43 percent), student magazines were published in a variety of types (79 percent were standard in size and format) and with a variety of frequencies (72 percent were published one, two, or three times a year).

After mailing a 37-question survey to more than 100 schools, I confined my 1993 study to 40 magazines affiliated with journalism programs. Respondents typically bore such titles as student publications director or faculty adviser, and their institutions reflected a wide range of size and location, from Saint Mary-of-the-Woods College to Northwestern, NYU, Ohio, Kansas, Missouri, and Syracuse. Topics included each publication's age and name and how the name was selected; physical specifications and frequency; the mix of black & white and color art; issue size; circulation; distribution (from campus only to nationwide); production systems (desktop vs. conventional paste-up, types of hardware and software[8]); problems and challenges; suggestions and solutions; and aspects of editorial content: issue-to-issue consistency vs. a start-from-scratch approach, subject matter (literary vs. journalistic), and editorial scope (from campus to international).

The study concluded: "A disparity is apparent among the basic structures of the programs, the diversity of which reflects the participants' differing needs, goals, and resources. Editorial models include: staff editors plus nonstaff reporter/writers; staffers who report, write, and edit with few if any freelance contributions; and a range of combinations.... Significant variations in the 40 magazines are also seen in issue size, readership (e.g., students vs. alumni), and distribution. The magazines begin to overlap somewhat in their physical parameters, with a conventional size and a frequency of either one per year or one per semester the favorites. Most are staffed by undergrads. Almost all employ some black and white processing, and most favor Macintosh-based desktop systems. Significant overlaps can be seen in preferences for issue-to-issue consistency, journalistic approaches to subject matter, circulations in the 1,000 to 5,000 range, freedom from censorship pressures, and the primary goals of providing hands-on experience and showcasing student work.... The most striking commonality is a lack of resources. Faced with budgetary challenges, respondents are creative and diligent but often exasperated."

Governing College Student Publications also addressed journalism laboratory and practicum projects, briefly, concluding that the programs may range from educationally effective to a waste of time, the publications from excellent to embarrassingly poor.

Curricular Structure

After noting "at journalism schools, the primary goals of student publications are to offer hands-on experience and an outlet for student work" (as opposed to, say, providing public relations vehicles), "Student Magazines at Journalism Schools" explored the structure of student staff: size; composition (grads vs. undergrads); methods of selection (e.g., competition); organization (class vs. extracurricular); and compensation (course credit, salary). The latter two categories are cross-referenced, with programs grouped under headings such as *class with course credit* and *extracurricular activity with monetary compensation*. Details of compensation are also cross-referenced to funding sources (for example, Florida A&M pays its two top staffers $400 per semester and is funded 5 percent from advertising revenue, the remainder from student government or student fees)[9].

The First Amendment

Although Kopenhaver and Click briefly explicated the First Amendment, their discussion of 1967's landmark *Dickey v. Alabama State Board of Education* decision (affirming the extension of press freedoms to student publications) must be viewed today as backdrop, a footnote to 1988's *Hazelwood School District v. Kuhlmeier*. McKee (1991) explained how *Hazelwood*, the first student press case to reach the Supreme Court, granted school authorities broad discretion in limiting student speech or exercising prior restraint, and how it was viewed as a turning away from the liberal interpretations of free speech granted in previous cases. After noting that opponents claimed it would stifle school publications, the author concluded that "the best protection for student rights may lie in adopting a school-specific written regulatory code and in forming a publication board of elected students, faculty and administrators that will administer the code."[10]

The use of parody in entertainment, social commentary or advertising was addressed by Paddon (1991), who offered useful guidelines on this topic of substantial interest to journalists, particularly students.[11] In "Student Magazines at Journalism Schools," respondents were asked, "Are there any topics

[your] magazine won't cover?" Most reported a freedom from censorship pressures, although others revealed why some stories were pulled prior to publication, how various dilemmas were resolved, and guidelines used by some advisers.[12]

Ethics

It was noted above that while few articles document what advisers do, many suggest what they *should* do. Nowhere is the contrast more apparent than in the field of ethics. Little has been written about the subject in terms of journalism school publications, although the ethics of publishing in general has been addressed at length, as regards both high school and college publications.[13]

The discussion of ethics in Click's *Governing College Student Publications* is helpful, and Kopenhaver and Click's *Ethics and Responsibilities* interprets various ethical codes in light of still-current journalistic conventions; their guidelines (warnings against accepting "freebies," for example) remain useful. The book includes the National Council of College Publications Advisers' Code of Ethics, as well as the Society of Professional Journalists' Code of Ethics and other statements of principles that can serve as models for journalism magazine programs.[14]

Funding

Heitschmidt (1979) examined the structure and funding of adviser positions through a questionnaire mailed to 306 faculty at post-secondary institutions. After documenting the publications' type, funding, and primary function, the author concluded that the major student publications were newspapers, yearbooks and literary magazines and that newspapers, and yearbooks were funded primarily by advertising and student fees, literary magazines by student fees and institutional subsidies.[15]

The 40 advisers participating in "Student Magazines at Journalism Schools" specified one or more funding sources—advertising, subscription fees, student fees, endowment, etc.—as well as the percentage of funding derived from each source. About half of the magazines were funded by a single source, usually described with terms such as *university subsidy*, *general college fund*, or *academic budget*. About half depended on advertising revenue for some of their operating costs, usually less than 50 percent.[16]

The Role of Faculty Advisers

Most articles addressing the role of advisers lack quantified foundation, but *Governing College Student Publications* draws upon substantial studies of policy statements in its useful discussion of an adviser's role in relation to the funding of his or her publication, and in its explications of codes of ethics and standards. A few sources, although not addressing journalism school publications, provide useful sketches.[17] Articles devoted to alumni periodicals are among the most helpful for journalism advisers,[18] and other articles examine aspects of advising such as editorial independence,[19] conflict resolution,[20] and grading.[21]

Although it does not focus exclusively on magazines, *Ethics and Responsibilities* is probably the most successful attempt to provide a comprehensive introduction. Prepared especially for advisers without much experience, it offers a philosophical underpinning as well as specific guidelines, such as: "The adviser is not a censor, nor a copywriter, nor a rewrite person, nor an editorial writer. The adviser does not lay out pages, nor edit any copy before it goes to the printer, nor act as an editor.... He advises and teaches these skills, but after giving guidance and the best possible judgment, defends—and observes—totally the right of the staff to make the final decisions." *Ethics and Responsibilities* reprints the National Council of College Publications Advisers Code of Professional Standards for Advisers (1974), which delineates responsibilities to the administration, students, and colleagues. The book also lists eight "basic models of advising situations" with brief commentary. The models: full-time adviser or publications director; load credit (reduced teaching load, generally one fewer class for each publication advised); extra compensation, "usually at the rate of one overload course per publication"; practicum course supervision; paid staff; unpaid staff; production responsibilities; and volunteer faculty with no direct responsibilities or compensation (an arrangement described as widespread).[22]

Heitschmidt's study documented the participating publications' number of advisers, as well as those advisers' primary assignments, direct superiors, titles, salary sources and compensation. Lanan summarized: "[Advisers] are there providing advice, setting policies, supervising, counseling, motivating, etc."[23] Additional details regarding adviser activities can be found in "Student Magazines at Journalism Schools," which reported that "advisers are typically involved in all phases of production from brainstorming to proofing bluelines, serving as a sounding board, teacher (writing, editing, design), critic, grader, motivator, counselor (particularly regarding legal, ethical and technical matters), and all around problem-solver." As reported in that 1993 study, decision making is accomplished under a variety of models. Responses to "Who calls the shots regarding topic coverage, graphics, and assignments?" were almost evenly divided between the chief editor and a consensus of student editors.[24]

Kopenhaver and Click pointed out that some magazines are advised by experienced professionals acting as managing editors with authority to approve, modify, or veto student decisions, an arrangement that could "stifle [students'] initiative, dampen incentive, and destroy staffer interest." They warn, "There is potential for great harm in such an approach." In its *Magazine Fundamentals, 3rd Ed.* booklet, cited in endnote No. 17, the Columbia Scholastic Press Association (CSPA) states: "Simply put, the adviser does not edit the magazine nor does he or she work as a staff member." Ball State's governing document, cited by *Governing College Student Publications*, asserts that "faculty advisers advise students but do not engage in actual editorial decisions."

But notwithstanding the proscriptions of various authors and codes, my study revealed that some advisers do indeed take active editorial roles. One respondent called the adviser a policy-setting editor in chief, another listed "edits all copy" among his duties, and others reported that positions filled by students at some institutions are assumed by faculty at others. Some emphasized that they are *not* de facto editors and allow—or rather require— students to make the decisions. Thus at journalism school magazines, the distribution of editorial authority seems to vary significantly, perhaps drastically.

Critiques, Suggestions for Further Research

"Student Magazines at Journalism Schools" was by no means a comprehensive study. Although it examined a largely unexplored field and surveyed a few dozen magazines' specifications and various programs' goals and practices, it tested no hypotheses and raised as many questions as it answered.

To what extent does existing literature meet the needs of journalism faculty and students who publish laboratory magazines? *Governing College Student Publications, Ethics and Responsibilities* and *College Media Review* provide helpful background, and "Student Magazines at Journalism Schools" and "How We Teach Magazine Journalism" are good starts. Still, the nature, curricular structures, and special problems of student publications in journalism schools remain largely unquantified. Important subjects awaiting further study include:

(a) The relationship between advisers and staffers, particularly regarding organization, the distribution of authority, mechanisms of decision-making and the extent to which advisers' practices conform to, say, Kopenhaver and Click's recommendations or professional codes.

(b) The extent to which advisers' attitudes towards ethics and their decisions in the face of ethical dilemmas conform to guidelines prescribed in various codes.

(c) The methods with which publication projects are integrated into magazine sequences (Are they required? Do all students participate? What are the prerequisite classes? How are staff selected?), as well as compensation to students (course credit, payment) and faculty (reduced teaching load, stipend).

(d) The extent to which laboratory magazines approximate or re-create real-world publishing environments.

(e) The relationships between funding sources and editorial freedom, production budgets, and compensation to staff and faculty.

(f) Creative responses to funding shortfalls.

Comprehensive data on these topics, if focused on journalism schools, could prove invaluable to faculty, administrators, and students alike who are engaged in the production of laboratory magazines.

Notes

[1] J. William Click, Governing College Student Publications (NCCPA Publications, School of Journalism, Lasher Hall, Ohio University, Athens, OH 45701, 1980). This monograph analyzes policy statements and codes formulated to assist in the production of student publications. "Governing," as used here, entails establishing a structure intended to provide orderly procedures for, say, selecting staff, reviewing editorial quality, and overseeing financial matters rather than providing guidelines for day-to-day operations. Sample policy statements are quoted, and a checklist for constructing a governing document is appended.

[2] Several sources that address problems faced by literary magazines contain potentially useful tips for journalism advisers. See Ann Hale, "Verbal and Visual—Together," Communication: Journalism Education Today, 18:3 (Spring 1985): 13, which suggests using written guidelines for all materials submitted to literary magazines; A. P. Colasurdo, "The Literary Magazine as Class Project," English Journal, 74:2 (February 1985): 82; J. Grady Locklear, "The Magazine: Its History and Present Status," Quill and Scroll, 62:4 (April-May 1988): 4; and John Cutsinger, "Undertaking a Creative Arts Magazine Requires Desire, Initiative, Insight," Quill and Scroll, 56:4 (April-May, 1982): 12.

[3] Lillian Lodge Kopenhaver and J. William Click, Ethics and Responsibilities of Advising College Student Publications (National Council of College Publications Advisers Publications, School of Journalism, Ohio University, Athens, OH 45701, 1978).

[4] The authors' recommended publications include College Press Review, Editor & Publisher, Columbia Journalism Review, The Quill, Community College Journalist, and Advertising Age. Although primarily targeting high school publications, the following sources, also recommended by Kopenhaver and Click, may prove useful: Scholastic Editor, Communication: Journalism Education Today, Quill and Scroll, Bulletin of the Columbia Scholastic Press Advisers Association (CSPAA), and The School Press Review.

[5] A. Lanan, "Student Magazines: Survey Reveals Few Common Policies in Student Magazines," College Media Review (Spring-Summer 1987): 10. A survey of 10 open-ended questions was mailed to a sample drawn from the 1986 College Media Advisers Directory of Members, and it garnered a "usable response rate" of 37 percent (32 responses). The author broke down funding sources such as the university fund, student fees, subscriptions, and advertising into two classifications: "those that assume there is a general benefit associated with the existence of these publications within a university community and those that attempt to assign a charge to the

users of these publications.... It appears that the use of general revenues and user revenues are both equally employed." She discussed categories of "users" ("private," "institutional"), distribution of revenues, and the allocation of authority to review budgets, approve expenses, etc.

[6] George J. Frangoulis, "How We Teach Magazine Journalism: An Analysis of Today's Magazine Curricula," a paper presented at the AEJMC national convention (Kansas City, MO, August 11-14, 1993). The author mailed 402 questionnaires to members of the AEJMC magazine division and ASJMC. The response rate was 44.8 percent from each group. Frangoulis cites Mary Kinville Seilo's "A Study of Magazine Journalism Education" (Master's Thesis, Ohio University, 1969), which considered 55 schools then accredited by ACEJ. Seilo found that producing a new magazine prospectus and dummy issue were considered important components in magazine programs. Ten of the institutions cited by Seilo had lab magazines; according to Frangoulis, "[M]ost were published once each semester or when the funds to publish the magazine were available."

[7] Tom Wheeler, "Student Magazines at Journalism Schools," a paper presented to the AEJMC Magazine Division Conference (Columbia, SC, November 5-7, 1993).

[8] For more on how computers are used in teaching magazine journalism, see Frangoulis [6].

[9] For more on staffing, see Click,[1], which discusses the necessity of a staff manual and a governing document, the editor's authority and responsibility, selection of staff, operations manuals, and censorship. Other sources discussing the staffing of student publications include: Curt Lader, "A Sharing of Natural Resources," School Press Review, 56:7 (February 1981): 5, which examines shared staff in the production of magazines, newspapers, and yearbooks; and Paul E. Burd, "You Gotta Have a Blue-Chip Magazine," College Press Review, 19:1-2 (1980): 47, which sketches how a periodical at Ohio evolved into the self-supported Athens Magazine, produced with "minimal" faculty supervision and by staff that changes each quarter.

[10] Kathy Brittain McKee, "Regulating High School Publications after Hazelwood: An Inclusive Model," a paper presented at the annual meeting of the Association for Education in Journalism and Mass Communication (Boston, MA, August 7-10, 1991), Part XVII: Misc. Studies, Section B. Although it concerned high school rather than university publications, Hazelwood seems to be the controlling case law at present. See also, J. William Click and Lillian Lodge Kopenhaver, "Few Changes Since Hazelwood," School Press Review, 65:2 (Winter 1990): 12, which surveys CSPA newspapers to gauge the case's influence.

[11] Anna R. Paddon, "Parody as Free Expression: A Unit for Magazine Classes (Approaches to Teaching Freedom of Expression)," Journalism Educator, 46:2 (Summer 1991): 42. The author introduced a parody component into her management and production class "to demonstrate that federal courts have granted constitutional protection to risque, irreverent, and outrageous parodies."

[12] Wheeler, "Student Magazines." Those interested in censorship issues in student publications should see other articles concerning Hazelwood, such as: A. Gynn, "Supreme Court Deals Blow To Student Journalists," Social Education, 53:3 (Mar. 1989): 175; as well as David Martinson and Debra Minick, "Future Advisers React," College Press Review, 17:3 (Spring 1978): 30, which discusses advisers' roles in relation to the First Amendment; and M. Ryan and D. L. Martinson, "Attitudes of College Newspaper Advisers toward Censorship of the Student Press," Journalism Quarterly, 63:1 (Spring 1986): 55.

[13] College Media Review offers several articles on ethics. The College Media Advisers' Code of Professional Standards for Publications Advisers, revised 1983, appears in 30:2 (Spring 1991): 12, and addresses the ethics of advisers as journalists, educators, and managers, as well as their responsibilities to students, administrators, and colleagues. Other pertinent articles from College Media Review include: College Media Advisers' Code of Ethics, 30:1 (Winter 1991); David Martinson, "Adviser Ethics: Answering ALL the Questions," 30:2 (Spring 1991): 14, in

which the author asserts that too much time is spent on considering what an ethical adviser is, and not enough on whether being ethical is important to the individual or whether he or she has the necessary will; and "Freebies, Ethics and Pizza," 30:3 (Summer/Fall, 1991).

[14] Regarding the Council for Advancement and Support of Education (CASE) statement of ethics for periodicals editors, see the LaSalle cite [18] below.

[15] Donnetta Lynn Heitschmidt, "The Organizational Structure and Funding of the Student Publications Adviser Position," Dissertation Abstracts International, 40 (July-December 1979): 1.

[16] Nineteen magazines had a combination of two or more funding sources, the most common of which was advertising plus student government or student fees; of the seven within that group, only one was funded primarily by advertising, and the others received only 5 percent to 25 percent of funding from ads. See also Ron Parent, "Good Friends Support Good Reading," Currents, 8:6 (July-August 1982): 22. In discussing the financial support of Notre Dame, an alumni magazine with an annual budget of $500,000, the author addressed overcoming administrator skepticism of the magazine's purpose and effectiveness, and the educator as fund raiser; includes an example of an editor's letter intended to solicit funding.

[17] The pamphlet Magazine Fundamentals, 3rd Ed. offers brief but useful advice on establishing a format, the role of the staff, content, design, and other matters. It is published by the Columbia Scholastic Press Association (CSPA; Box 11, Central Mail Room, Columbia University, New York NY 10027), which evaluates magazines and presents awards. See also, "The Game Plan," Communication: Journalism Education Today, 19:2 (Winter 1985): 2, which provides guidelines for advisers working on newspapers, literary magazines and yearbooks; E. J. Sullivan, "The School Literary Magazine: History, Form, and Function," Teachers and Writers Magazine, 18:4 (March-April 1987): 4, which addresses the role of faculty advisers among other topics; and S. J. Hagen, "Internship Problems and the Academic Advisor's Role," a paper presented at the annual meeting of the Speech Communication Association (67th, Anaheim, CA, November 12-15, 1981); its discussions of task instruction and feedback could prove useful to magazine advisers.

[18] For example, see Patricia Ann LaSalle, "College and University Magazines: Building Credibility to Advance Your Institution," CASE, Washington, D.C., 1991. This monograph addresses magazines intended to promote the school and enhance its image. Topics include history, information giving vs. image building, policies and practices, decision making, fund raising, dealing with authors, plagiarism, management, and staffing. Several articles from Currents magazine are reprinted; sample mission statements and the CASE statement of ethics for periodicals editors are appended. See also, Walton R. Collins, "What's Wrong With Alumni Periodicals," Currents, 11:6 (June 1985): 34, in which several editors provide advice on improving publications. Weakness of design, failure to establish an identity, and other topics are very briefly discussed. Several tips are obvious (remember your audience, be credible), but this is nevertheless a useful article for advisers.

[19] Marshall Ledger, "Who's in Charge Here?," Currents, 13:3 (March 1987): 10, which surveys 35 editors about restraints on their independence and discusses getting the authority necessary to edit an effective alumni magazine; tips for covering controversy are offered.

[20] Mary Anne Higgins, "Defining The Adviser's Role," Scholastic Editor, 59:2 (November-December 1979): 4, discusses conflict between an adviser and student newspaper staffers who wanted to print a statement the adviser considered unfair to the school administration. Conflict resolution procedures were discussed.

[21] Mary Kahl Sparks, "The Grading Systems of Award-Winning High School Journalism Teachers in Production-Oriented Classes," a paper presented at the annual meeting of the Association for Education in Journalism and Mass Communication (Corvallis, OR, August 6-9, 1983). Self-evaluation, peer evaluation, point systems and other methods are discussed by 27 teachers.

[22] See also, Heitschmidt (cited in endnote [15]), which discussed five types of advising responsibility: budgets, newspapers, bid specifications, yearbooks, and literary magazines. Eleven descriptive models were discussed, such as adviser-instructor, adviser-PR official, adviser-administrator, volunteer, and professional journalist as consultant.

[23] Lanan grouped adviser roles into three activity categories (oversees general operation, oversees production, and provides quality control). The author admitted that the groupings were "a bit arbitrary and the assignment of the individual roles to these categories even more questionable," but suggested that the system did reveal the variety of job descriptions. See also D. Martinson, and M. Ryan, "The Adviser's Role: What Is the Adviser's Obligation to Students?," College Media Review, (Summer 1986): 8, which describes the adviser's "schizophrenic nature."

[24] Wheeler, 1993. One respondent named the adviser alone, one indicated that the class made decisions as a group, and others selected different combinations of chief editor, staff editors' consensus, and adviser. Nine participants described details of their jobs or of the decision-making apparatus in their programs.

Acknowledgements

The author wishes to acknowledge the advice of Assistant Professor Wayne Wanta, School of Journalism and Communication, University of Oregon, in the preparation of this article.

9

Research Review:
Issues in Magazine Journalism Education

Elliot King

ABSTRACT

Hobbled by an impoverished underlying model and a lack of resources, very little empirical research has explored magazine journalism education. The underlying paradigm is investigated, the research that has been conducted is reviewed and an optimistic assessment about the possibilities of future research is offered.

Introduction

Magazine education holds a marginal position within the journalism and mass communication academy. A 1989 census of journalism and mass communications programs reported that only 47 schools offered students the opportunity to specialize in magazine journalism. In contrast, 242 schools offered concentrations in a news-editorial sequence, 199 in public relations, 178 in broadcasting and 128 in advertising. Fewer than two percent of the graduates of those journalism and mass communications programs specialized in magazine journalism.[1] Of course, the 42 specialty programs do not represent the complete presence of magazine journalism within colleges and universities in the United States. Of the 110 schools responding to a 1976 survey, 92.5 percent indicated that they offered at least one magazine journalism course although only 22 percent had sequences of magazine journalism courses.[2]

With relatively few courses in magazine journalism offered, relatively few faculty members are needed to teach them. The 1976 survey indicated that of the schools which offered one or more courses in magazine journalism, only 30 percent had at least one faculty member who dedicated at least one third of his or her efforts to magazine journalism and only 15 percent had two faculty members devoting one third of their time to magazine journalism. More than 50 percent had less than one person devoting one-third of their time to magazine journalism. Moreover, at that time, only 26 percent of the primary instructors in magazine courses and sequences held a Ph.D.

Though the landscape for magazine journalism education surely has changed to a degree in the ensuing 17 years, that constellation of factors—few courses to support faculty and few research-oriented faculty within that small pool—has meant that very little academically oriented research has been published about magazines in general and even less about magazine journalism education. From 1964 to 1983, for example, only six percent of the articles in *Journalism Quarterly*, or 116 articles, examined magazines at all and only one percent explored magazine journalism education.[3] Since then, no articles primarily about magazine journalism education have been published in *Journalism Quarterly*. And while articles concerning magazine journalism have appeared from time to time, since 1985, fewer than 20 people have published on that topic in *Journalism Educator*.[4]

Nor has the related academic field of composition shown much interest in magazine journalism education. In the 1980's, only one article in *College Composition and Communication* addressed issues possibly of interest to magazine journalism educators.[5] Why has not more research into magazine journalism and magazine journalism been published? The few researchers who have been active in the field offered the following reasons. Magazine publishers themselves conduct a lot of research; the researchers lacked time, money, or support; and few of them considered themselves primarily magazine specialists.[6]

The small body of research about magazine journalism education that has been published or archived in ERIC can be roughly categorized in three ways. First, some researchers have examined the relevance of what has been called the revolution in college composition to magazine journalism educators. Several people have provided teaching tips, suggestions, and accounts of what they do in their classroom. Finally, a handful of reports on miscellaneous subjects have been published. Not everybody agrees with the one scholar who described research into journalism education in general as "little more than ritualistic articulations of the obvious."[7] But even those most active in the field believe that most research into magazine journalism in general has been unsatisfactory.[8]

Working from this landscape, I will first suggest that in addition to the lack of resources and personnel, research into magazine journalism education has been impeded by an implicit and impoverished notion of the scope of magazine education. Next, I will review what little has been published about magazine journalism education. Finally, I will suggest areas of potential exploration in the future, including integrating magazine research into magazine journalism education.

The Theory of Magazine Journalism Education

In virtually all academic disciplines, research is driven by an underlying set of assumptions. These assumptions shape the way questions are asked; the methods through which data is gathered; and the criteria and standards for evaluating the validity of the work. Within mass media research in general, at least three different paradigms—which some scholars have categorized as social scientific, interpretive, and critical theory—are in operation.[9]

Though clearly a niche within the mainstream of mass media research, research into magazine journalism education does not fall neatly into any or all of those categories. And while in most academic disciplines what is taught in the class room is determined by theory and the research to which that theory leads, what is generally taught in the magazine journalism classroom is, as John Henningham puts it, a "distilled version of what is practiced by media professionals." Moreover, he adds, journalism education is looked at as technical training that does not lend itself to research.[10] And there can be little doubt that magazine journalism education is dominated by a professional orientation. For example, in its section of a report about the future of journalism and mass communication education, the magazine task force concentrated its attention on the skills students will need to get a job and to advance in their careers.[11]

Of course, the degree to which journalism education should be tied to the needs of the media industry is a debate which is reverberating throughout the field.[12] But the problem runs deeper within magazine journalism education than elsewhere in the journalism academy. In this arena, not only are the goals of education closely linked to the needs of the industry—i.e. train entry level professionals—the most commonly held notion in the JMC academy of what the industry is does not reflect the full range, variety, and richness of magazine journalism. Though magazine journalism educators give lip service to the impressive scope of magazine journalism,[13] based on the research surveyed for this article, the implicit and privileged model for most magazine journalism classes is the long-form feature story assembled through extensive reporting with human sources and aimed at middle- to high-brow, general-interest, consumer audiences—articles that would appear in magazines like the *New Yorker*. Moreover, these magazines are not seen as medium of communication but simply as markets to which students can sell a commodity—their articles.

This implicit model can be seen in two ways. First, a traditional paradigm in an area can usually be found in its text books.[14] Though no systematic examination of the textbooks used in magazines has been conducted, in one study, magazine textbooks were found to adhere strictly to a narrow range of genre expectations.[15] Surveying three popular texts which have had multiple editions, one indicates that much of its advice comes from winners of the Pulitzer Prize for journalism.[16] Another relies on the words of wisdom from the likes of David Halberstam, Joyce Carol Oates and Gay Talese. It also argues that most newspapers now publish stories running over 3,000, the kind of story this text teaches students to produce.[17] The third holds up *Reader's Digest* and *TV Guide* as eventual markets for aspiring freelance magazine writers.[18]

The notion that the model for magazine journalism education should be long features for consumer magazines and consumer magazine themselves is so dominant that after surveying the readers of the *Argus Journal*, a magazine of an association of the cattle industry, in 1990, Jeffers argues that magazine educators should consider moving more towards "service journalism" rather than general features in their course. Almost to his surprise, he found younger readers of the magazine liked how-to articles with management information.[19] In other words, he argues that perhaps students should be trained to create a different type of commodity.

Broadening the range of products students are trained to develop is a small step. The idea that students are being trained to produce a specific commodity—the implicit paradigm informs many of the teaching tips and research that has been conducted—at times leads the discussion of research results away from potentially more interesting avenues. For example, Mandelbaum observed that student expectations of magazine courses were shaped by what they read, such as first person personality pieces in teen magazines. But instead of exploring the implications of working with immature readers, he describes how he shared his experience of writing an article for the *New York Times Magazine* with them.[20] The implicit attitude is that the objective of his class is to train students to write not for *Seventeen* but the *New York Times Magazine*.

Along the same lines, Reuss introduced her analysis of the use of quotations in different magazine stories by arguing that students do not read the publications they have targeted as potential markets for their stories closely enough and don't understand the techniques they must use to create saleable articles.[21] Her assumption apparently is that the extensive use of vivid quotation from a variety of sources is an essential element of a saleable article. That assumption leads her to dismiss her provocative findings: the article with the greatest number of quotations and the article with the fewest number of quotations both appeared in the largest circulation magazines in her sample. For the two articles with the fewest number of quotes, she opined that "Perhaps the editors were interested in the author and his declarations on the subject."[22]

Perhaps they were. Or perhaps the amount of quotation needed for a saleable article depends largely on the type of article written. But even more interestingly, if magazines were conceptualized not as "markets" but as a medium of communication, a study of the use of quotations could lead to interesting insights about the relationship of presentation, substance, and audience.

Along the same lines, perhaps blindered by the dominant model, Jolliffe ignored an intriguing result in her study of the way editors, regular contributors, and novice writers evaluated query letters. The objective of the study was to help novices write better query letters so they could place their articles.[23] The results represented a provocative study in persuasive communication. Editors primarily cared about the quality of the idea and the demonstrated writing skill. They did not care about the writer's experience or expertise, or minor grammatical mistakes in the letter. Evidence of extensive research led to letters being ranked lower. While unpacking the implications of those results is beyond the scope of this paper, they are far richer than simply guideposts for writers of query letters. Those results could be seen to have more meaning if they had not been thought of basically as sales letters to sell a commodity.

Indeed, one of the reasons research in magazine journalism education is so sparse is that the theory is impoverished. Based on an analysis of textbooks and the assumptions of selected studies, it is clear that the dominant paradigm in magazine journalism education is extremely narrow. The goal apparently is not just to train students to enter the professional magazine world but to prepare them to write for a select group of elite magazines—those magazines which publish long-form features for a consumer audience.

Given the relationship between theory and research, it is not surprising that this market model has narrowed the scope and substance of research driven by it. The two most interesting questions stemming from this model is what are the attributes of what sells, and how to be able to get students to create commodities with those attributes. Those questions have been at the center of most of the research into magazine journalism education. Other interesting questions, however, can be and from time to time are asked.

The Composition Revolution Meets Journalism Education

Among the most interesting studies in magazine journalism education research are generated by what has been called the revolution in composition studies. Since the early 1970s, scholars have argued that old methods of teaching composition which focussed on the formal attributes of the end product and formalized instruction to create end products with those attributes were inadequate. For example, Hairston argued that the traditional paradigm in composition studies "did not come out of research or experimentation" but instead represented "an idealized version of what professional writers think or imagine what an efficient writing process should be."[24]

Instead of the end product, proponents of the composition revolution argued that the central concern of instructors should be the writing process. Researchers should identify through empirical research how accomplished and novice students write. Then instructors could work with student writers at every stage of the process.[25] As with all revolutions, different researchers used slightly different terms to describe the various stages of the writing process. Among the steps in the process are the conception of the idea or the stimulus; the incubation of the idea; and then the production of the idea, which includes writing and revising. The process was seen as recursive and in some versions discovery through the act of writing was emphasized.[26]

Although much of the writing-as-process research has been conducted with students engaged in reflexive writing in which the writer is posited as the chief audience, at least four scholars have argued that the ideas contained in the writing-as-process revolution could be relevant to journalism education. In 1986, Zurek argued that the shift in emphasis represented by the revolution in composition studies could be useful to journalism instructors. The old emphasis on the product rested on a philosophy that reality was static, waiting to be reported. The new approach would emphasize meaning, discovery, and revision. No longer would students be advised to begin to write only when then knew what they wanted to know.[27] Zurek's sentiments about writing as process were generally applauded by Olsen the following year.[28] Since then, two empirical studies have been reported based on the ideas of writing as process. Arguing that the insights gained in the composition revolution had not yet penetrated journalism research, textbooks, or teaching methods, Pitts studied eight working reporters and five student journalists as they worked in their regular environment. She then developed a model of how those writers actually worked.[29]

Among Pitts' more interesting findings were that the lead was often written independently of the rest of the story and took as much as one third of the total writing time. The remainder of the text was then set against the lead, and if they didn't cohere, one or the other was revised. Reporters also used editing both for fundamental revision and for polishing minor errors. But perhaps Pitts was overly harsh in her assessment of the degree to which the writing-as-process philosophy has penetrated journalism education. Observing that the steps outlined in the writing-as-process sequence—particularly those describing writing as discovery and the need for multiple revisions—were more suitable to magazine writing with its longer deadlines and more complex nature than basic newswriting, Schierhorn and Endres surveyed magazine instructors to see which approach to writing they used.[30]

They found that regardless of which method instructors professed to employ—product versus process—they all worked closely with their students. Moreover, both camps identified similar advantages and disadvantages to the methods they used. The advantages claimed by instructors using both methods included better story development, the replication of a real world environment, and helping students identify their own writing problems. The disadvantages involved the students becoming dependent on teacher or peer feedback and students waiting for the last minute to complete their assignment. The process method also seemed to lead to grade inflation. In a related study, Schierhorn and Endres found little gender differences among instructors using each method.[31]

While the revolution of the 1970's was old news in composition studies by the early 1980's, it was not without its critics in journalism education at least through the late 1980's. In a trenchant article dripping with disdain for composition teachers who he characterized as "creatures of arduous slogging...on their wearying path from B.A. to M.A. to Ph.D.," Mencher warned against privileging writing in a basic journalism class. Each story type, he argued, had certain nonnegotiable necessities and teaching writing as process can be insidious.[32]

Nevertheless, at least some of the ideas contained in the writing-as-process approach seem to be penetrating the journalism academy under the rubric of the writing coach. For example, in a review of *Coaching Writers: Editors and Reporters Working Together* by Roy Peter Clark and Don Fry, August Gibbon noted that the book introduced the concept of writing coach into the literature of journalism instruction.[33] While he does not link coaching explicitly to writing-as-process principles, Schierhorn does when she describes the techniques used by 10 instructors using coaching methods in magazine writing classes. While commenting that there had been virtually no reported research on the coaching method previously, she demonstrates how coaching cleanly maps onto the writing-as-process model of writing.[34]

Consciously or not, the composition revolution is slowly infiltrating magazine journalism education. To date, however, it has not been unshackled from the professional model which still dominates instruction. To date, within the journalism academy, writing as process has been seen as an instructional approach and not as a framework for empirical research.

Other Empirical Research and Teaching Tips

Other than the studies based on writing as process, there are very few empirical studies of what transpires in magazine journalism classrooms. In a very limited study in a related area, Renfro and Maittlen-Harris suggested that increasing the amount of time students spend using a computer in class from one hour to three hours a week did not measurably improve their ability to produce more copy under deadline, write tighter or organize their work better.[35] And in a well-crafted paper that at least acknowledged the need to assess student responses to new teaching methods, Prior-Miller, Terry, and Dove described how they integrated quantitative research skills into their magazine class.[36]

In fact, most of the literature about magazine journalism education can be best described as teaching tips. Instructors share the techniques that they use in class, often concluding that the students seem to enjoy them. For example, Smith uses a "screw model" to describe the organization of a story.[37] Nelson teaches article writing using a train metaphor.[38] Lieb helps students reclaim a subjective voice appropriate for magazine journalism by having them write editorials on both sides of a single issue.[39] Rowan has devised a series of questions to help students discover ideas about which they can write.[40] Paddon uses copyright and trademark law about parodies to teach editorial decision making and legal and ethical issues in a magazine management class.[41] Grow has developed a checklist to rate good magazine articles.[42] And Wheeler has effectively simulated the writer-editor relationship in his magazine journalism classroom.[43]

While articles of this type are generally interesting and contain the explanations and reasoning which led to the development of the techniques described, they are not intended as serious research. Nor do they fill the research void in magazine journalism pedagogy. Instead, they are all tips about ways to cajole students to write saleable magazine articles.

Future Directions

Magazine journalism educators face two main challenges if they hope to construct a framework for systematic research. Minimally, they must broaden the professional model they use to include non-long-form feature articles for general interest consumer publications. They must widen their vision of reality and see the magazine industry as more than a dialogue between the potential writers and imaginary editors. Magazine journalism educators often claim they want to simulate reality.[44] But the narrow model underlying their educational strategies belies that claim.

While broadening the scope of market orientation of magazine journalism classes would not insure theories which could drive interesting research would develop, it would open up a wider space for that to happen. Magazines could be seen as a complex channel of communication. Ironically, most of the dynamic growth in magazines has not been in general interest magazines but in specialized magazines. Articles in hobbyist magazines like *PC* and *PC World*, for example, do not rely on long-form features with lots of quotes from lots of people. They often consist of overviews of different kinds of products in specific categories. Articles in trade magazines often do extensively use quotations, but they do not devote much space to colorful details and scene-setting. Company magazines use different kinds of articles than technical publications. Moreover, only very few magazines—perhaps the 50 to 150 largest—can afford extensive rewriting by authors. For their part, in the real world freelancers generally chafe at revisions.

Broadening but not relinquishing the professional model implicit in magazine journalism education would open several possibilities for educators. They could begin to incorporate interesting research into magazines which do not necessarily have a specifically pedagogical intention. For example, classes could explore the nature of the audience looking at uses and gratification research.[45] Or students could study how advertising influences editorial content in magazines.[46]

In addition, by widening their vision, magazine educators could begin to systematically explore the different forms of magazines and how those magazines change over time. Students could study how the form of saleable magazine articles change over time and how they remain the same.[47] A broader, professional, commodity-oriented model could lead to a more systematic study of media economics; of who actually becomes magazine writers and why; and how magazines negotiated the same kind of demassification process that seems to be confronting television today.

A more radical approach would be for magazine educators to replicate the revolution in composition studies and end their fixation with the final product—the creation of young graduates prepared to produce saleable commodities to specific markets—and instead focus on the process of student education. They could conceive of magazine journalism education as a process of teaching people to communicate through specific forms within specific real world contexts.

In that framework, in addition to research into those real world contexts, a whole range of student-centered questions which could be important to magazine journalism education could come into focus. Those questions can be summarized along these lines. What do students know; when do they know it; how do they do it; why do they know it; what do they do with that knowledge; what do educators believe they should know; and what are the communication processes available to achieve those ends? To date, questions of that kind have rarely been asked, much less answered.

Conclusion

Although not every article or paper concerning magazine journalism education has been reviewed in this article, the research cited here is a fair and representative sample. The inescapable conclusion is that research into magazine journalism education has yet to produce much insight into classroom processes. The field is hobbled by a lack of resources including too few research-oriented faculty as well as an impoverished model underscoring common teaching methods. Indeed, the dominant paradigm sometimes deflects researchers from recognizing interesting aspects in the results of the few empirical studies which have been conducted.

Some would be tempted to call research into magazine journalism education a barren terrain. It's not. It is virgin territory waiting for a conceptual framework which will point researchers to significant questions. From those questions, significant answers will emerge.

Notes

[1] Lee Becker, "Enrollments Increase in 1989, But Graduation Rates Drop," Journalism Educator 45:3 (Autumn 1990): 4-15.

[2] Donna J. Schnadel and Byron T. Scott, "A Survey of Magazine Journalism Education," Paper presented to the Association for Education in Journalism and Mass Communication, College Park MD., August 1976, ERIC ED 149372.

[3] Peter Gerlach, "Magazine Research in Journalism Quarterly," Journalism Quarterly 64:1 (Spring 1987): 178-182.

[4] I reviewed nearly all the issues of Journalism Educator from 1985 forward in researching this article.

[5] "Student as Staff Writer, Instructor as Editor: A Situational Context for Teaching Writing," College Composition and Communication 32: 327-329.

[6] Peter Gerlach, "Magazine Research."

[7] Enn Raudsepp, "Reinventing Journalism Education," Canadian Journal of Communication 14:2 (May 1989).

[8] Peter Gerlach, "Magazine Research."

[9] W. James Potter, Roger Cooper, and Michel Dupagne "The Three Paradigms of Mass Media Research in Mainstream Communication Journals," Communication Theory 3:4: 317-335.

[10] John V. Henningham, "An Australian Perspective on Educators as Researchers," Journalism Educator 41:3 (Autumn 1986): 8-12.

[11] "Challenges and Opportunities in Journalism and Mass Communication Education: A Report of the Task Force on the Future of Journalism and Mass Communication Education," Journalism Educator 44:1 (Spring 1989): A14-15.

[12] Robert O. Blanchard and William G. Christ, Media Education and the Liberal Arts: A Blueprint for a New Professionalism (Hillsdale, NJ: Lawrence Earlbaum Associates, 1993).

[13] Lee Jolliffe, "How Editors, Regular Contributors, and Novice Writers Rate Query Letters," Paper presented to the Association for Education in Journalism and Mass Communica-

tion, Washington DC, August 1989, ERIC ED 311507.

[14] Maxine Hairston, "The Winds of Change: Thomas Kuhn and the Revolution in the Teaching of Writing," College Composition and Communication 33:1 (Winter 1982): 76-88.

[15] Monica Johnstone, "A Rhetorical Approach to Journalistic Writing," 1992, ERIC ED 352648.

[16] Edward Jay Friedlander and John Lee, Feature Writing for Newspapers and Magazines, 2nd Edition (New York: HarperCollins College Publishers, 1993).

[17] William L. Rivers, Freelancer and Staff Writer 5th ed. (Belmont CA: Wadsworth Publishing Co, 1992).

[18] Betsy P. Graham, Magazine Article Writing, 2nd ed. (Fort Worth, TX: Harcourt Brace Jovanovich, 1993).

[19] Dennis W. Jeffers, "Magazine Educators Consider 'Service Journalism' Orientation," Journalism Educator 45:1 (Spring 1990): 47-50.

[20] Paul Mandelbaum, "Preaching Our Practice: On Sharing Professional Work With Magazine Students," Paper presented to the Association for Education in Journalism and Mass Communication, Montreal, Quebec 1992, ERIC ED 350607.

[21] Carol Reuss, "Quote Analysis and Article Improvement: A Teaching Technique," Paper presented to the Association for Education in Journalism and Mass Communication, Madison, WI, 1977, ERIC ED 154380.

[22] Carol Reuss, "Quote Analysis," 6.

[23] Lee Jolliffe, "How Editors."

[24] Maxine Hairston, "The Winds," 8. [25] Janet Emig, The Composing Processes of Twelfth Graders (Urbana, IL: National Council of Teachers of English, 1971).

[26] James Britton et al, The Development of Writing Abilities (11-18) (Houndsmills Basingstoke Hampshire, England: Macmillan Education Ltd. 1975).

[27] Jerome Zurek, "Research on Writing Process Can Aid Newswriting Teachers," Journalism Educator 41:4 (Spring 1986): 19-23.

[28] Lyle Olsen, "Recent Composition Research is Relevant to Newswriting," Journalism Educator 43:3 (Autumn 1987): 14-18.

[29] Beverly Pitts, "Model Provides Description of Newswriting Process," Journalism Educator 44:1 (1988): 12-19.

[30] Ann B. Schierhorn and Kathleen L. Endres, "Magazine Writing and the Composition Revolution," Journalism Educator 47:2 (Summer 1992): 57-63.

[31] Ann B. Schierhorn and Kathleen L. Endres, "Closing the Gap: An Analysis of Genderbased Differences and Similarities in Magazine Writing Instruction," Paper presented to the Association for Education in Journalism and Mass Communication, Montreal, Quebec August 1992, ERIC ED 349565.

[32] Melvin Mencher, "Truth, Beauty and Journalism," Journalism Educator 42:1 (Spring 1987): 11-17.

[33] August Gibbon, "Review of Coaching Writers: Editors and Reporters Working Together," Journalism Educator 47:3 (Autumn 1992): 81.

[34] Ann B. Schierhorn, "The Role of the Writing Coach in Magazine Journalism," Journalism Educator 46:2 (Summer 1991): 46-53.

[35] Paula C. Renfro and John Maittlen-Harris, "Computer Time Won't Help Writing," Journalism Educator 41:3 (Autumn 1986): 49-51.

[36] Marcia Prior-Miller, Janet Terry, and Susan Dove, "Broadening Undergraduate Education: Using Readership Studies as a Teaching Tool in Magazine Journalism," Paper presented to the Association for Education in Journalism and Mass Communication, Portland, OR, July 1988, ERIC ED 295177.

[37] Edward J. Smith, "Screw Model has Advantages Over Inverted Pyramid," Journalism

Educator 33:4 (Summer 1979): 17-19.

[38] Jack A. Nelson, "Use Choo Choo System to Teach Article Writing," Journalism Educator 43:2 (Summer 1988): 95-97.

[39] Thom Lieb, "Two Faced Exercise Reinforces Lessons in Magazine Class," Journalism Educator 41:3 (Autumn 1986): 29-30.

[40] Katherine E. Rowan, "No-ideas Students Learn to Find, Research Stories," Journalism Educator 42:4 (Winter 1988): 38-40.

[41] Anna R. Paddon, "Parody as Free Expression: A Unit For Magazine Classes," Journalism Educator 46:2 (Summer 1991): 42-45.

[42] Gerald Grow, "Criteria Checklist is Helpful in Magazine Writing Course," Journalism Educator 42:3 (Autumn 1987): 22-24.

[43] Thomas Wheeler, "Teaching the Writer-Editor Relationship," Journalism Educator, forthcoming.

[44] Lee Young, "The Prototype Magazine: An Instructional Device For Teaching Magazine Journalism," Paper presented to the Association for Education in Journalism and Mass Communication, 1976, ERIC ED 149337.

[45] Gregg A. Payne, Jessica Severn, and David Dozier, "Uses and Gratification Motives as Indicators of Magazine Readership," Journalism Quarterly 65:4 (Winter 1988): 909-913, 959.

[46] James W. Tankard and Kate Pierce, "Alcohol Advertising and Magazine Editorial Content," Journalism Quarterly 59:2 (Summer 1982) 302-305.

[47] Ron Marmarelli, "William Hand: A Not 'Half Bad' Candidate and Artful Pilot on the Rolling Rapids of Monthly Ink," Paper presented to the Association for Education in Journalism and Mass Communication, August 1983, ERIC ED 230946.

10

Magazine and Feature Writing Unbound: A Critique of Current Teaching Paradigms and a Case for Rhetoric

Monica Johnstone

Andrew Ciofalo

ABSTRACT

In this article, the authors argue that many of the most widely-used text-books for magazine and feature writing courses display a remarkable influence from news writing textbooks. Not all of this legacy is appropriate or, ultimately, helpful. Magazine and feature writing has special qualities that can be profitably discussed and taught using a vocabulary that some have called for devising, but which is, in fact, already largely in existence. This vocabulary is drawn from the ancient and persistent field of rhetoric. Making use of the longstanding rhetorical tradition not only provides a helpful vocabulary for teaching magazine and feature writing courses, but also increases the possibility of useful interdisciplinary discussions with composition and rhetoric teachers.

Introduction

Many journalism curricula, including their magazine courses, use a model of the discipline whose theoretical underpinnings lie in the social sciences. Most of the rest have a rigorously professional orientation which places a premium on marketability and learning the "ropes" of the profession. But the increasing emphasis on writing in most media curricula and in the profession suggests that there are other relevant theoretical models which approach communication as process, and as such are "more closely allied to...theoretical studies in writing and rhetoric than in mass communications."[1] James W. Carey takes it farther:

> We ought to think of journalism not as an outgrowth of science and the Enlightenment, but more as an extension of poetry, the humanities, and political utopianism. What would journalism look like if we grounded it in poetry, if we tried to literalize that metaphor rather than the metaphor of objectivity and science? It would generate, in fact, a new moral vocabulary that would resolve some current dilemmas.[2]

In that direction, we, the authors, write together, one rhetorician and one journalist, finding a common path in a program of approximately 300 majors, the department of Writing and Media at Loyola College in Maryland. It is our intention to show that a grounding in rhetoric is especially applicable to the teaching of magazine and feature writing, and that this model has some advantages over the prevailing models represented by magazine writing texts which demonstrate a strong influence from newswriting texts.

It is not just a minor change in a single course that we have made or that we seek to have others consider. The roots of our concerns are in the basic news writing course because, as we will show, its pedagogical style tends to influence both the texts used in magazine and feature writing courses and students' expectations of courses.[3]

We acknowledge at the outset that actual courses have the breath of life that cannot be re-created in textbooks by even the most brilliant teachers. Problems that we see in some texts may not be translated into well-conceived courses. We also acknowledge that increasing class sizes tends to work against the teacher who wants to increase the stress on writing in his or her course. With those caveats in mind we still contend that even a good course can be made better and that an overburdened course can be reworked in ways that are not necessarily harder on the instructor.

News Influences in Feature and Magazine Courses

One survey of the content of the basic news writing course in journalism programs revealed that one-third of the time spent in class was devoted to the teaching of writing. If one discounts the time spent on grammar and wire service style, only about 21 percent of the class time is devoted to the writing process. In the Writing and Media Department at Loyola College closer to 70 percent of the introductory course is spent on journalistic writing and related rhetorical concerns. Reporting and interviewing are reserved for a second course.

While both models may be equally valid bases for an introductory news writing course, the predominant approach is less applicable as the curriculum moves to more complex journalistic writing—feature stories, magazine articles and opinion pieces. The shift from courses in which writing does not predominate to a rhetorical approach which is writing-centered requires redirecting our pedagogy "from a concern for the effects of messages and how to manipulate them" to a concern that also includes the process that creates that message.[4]

An examination of the text books in journalism and magazine writing reveals that magazine writing courses lean heavily on sociological and "rigorous professionalism" models borrowed from journalism, which are not the only, nor necessarily most advantageous, models to apply to magazine writing. Though necessarily reductive of the actual complexity of teaching in any field, textbooks do at least provide us with something concrete.

To illustrate this influence, it is helpful to review how journalism texts are configured. One of the best established and widely used texts in newswriting courses is Melvin Mencher's *News Reporting and Writing*. An abbreviated version of its table of contents follows[5]:

The Reporter at Work
    On the Job
The Basics
    Components of the News Story
Writing the Story
    What is News?
    The Tools of the Trade
    The Structure of the News Story
    The Lead
    The Writer's Art
    Features, Long Stories and Series
    Broadcast Writing
Reporting Principles
    [Eight chapters including interviewing, digging for information, use of sources, etc.]
Covering the Beat
    [Seven chapters including accidents and disasters, obituaries, sports, courts, business, local government]
Risks and Responsibilities
    [Three chapters including reporters and the law, taste, and morality]

A basic assumption of this text, typical of most newswriting texts we have examined, is that finding subject matter is not particularly difficult once one understands news values, starting with the question, "What is news?" News is out there waiting to be reported on, and how one writes up the facts is simply a matter of applying the rules and guidelines governing journalistic style. His chapter on The Writer's Art (new to this edition) gives classic warnings to show rather than tell, promotes accuracy and clarity and appropriateness, and suggests revision. In this same chapter, Mencher provides Ten Guidelines for Writing the News. He also points out that storytelling is an important technique: "Readers hunger for a good story—plenty of detail, lots of quotes, interaction between a major figure and other characters, and a climax at the end."

All of these points are helpful to a beginning writer—to a point. Unfortunately, over the last twenty years, all of the advice provided has been critiqued as reductive and overly formulaic by scholars in composition.[6] Dobler warns that such a formulaic approach to writing impinges on creativity:

> There is a middle ground between giving students formulas for invention and cutting them adrift in a sea of ideas. Either of the extremes will tend to undermine a student writer's motivation. Formulaic writing becomes too easy and mechanical. Completely aimless drifting will undermine self-confidence and creativity.[7]

The implied middle ground here is approachable. A student must not be hampered by the idea that writing is formulaic, though. The mediating concepts are just those the texts neglect: voice and audience.

A notable omission in Mencher's *News Reporting and Writing* and other news texts[8] is the lack of any chapter or subheading on the concept of a writer's voice. Mencher's *News Reporting and Writing*[9] does include a chapter on writing "Features, Long Stories and Series" which seems conscious of these genres' special needs. For instance, it briefly considers how to put elaborate data in "human terms." But instead of developing the concept that rhetoricians call voice, "brevity and clarity" are touted as supreme stylistic virtues. Since Mencher argued in *Journalism Educator*[10] that "After all, students are supposed to learn composition in their English classes," we might not expect a fully-rendered discussion of style. Some might even argue that these matters are outside the scope of the basic course in journalism. It is helpful to recall that journalism courses are often the springboard to the rest of the courses in a program and are highly influential.

Thus it is still worth examining what *is* offered: brevity and clarity. In composition studies these very ideas are attacked both in the theoretical literature and pedagogical practice.[11] In other words, "brevity and clarity" have been shown to be less than effective rallying cries when the goal is better writing. Two leaders in the field of composition provide an illustration of what is advocated: both Donald Murray and Peter Elbow spend entire chapters on voice.[12] Murray writes:

Voice is the quality in writing, more than any other, that makes the reader read on, that makes the reader interested in what is being said and makes the reader trust the person who is saying it. We return to the columns, articles, poems, books we like because of the writer's individual voice.[13]

Voice should be an important aspect of professionalism (not to mention an important consideration for those interested in message effectiveness). But in journalism texts professionalism is defined through integrity, thoroughness of research and reportorial technique, and knowledge of (and adherence to) genre expectations—without reference to "voice" or any similar concept. Even a concept as basic to composition studies as "audience" is hard to find in a newswriting text, as Olson[14] reports after analyzing 14 such texts. Most texts simply ignore the literary devices that good writing requires.

Our non-media colleagues in Loyola's writing-intensive program tell us that it is difficult to wean students away from the news story form to other genres of prose writing. There is no doubt that the journalistic perspective enables students to distill the main point out of complex material, a skill that carries over well into other disciplines where analyzing and understanding content are critical to effective learning and test taking. But in disciplines such as writing, where process is considered as well as content, structural strictures can be devastating to the student's ability to progress and grow.

While the training of beginning news writers may strategically require fewer overt rhetorical devices to meet the limited objectives of accuracy, brevity and clarity—and demand adherence to prescribed structures—this journalistic mode has little to do with the concerns of magazine and feature writing and can even hamper the teaching of these courses.

Oddly enough, despite the differences between news and feature or magazine writing, many texts on magazine and feature writing strangely echo the news writing texts. For instance, Peter Jacobi's *The Magazine Article: How to Think It, Plan It, Write It* promises us a "four-step writing process, ...ten rules to write by, [and] eight techniques from poetry that will improve your magazine writing." In essence, students get very prescriptive advice in handy enumerated bits. To be fair, Jacobi is concerned with idea generation, structure, and narrative techniques. But under all these rubrics, invention, arrangement, and style remain information driven.

For example, his chapter "Narration and Description" promises that "using storytelling techniques will humanize your information"—assuming that the devices of fiction support the purposes of the piece. Dobler sees this approach as a very limited view of the possibilities:

For any writer whose work is worth reading, invention is rather critical to the writing of the piece. Our inventions come from that self which is uniquely our own. Invention comes in several forms. Rhetorical invention has been discussed and taught since the early Greeks. There is also perceptual invention, based in twentieth-century psychology. Perceptual invention assumes that facts are useless without a way to relate them to one another, without an angle of vision that connects them together. Perceptual invention also implies that what we identify as "creative" often involves a change of angle, a new way to look at or connect old facts. The problem is that we have perceptual habits which allow us to function rather automatically in the world but which also keep us from experiencing the world as freshly as we did when we saw it for the first time.... A writer needs not only to be able to find a new angle, that new viewpoint to illuminate the old, but also be able to communicate that fresh vision in fresh language so that the readers too will be able to perceive its uniqueness.[15]

Students trained in journalistic writing conventions rarely have at the center of their writing a wonderful original idea; more frequently they write about something in the external world. Some might argue that it is pie-in-the-sky pedagogy to promote anything but information-driven writing, especially when magazine texts such as Jacobi's confront students with "proven article writing techniques, including: hooking readers with style and technique, compressing lots of information in a small space to make a big impression on readers, and using fictionalization to heighten impact or lend universality."[16]

Jacobi seems to want to give students valuable practical knowledge—tricks of the trade—without insight into the writing process, and he could be faulted for a presentation that implies students can become successful professional writers by putting one over on their readers. And Jacobi isn't alone in this. Myrick E. Land's *Writing for Magazines*[17] shares the journalistic penchant for information, interviewing techniques, limited and limiting sense of genre, legal concerns, professionalism, and reducing style to matters of clarity. Barbara Kevles's *Basic Magazine Writing: How to master the seven most important article forms and get published in the leading national magazines*[18] is, not surprisingly, similar.

Both of these books, like many magazine writing texts, show their journalistic roots in their prescriptiveness, their assumption that even beyond news writing all journalistic forms are information driven, their questionable relationship to audience, and their concern with professional issues over issues of creativity.

One book that has attempted to break away from this constraining pattern is Friedlander and Lee's *Feature Writing for Newspapers and Magazines*[19], which makes use of many prize-winning pieces of professional writing and even briefly teaches analysis of a feature story. However, it does not meet our hopes of a rhetorically based text because it still stresses avoiding mistakes and strict adherence to existing structures. Similarly *Magazine and Feature Writing* by Hiley Ward[20] stresses a "personal style" but does so prescriptively.

The Challenge of the "New" Journalism

In some ways the literature of and about the New Journalism, despite all the questions about whether it is in fact "new", is somewhat better. Dennis and Rivers's *Other Voices*[21] provides a definition of New Journalism (by its nature intended as feature and magazine writing) as "dissatisfaction with existing standards and values" not only in society at large but also more specifically in mainstream journalism. This defining feature is echoed in the work of several others.[22] No matter what we see as the contributions or deficiencies of the New Journalism, it presses us to ask ourselves what the differences are between "hard" news (and its pedagogy) and that of other types of newspaper and periodical writing.

Perhaps because of his interest in the New Journalism, William L. Rivers's text, *Free-Lancer and Staff Writer* takes a different tack than the books surveyed above.[23] Though retaining a very professional emphasis (on the writing scene, editors, "breaking in," and a checklist of rules for magazine writing), Rivers also includes a chapter on invention, "Generating and Developing Ideas for Articles." He also frames his remarks about journalistic forms in such a way that students would be likely to see that these are some of the possibilities, not the one or two models to be followed. He even includes a chapter on "Voice and Flow." Though not overtly rhetorical, this text brings into the discussion several of the concerns missing in other major textbooks.

The Case for Rhetoric

Aristotle defined rhetoric as a way of finding the available means of persuasion in a given case. His notion of rhetoric was that it served the real world in the way philosophy serves the theoretical realm. Modern rhetoricians work in areas that go far beyond finding available means (invention) or the study of persuasive discourse. What both the ancient and modern rhetoricians share is a vast vocabulary for the techniques used to convey meaning in a very wide variety of discourse. Rhetoricians (which now includes composition scholars) study both the process and product of composing by students and professionals in all genres.

As an illustration of the way a rhetorician might operate, it is useful to recast basic news writing within a rhetorical context so that it becomes part of a continuum that connects all forms of writing. Such a reconfiguration would require "media rhetoric" as a prerequisite survey course, along with "introduction to mass communications," to provide students with a deductive framework for shaping their comprehension of genres of journalistic writing and other forms of prose writing.

Westfall feels that until we learn how to read critically magazine non-fiction, we will never escape the ties that bind us to the formats of news writing. She calls for a separate line of scholarly inquiry into non-fiction prose. Westfall's contribution sets the premise for the discussion to follow:

> There are few terms or methods dedicated exclusively to magazine journalism. We borrow language from social science, literary studies, psychology, even the newsroom. I think we need a language of our own.... If we could develop our own critical tools and hone them with the rigors of scholarship, I think we could begin to truly "read the magazine."[24]

In a sense her call has already been heeded in the considerable theoretical literature emanating from rhetorical studies.[25] A vast vocabulary exists, since classical times, for critical reading.[26] Westfall did magazine non-fiction a favor by calling for critical analysis of these texts so that those already deeply saturated by an existing methodology could begin to adapt existing vocabulary and methods in order to make them helpful for the magazine non-fiction teacher. Westfall builds her teaching of magazine article writing "around six ideas: focus, format, structure, authority base, evidence, and voice." If not the beginnings of a specialized rhetoric, this is at least a rhetorical stance. What we propose is to utilize the work already done by others rather than to reinvent it.

Wyatt and Badger[27] also call for a new typology, rhetorical in nature, to address the variety that exists in journalistic genres. They suggest borrowing and introducing categories (description, narration, argumentation, exposition, and criticism) to "provide a more definitive classification scheme for contemporary journalism than the old news/feature/editorial trichotomy or the news-opinion continuum." This seems to us a move in the right direction. In fact, we would go further.

Because the news story is information or event driven, it relies on structure or format to present that information effectively to as broad an audience as possible. By contrast, the magazine article is perceived as audience driven, and therefore narrowcasts its information according to the tastes of editors who are stylistic gatekeepers for their markets. In both instances, the role of the writer is minimized and concerns external to the creation of the work are viewed as paramount. Westfall acknowledges the lure of structure as a defining element in magazine prose when she observes two types of articles and cleverly maps them: the rigidly structured article and the intertwining article. This acknowledges that some variety of approach already exists in practice. Wyatt and Badger take the discussion beyond structure to types which they number five. Both articles point in the same direction: to the often unacknowledged variety in existing practice.

Nelson blames the "enshrinement of objectivity" for young journalists' timid adherence to facts at the expense of "interpretive, colorful, and compelling writing." He decries the "sterile, formula-ridden writing" that results when "the major task of newswriting classes is to rid students of the passion of opinion...."[28] It is precisely in this "passion" that the voice of the writer resides. While one must be very careful about coaxing it out in a news story, it can and often should be heard loud and clear in newspaper features and might profitably dominate the entire thrust of a magazine article.

At this juncture, let's recast the Mencher text, our exemplar of current pedagogy in both news and magazine writing, in terms of what are known as the five offices of rhetoric. These offices—Invention (brainstorming and material gathering), Distribution (arrangement and structuring), Elocution (style), Memory, and Delivery—were what Aristotle in the *Rhetoric* considered the primary areas of concern in the process of composition of a speech. Most of them also apply well to written works. Through this recasting we see the conventions of journalistic writing are confined to a very particular band of concerns. In *News Reporting and Writing* we find little exploration of "invention," prescriptive rules for "arrangement," a minimal account of acceptable "style," a brief nod to "memory" (note taking), and an implied attention to "delivery" in the section on Broadcast Writing.

There are significant differences in the constraints faced by news writers and magazine writers. The feature and magazine writer has greater freedom of subject matter. Length is less restrictive. Preparation time is longer. Voice is a more relevant concern. And for all these reasons, structure should be less strictly dictated.

Changing our teaching and texts to reap the benefits of rhetoric and her modern offshoot, composition studies, will offer the feature and magazine writing student and scholar a wide and versatile vocabulary, a long tradition of descriptive analysis and critical thinking, and elastic notions of structure and genre based on occasion and audience. We need to disengage our students from the erroneous notion that all journalistic writing is only about information processing. Instead, it is about writers and readers and the many ways they can productively connect.

In describing that connection we, as teachers and text writers, have confused the needs of editors with the requirements of scholarship. Westfall explains how professionalism muddies our cognitive faculties:

> In many magazines, the main determiner of form is audience, or rather an editor's interpretation of audience. What writers or editors consider good or bad writing is, bluntly, irrelevant, at least outside the pages of that editor's magazine. One editor's literature is another's trash. Taste is not perception—it is value judgement. I tell my students I don't think they can be human

without values, but they cannot be writers or editors if they confuse values with perceptions, or taste with critical skill.[29]

Current texts assume that the magazine article, like the news story, exists only to tell readers about some event or thing or person of note. Under this model, the writer sees his or her "job" as one of presenting clearly and palatably information, say, about a factory closing. Which would make a better article:

(a) One resulting from a week of interviews, time spent with management and workers making observations on the job and in the home, and extensive background research into the economics and politics behind the closing, or

(b) One resulting from a personal perspective by an individual who recently quit his high-paying consulting job because he felt it was unethical to produce the studies which he knew would be used as justifications for sending jobs overseas?

Traditional journalism would tend to choose the first scenario, given an objective observer with access to both sides of the story. It could appear as news. The second model, which was actually written by a former student (who had taken courses in rhetoric), brought out the kinship he felt with the men on the line and his alienation from his co-workers at the home office. The first writer is unlikely to seek an individual voice and most likely will invoke all the stylistic paradigms of her magazine or newspaper, be it *Time* or the *New York Times*. The second writer's point of view, born of involvement and enhanced by his rhetorical sophistication, enables him to develop his own voice. Though we might hope that both articles might deserve our attention, it is unlikely under the prevailing pedagogy that we would encourage both as viable articles in the same course. A course with a rhetorical bent would discuss these different approaches to the same basic subject as difference in voice and intended audience. Students would then be less apt to think one kind of writing "right" ("objective," "newsworthy") and the other "wrong" ("subjective," "biased," "too personal"). After all, contemporary newspaper and magazine practice is quite varied—our students should not be under the misapprehension that some strict model is enforced in practice.

Dobler describes how critical it is for the magazine writer to write from within and escape the tyranny of facts:

At the same time that we are discovering or inventing, we're also making something new. We've had this crazy notion that we can actually be creative. Instead of finding something on the outside [like the first writer], we're causing it to grow within ourselves [like the second writer]. In other words, when we are creative, we're creating a new original thing from bits and pieces we've had floating around in our brains, the flotsam and jetsam of our experiences.[30]

Of course, the first writer's approach will rightfully continue to dominate the way newspaper and newsmagazine journalism is practiced and taught, but a model that wouldn't allow for or encourage the second approach is impoverished. Information can have an important place in this scheme, but it cannot be mistaken for the scheme itself. As so much of twentieth-century literary criticism reminds us, the subject is frequently the writer and his or her thoughts rather than something that is "out there." Part of what is so engaging about feature and magazine writing is that it isn't just news writ large.

What would a new, more rhetorically-minded magazine writing text look like? It might begin by examining a range of examples, stressing their differences rather than seeking commonalities in a few underlying structures for students to emulate easily. Rather than encourage an overall reportorial tone, we would note how distinct their voices are from one another as the authors strove to create a meeting of the minds with their readers.

For instance, selections might include Bill McKibben's extensive article for the *New Yorker*, "The End of Nature" with its personal insights into the disappearance of wilderness, and Dinesh D'Souza's polemical "Illiberal Education" which caused a sensation when it appeared in the *Atlantic Monthly*. Pieces by such writers as Agee, Mencken, Wolfe, and McPhee, with their distinctive voices (as opposed to a slick but generic "professional" style) would have a definite place. So would a Pulitzer Prize-winning profile such as Ann O'Hare McCormick's 1937 *New York Times* piece, "A Portrait of a Pope," which describes the pontiff using an extensive vocabulary drawn from painting. In the face of this sort of breadth, the lists of "rules" shrink away.

In our new rhetorical text, discussions of techniques would be open-ended rather than inclusively numbered. The editor-writer relationship would be discussed as an important subset of audience concerns and would avoid discussions of audience that smack of pandering. Professionalism would be noted as an important feature of the writer's ethos and ethical responsibility rather than as a guideline for avoiding lawsuits. Rhetoric's millennia-old preoccupation with logical argumentation would help ingrain the habit of providing assentworthy reasons for assertions.[31] Authorial credibility, and concomitant public trust, would be presented as positive values rather than the tacit promotion of the idea that the only line not to be crossed is the one that leads to financial loss, diminished circulation or lawsuits.

All the discussions of style would note the limits of mere clarity. Students would do exercises that drive home the point that "style" that creates the writer's voice isn't an afterthought or add-on; rather it is a clue to the mind at work. As Lakoff and Johnson put it in *Metaphors We Live By*, "the way we think, what we experience, and what we do every day is very much a matter of metaphor."[32] Beyond tired discussions of simile and metaphor, this rhetorical text on magazine writing would show students that the discovery of underlying tropes, figures of speech and thought, can be a principle of organization, a point of departure, or the key to the door of invention.[33]

This new descriptive, elastic, organic, ethically complex textbook wouldn't be easy to write. True, it departs from tried and true formulas and easy class preparation. It wouldn't provide easy to memorize rubrics. But it would engage the students and the teachers and the best of the published magazine writers in a realistic dialogue. It would answer the interdisciplinary calls for emphasis on critical thinking in instruction. It would teach the composition and communications faculties to speak a common language. And it would give students a more coherent experience as they go from freshman composition to basic news writing to advanced prose and opinion writing.

Journalists are trained to look at the world in terms of events or oddities worth writing about, and in its more complex aspects, worth interpreting or analyzing. On the other hand, the writer looks for opportunities to write, driven by a creative urge that connects his experiences to unique ways of looking at the world. The writer weaves a web of universality through disparate events and situations that sharpen their meaning for the reader. If we continue to impose the limitations of current journalistic conventions and practice on our students, they will rarely move beyond what they have been professionally and culturally conditioned to accept as important and worth writing about.

Notes

[1] Andrew Ciofalo, "A Journalism Education Model in the Jesuit Tradition," ERIC ED323558, 1991.

[2] James Carey, "The Press and the Public Discourse," Kettering Review (Winter 1992).

[3] R.O. Wyatt and D.P. Badger, "A New Typology For Journalism and Mass Communication Writing," Journalism Educator 48:1 (1993): 3-11.

[4] Ciofalo, "A Journalism Education Model."

[5] Melvin Mencher, News Reporting and Writing, 5th ed. (Dubuque: Wm. C. Brown, 1991).

[6] Richard Lanham, Style: An Anti-textbook (New Haven: Yale, 1974).

[7] Judith Dobler, Panel: Making Writing Central to the Journalism/Magazine Curriculum (unpublished), AEJMC Magazine Division (Spring 1991).

[8] Mencher, News Reporting. The Missouri Group: B. Brooks, G. Kennedy, D.R. Moen, D. Ranly, News Reporting and Writing, 4th ed. (New York: St Martin's, 1992). William Metz, Newswriting From Lead to "30" (Englewood Cliffs: Prentice Hall, 1991). Gerald Stone, "Measurement of Excellence in Newspaper Writing Courses," Jounralism Educator 44:4 (1992): 4-19. Julian Harriss et al, The Compete Reporter, 4th ed. (New York: MacMillan, 1981). William L. Rivers, News in Print: Writing and Reporting (New York: Harper & Row, 1984). Conrad Fink, Introduction to Professional Newswriting: Reporting for the Modern Media (White Plains: Longman, 1992).

[9] Mencher, News Reporting and Writing.

[10] Mencher, "Confronting Critics and Ourselves," Journalism Educator 44:4 (1992): 64-67.

[11] Lanham, Style. Nevin Laib, Rhetoric and Style (Englewood Cliffs: Prentice Hall, 1993).

[12] Donald Murray, The Craft of Revision (Fort Worth: Holt, Rinehart & Winston, 1991). Peter Elbow, Writing with Power (New York: Oxford, 1981).

[13] Murray, The Craft of Revision.

[14] L.D. Olson, "Technical Writing Methods Show Ways to Consider Audience," Journalism Educator 44:2 (1992): 3-6.

[15] Dobler, Making Writing Central.

[16] P. Jacobi, The Magazine Article: How to Think It, Plan It, Write It (Cincinnati: Writer's Digest Books, 1991).

[17] Myrick E. Land, Writing for Magazines, 2nd ed. (Englewood Cliffs: Prentice Hall, 1992).

[18] Barbara Kevles, Basic Magazine Writing: How to master the seven most important article forms and get published in the leading national magazines (Cincinnati: Writer's Digest Books, 1987).

[19] E.J. Friedlander and J. Lee, Feature Writing for Newspapers and Magazines (New York: Harper & Row, 1993).

[20] Hiley Ward, Magazine and Feature Writing (Mountainview, CA: Mayfield Publ., 1993).

[21] Everette E. Dennis and William L. Rivers, Other Voices (San Francisco: Canfield, 1974).

[22] T. Wolfe, The New Journalism (New York: Harper & Row, 1973). Ronald Weber, ed. The Reporter as Artist (New York: Hastings House, 1974).

[23] William L. River, Free-Lancer and Staff Writer, 5th ed. (Belmont, CA: Wadsworth, 1992).

[24] P. Westfall, "Teaching Magazine Students to Read," Magazine Forum-A Publication of the AEJMC Magazine Division 1:1 (Winter 1990): 4-9.

[25] Roderick P. Hart, Modern Rhetorical Criticism (Glenview, IL: Scott, Foresman, 1990). Bernard Brock, ed. Methods of Rhetorical Criticism, 3rd ed. (Detroit: Wayne State Univ., 1980). Sonja Foss, Rhetorical Criticism (Prospect Heights, IL: Waveland, 1989).

[26] Arthur Quinn, Figures of Speech (Salt Lake: Gibbs M. Smith, 1982). Lanham, Handlist of Rhetorical Terms (Berkeley: Univ. of California Press, 1968). Edward P.J. Corbett, Classical Rhetoric for the Modern Student (New York: Oxford, 1990).

[27] Wyatt and Badger, "A New Typology."

[28] J. Nelson, "Are We Failing to Educate Reporters who Can Write?" Journalism Educator 44:4 (Winter 1990): 20-25.

[29] Westfall, "Teaching Magazine Students to Read."

[30] Dobler, Making Writing Central.

[31] Wayne C. Booth, Don't Try to Reason with Me (Chicago: Univ. of Chicago Press, 1970) and Modern Dogma and the Rhetoric of Assent (Chicago: Univ. of Chicago Press, 1974).

[32] George Lakoff and Mark Johnson, Metaphors We Live By (Chicago: Univ. of Chicago Press, 1980).

[33] Monica Johnstone, "Figures to Teach: Tropology and The Speech Classroom," Iowa Journal of Speech Communication 24:1 (Spring 1992): 30-41.

11

Preaching Our Practice: On Sharing Professional Work with Students

Paul Mandelbaum

ABSTRACT

This paper describes my classroom use of interview samples, editors' comments, and other materials from my own article-then-in-progress for the *New York Times Magazine*. Students, who were creating their own in-depth magazine articles, could see the same principles and techniques we had discussed in relation to their work applied on a professional level. This improved understanding and motivation and clarified the relevance of the course's rigorous expectations. The paper provides a framework and encouragement for journalism teachers to bring more of themselves and their professional work into the classroom.

Introduction

Many an undergraduate's expectations of magazine writing are shaped by those genres to which the student has had the greatest exposure: how-to or first-person accounts in teen magazines, record reviews and interviews in music magazines, beauty and fashion nuggets in *GQ* and *Vogue*. Often these specimens of magazine writing are marketed in such a flashy, chatty format that the aspiring writer may conclude that magazine writing is a breeze.

A university-level class in magazine writing, and especially one in advanced magazine writing, if it is to broaden students' vision of the craft's possibilities, should reach beyond the more lightweight modes of magazine expression. Many of my advanced students at Drake University in spring 1991 were a bit anxious when I asked them to create a 4,500-word article that included reporting from a variety of written and oral sources, that shaped and selected weeks' worth of gathered material into a cohesive form, that had a sense of movement and climax without degrading the integrity of the reporting, and that achieved a style and quality of language worthy of holding a sophisticated reader's attention for a half hour. This sort of task is not for the timid. It is difficult for students to sustain the kind of driving passion required to *finish* such a project in a classroom setting. And it is difficult for teachers (not to mention unreasonable of them) to demand of students that, as part of their reporting, they interview at least ten sources and then use only the best ten to fifteen percent of that material, if it is suspected, even for a second, that the teacher would not be willing to do the same.[1]

For this reason, the timing of a profile I was writing for the *New York Times Magazine* [2] was propitious. During my visiting appointment at Drake during the 1990-1991 year, I was revising this profile, adding to and re-examining my reporting materials, and negotiating with editors. In class, I could not only tell my students about the hard work involved in attempting to create a magazine piece of quality, I could show them. This process was not a display of egotism, and there were enough self-deprecating lessons worth sharing to insure it wouldn't be. (Also there was the ever-present risk that, until it was at last published, the entire piece could have been killed by the *Times*, which in itself would have offered its own valuable, if painful, lessons.) Rather, the process was an attempt to improve understanding and motivation, as well as to clarify the relevance of the course's rigorous expectations.

Journalist-teachers have plenty of lessons to share from their own clips. In *Writing for Story*, [3] to mention just one example, Jon Franklin annotates two of his articles in detail to explain some of the many journalistic choices made in their creation. This paper focuses on how I incorporated my own annotated article and my own behind-the-scenes work in a classroom setting, and provides a model for teachers to bring more of themselves and their work into the classroom.

In our discussions of my ongoing project, students and I were able to handle bundles of notes, files, and discards that formed a still warm and changing paper trail of the writing process and the author's own education. This emphasis on process reflects reported trends in composition education and similar approaches reported in journalism education.[4] Students could see the same principles and techniques we often discussed in relation to their own researching, interviewing, organizing, writing, and revising applied on a professional level. They were given something to shoot for, I was kept in touch with the demands the course was making, and greater empathy was attained all around.

Interview Preparation Demonstrated

On three or four occasions during the academic year, I would bring materials to class from the article I was writing: a 4,000-word profile on controversial film maker John Waters. Early in the spring semester, when the advanced
class was, in accordance with our syllabus, feverishly engaged in research—
casting about for angles, questions, follow-up questions, anecdotes, kernels of
narrative—I lugged in a stack of files containing my own research. Before
passing the folders around, I spent some time discussing their organization.

First came the clippings: a folder of reviews of the director's work, a folder
of previous major profiles about him, smaller articles about him, some pieces
written by him, a separate folder on an obscenity case out of Florida that interested me as a timely peg—perhaps a hundred clippings in all, about half of
which had been provided to me by the *Times*; the other half I had collected.
My students, who had been asked to dig up a number of clippings pertaining to
their own subjects and to discuss their relevance, could see (by looking through
the folders I had brought) the circled passages that had interested me and the
questions those passages sometimes inspired, jotted in the margins and then
organized in computer files.

Weeks in advance of my in-depth interviews in Baltimore—as I explained,
leading my students through the files—I had been cultivating and organizing
questions. Whenever I would conduct a preliminary phone interview with any
of a dozen co-workers, friends, and relatives of Mr. Waters's, I would learn of
new anecdotes, new themes, new ideas—and the questions that these inspired
I would tuck away in a separate file to ask Mr. Waters himself. This list of
questions spanned eight single-spaced printed pages, subdivided into categories of "family and childhood," "religion," "friendship and love," "making
movies," and "general."

That I rarely referred to the actual list of questions during my eight hours
of interview time with Mr. Waters undoubtedly struck some of my students as
ironic and imprudent. But, as I tried to explain in class, I'd become fairly
familiar with the list before the interviews began, and after my first four-hour
interview was over, I consulted the list to note what had been covered, what
had not, and what new ideas deserved to be added, before returning for the
second four-hour interview, during which the list was again only minimally
consulted. And yet, I ended up covering virtually all of the questions on it, and
a good deal more. In my interviews I had wanted the security and knowledge
that one derives from preparation as well as the relaxed, encouraging atmo-
sphere that comes with spontaneity, or at least the illusion of spontaneity.[5]
This combination requires even greater preparation; so went the thrust of my
classroom argument, and being able to pass around the actual lists lent it an
added measure of credibility.

Great classroom emphasis was placed on being able to observe one's subject in natural surroundings—ideally, interacting with other people—so that
the interviewer learns what the subject is like outside of the potentially inhib-
iting interview process. I asked Mr. Waters on several occasions what he had
planned to do during the week I'd be in town, and he suggested that he throw
one of his traditional summer barbecues for his long-time friends and co-workers. The barbecue scene became an anchor for the piece, as it was useful narra-
tively and thematically. Class time was spent discussing the various ways to
cover such an event, ground rules about quoting participants, and the ethical
considerations in arranging such an event so as to avoid creating scenes that
have more to do with the reporter's imagination than the reality of the subject.

Even a reporter's most carefully considered plans fall flat—as evidence I
could produce the morning wasted driving around with one of Mr. Waters's
childhood friends as she tried to point out for me various sights of their teenage misbehavior. The results, which were deadly dull, were not all her fault.
After all, I had asked for the tour. The important lesson for students, however,
was to have a few potential narrative scenes in mind as backups. And when my
students' own scenes sometimes fell through, they knew they could count on
their instructor's commiseration (even as I insisted they get back out there).

I was amazed at how resourceful these students were at arranging and
reporting narrative scenes. One student, in fact, spent at least a half dozen
afternoons and evenings visiting and interviewing the residents of a half-way
house for recovering women alcoholics, observing her subjects as they shared
meals, as they listened to a guest speaker, as they joked with and confided in
one other.

Our classroom discussions about the John Waters piece, this student remarked after the semester was over, "taught me not to think so rigidly about
interview settings."[6]

Hearing the Interviews

On several occasions I played taped interview excerpts for my students.
The first was from a phone interview with one of John Waters's producers,
Brian Grazer, who was discussing how the overweight protagonist of Mr.
Waters's movie *Hairspray* charmed him and what a surprise this was, because,
as he put it, "I pretty much only like attractive people." Concerned that he
would sound superficial, he immediately followed this revealing pronounce-
ment, which had said as much about Hollywood in general as it said about him
specifically, with three of the most common and dreaded words that sources
say to reporters: "Don't write that."

While not involving Hollywood producers, similar situations had rankled most of the students in class at some point in their young careers. Listening to the taped excerpt led to class discussions about what a reporter's options might be under such circumstances: refuse and perhaps alienate the source, strike some deal of anonymity, roll over, to name several possibilities, and we'd ranked their order of preference to the reporter and to the source.[7] We also examined the option I had exercised on tape: while stumbling for the right words, I was able to convince Mr. Grazer that it was an important quote (which I truly believed, and which I ended up using). Our little dance went like this:

Source: "I pretty much only like attractive people. [Laughing] That's terrible to say."
Reporter: "Well, hey, it's an honest thing to say."
Source: "You know, I mean [pause] don't write that. That's just so superficial."
Reporter: "Well, it's not necessarily superficial, if ah, put in the context of how—"
Source: "All right."
Reporter: "Of how, ah, you know—it means something."
Source: "Yeah, it means something."

That the professional reporter was, in this case, fumbling for the right words proved as valuable a lesson as the exchange's happy resolution, because it demonstrated for students that their anxiety, their difficulty with such situations, is normal and shared by people with much more experience, and that it need not undermine the final product. A colleague of mine at the University of Iowa once told me that teachers sometimes should play the role of the fool. And although I admit to having been perplexed by his meaning at the time, it became clear to me as students and I laughed together at my crudely phrased: "Of how, ah, you know—it means something."

Students were also privy to some of the awkward pauses, the searching for words, and the reporter's twice and thrice asked questions, as he tenaciously, and at times obnoxiously, returned to topics that he believed might serve some thematic instinct of his, if only the source would cooperate with the right answers. One moment on the tapes I enjoyed sharing was an excruciatingly long silence between my subject's less-than-complete answer and my own follow-up question. Many student reporters, when faced with the prospect of an awkward silence, would move on to the next question on their list and forget about the train of thought that had proved so difficult. When the interviewer does this, of course, he or she has lost control of the interview and is merely taking dictation. The lesson in those long seconds of silence is this: don't be afraid of it, you can edit it out later. Just gather your thoughts and consider your response. When it comes to their experience with *hearing* interviews, students are perhaps most used to the broadcast variety. And in comparison, the fumbling print-reporter's research interviews must sound horribly unprofessional. So getting used to a new type of sound is valuable.

Learning about these kinds of interviewing problems and issues can be sterile on the textbook page and tend to loom larger than life when they crop up in the student reporter's actual experience. On the other hand, my interview tapes provided a context that offered immediacy without being threatening.

Cutting and Revision

Culling and organizing material seem to be the most difficult processes for even advanced magazine-writing students to grasp and master. Because the elements of a coherent magazine feature story should conform, however subtly, to some theme or structure, without degrading the accuracy and fairness of the reporting, far more information must be gathered than is ultimately used. The average undergraduate journalism major has trouble conceiving the amount of labor involved in such a process on the professional level. But a clear picture of this is necessary if one is to aspire to it. The process was made graphically clear, quantitatively and qualitatively, by comparing partial transcripts (more than 20,000 words from just Mr. Waters's interviews) with my first draft (7,000 words) and again with my second draft (5,000 words).[8]

Two important lessons were potentially derived from this: a) There exist vast amounts of material that, while being somewhat interesting, are ultimately not interesting or pertinent *enough*, and b) Quotations must be carefully selected—or paraphrased—rather than transcribed at great length into the article. (Predictably enough, much student magazine writing turns control of the story over to the subject's long, unfocused quotes.) In this case, students could see for themselves how entire pages of amusing, engaging quotations were completely left out, and, elsewhere, how rambling anecdotes that required many paragraphs of conversation to elicit all the important details had been boiled down to a brief recreated scene.[9]

A brief aside: with other magazine articles of mine, I've distributed copies of my first and second full drafts, marked as vividly as possible to show the great copy migrations (scenes and issues moved from after a forced transition to a place in the story where they fit more organically); catchy anecdotal material that didn't really serve a larger purpose and so was cut; bursts of inspiration that evolved into more coherent passages after much experimentation and examination—all changes that graphically represent the vital lesson that just because one has written something, doesn't mean it's ready to be published.

Finally, students were surprised at the amount of time I spent on the phone refining the story with my editor. That March, I spent more than a dozen hours so engaged, including a fair chunk of time discussing the Florida obscenity case which, as less-than-ideal luck would have it, was scheduled to go to trial a week before we were to publish, yet too late for us to make changes to the story. Had the reporter been a little more on the ball, went the slightly embarrassing theme of this classroom lesson, the article might have had a better peg. As things stood, students and I engaged in an impromptu discussion on "finessing it."

When considering my dealings with the *Magazine*'s editors, students seemed particularly intrigued by the notion that I was answering to someone—indeed to *someones*—in much the same way that the students were expected to answer to me. How copious were the revisions their teacher was asked to make! How he had squirmed upon hearing one editor's reaction (the freelancer's nightmare) to his first draft: "Why are we writing about this guy?!"

One student remarked after the semester's end that she especially enjoyed learning about the "frustrations of working with editors—making new changes for different editors, having editors change things for you that you had been happy with."[10] Able to see me in their shoes, my students learned that we were in this process of magazine writing together.[11]

Rewards

Certainly the most enjoyable aspect of magazine writing that I was able to share in the classroom was the thrill of publication. Lab magazines can provide students with some motivation, and Drake has a couple of fine ones, but many magazine students are lured into this field by the promise of publication in high-profile consumer titles. The prominent by-line, the colorful photos, and the mouth-watering, albeit abstract, concept of the Sunday *Times'* 1.6 million circulation, were a handy reminder of the potential rewards of such hard labor.

Some disillusionment, however, had set in, as well. As my students watched me age three years in our nine months together, at least one of them came to the conclusion that it was not worth it. On the other hand, I can name one other who was inspired to buy a copy of Norman Sims's *The Literary Journalists* for summer pleasure reading.

And there was inspiration evident in the work that the class wrote that semester—a fringe benefit from the land of *product*: more than half of my students wrote stories that were great.

Notes

[1] "To maintain credibility with students," among other reasons, Brigham Young University's Alf Pratte has served as a stringer for local daily newspapers. "I find it difficult to preach what I don't practice on a regular basis...Rather than relying on textbooks...I can refer to speeches or meetings I attended the same day or day before." Alf Pratte, "Teacher Benefits as a Part-Time Correspondent," Journalism Educator 42 (Autumn 1987): 25-26.

[2] Paul Mandelbaum, "Kinkmeister: Film Maker John Waters Is Living Proof That Nothing Exceeds Like Excess," The New York Times Magazine, 7 April 1991, 34-38, 52.

[3] Jon Franklin, Writing for Story: Craft Secrets of Dramatic Nonfiction by a Two-Time Pulitzer Prize Winner (New York: Atheneum, 1986). See also Donald M. Murray, Read to Write: A Writing Process Reader (Fort Worth: Harcourt Brace, 1990) and Carole Rich, Writing & Reporting News: A Coaching Method (Belmont, Calif.: Wadsworth, 1994).

[4] Lyle Olson, "Recent Composition Research is Relevant to Newswriting," Journalism Educator 42 (Autumn 1987): 14-18; Ann B. Schierhorn, "The Role of the Writing Coach in the Magazine Curriculum," Journalism Educator 46 (Summer 1991): 46-53; Ann B. Schierhorn and Kathleen L. Endres, "Magazine Writing Instruction and the Composition Revolution," Journalism Educator 47 (Summer 1992): 57-64; Jerome Zurek, "Research on Writing Process Can Aid Newswriting Teachers," Journalism Educator 41 (Spring 1996): 19-23.

[5] On the other hand, Janet Malcolm compares her interviews with Fatal Vision author Joe McGinniss and convict Jeffrey MacDonald to those conducted by Newsday reporter Bob Keeler and finds the results surprisingly similar. "It hadn't made the slightest difference that Keeler had read from a list of prepared questions and I had acted as if I were passing the time of day." Janet Malcolm, The Journalist and the Murderer (New York: Knopf, 1990), 98

[6] In his book on interviewing, Ken Metzler devotes a chapter to "Journalistic Observation," in which he discusses the value of "showing" the reporter's subject in action. In her book Reporting, Lillian Ross, one of the masters of the technique, provides students with a wonderful example. Her 1960 New Yorker article "The Yellow Bus," in which she glues herself to the Bean Blossom Township High School senior class on their trip to New York, is one of my favorite examples of narrative reporting, and one that has proved accessible and interesting to magazine writing students. Ken Metzler, Creative Interviewing: The Writer's Guide to Gathering Information by Asking Questions (Englewood Cliffs, N.J.: Prentice Hall, 1989), 94-105; Lillian Ross, Reporting (New York: Simon and Schuster,1969), 11-30.

[7] In her investigative piece "Let Us Now Appraise Famous Writers" and in the commentary that follows it, Jessica Mitford shows how she handled a similr interviewing situation involving Bennett Cerf. The book is filled with useful and entertaining tips and behind the scenes information. Jessica Mitford, Poison Penmanship (New York: Noonday, 1988), 156, 174.

[8] "In talking to the best reporters, we find that only about 5 percent of their notes eventually appear in the story in some form," write Roy Peter Clark and Don Fry, Coaching Writers: Editors and Reporters Working Together (New York: St. Martin's Press, 1992), 67. As part of taking readers through his process of writing a speech story (pp. 60-76), Fry shares his actual notes, providing some visual lessons on notation and organization.

[9] A striking example of narrative effectively recreated from interviews and other sources would be Ramsey Flynn's National Magazine Award-winning overview of the fatal Amtrak crash

in Chase, Maryland. Ramsey Flynn, "On the Wrong Track," Baltimore Magazine, November 1987, 76-93, 124-131.

[10] In other words, all the usual writer-editor stuff. Actually, I would have to say that most of the Times' input on this piece was very much appreciated.

[11] "Turnabout can be not only fair play but also invigorating education," writes John Palen, who describes how he interviews a student in class, writes a 750-word feature on the interview, and then takes his class through the process he used. John Palen, "Teacher as Writer Highlights Writing, Interviewing Skills," Journalism Educator 42 (Spring 1987): 52-53.

Acknowledgments

The author would like to thank Lee Jolliffe of the University of Missouri, Columbia for her comments and suggestions.

IV

Global and Local
Issues in
Magazine Journalism

12

Research Review:
An International Perspective
on Magazines

Leara Rhodes

ABSTRACT

A limited number of studies have been performed on magazines published outside the United States. The approach of this paper is to describe some of these studies and their methodologies, to review articles found to be important in discussing international magazines, and to offer some suggestions of types of studies that could be performed and why. When the type of scholarship being published about international magazines is examined, several conclusions emerge: First, there appears to be little linking of data to theory. Second, there seems to be little research on how to disseminate ideas. And third, there is a real void in many areas of magazine publishing; for example, looking at magazines as vehicles for sociological study, examining content categories, and investigating types of specialized magazines.

Introduction

Magazines published throughout the world find their way onto our major city newsstand racks and bookstores, or they come through the mail for the subscription price. In ethnic communities, the presence of foreign periodicals is greater than in other communities. These magazines bring a new voice to our culture, a new way of looking at similar issues. So how do American scholars use these periodicals in their research? The purpose of this paper is to survey the literature as to the types of methodology used in magazine research, offer some insights as to relative theory or methodologies magazine research can use, and suggest a direction for future magazine research.

Historically, there have been two approaches to the study of magazines: one approach defines magazines in terms of form as physical commodities, and the second approach defines magazines as vehicles for ideas, understanding, and reader service. The first approach is often found in our trade publications, the second is found among our scholars, for the latter often view magazines as agents of socialization and as media for dissemination of popular culture. If then magazines are seen as reflective of culture, studies should also mirror that culture. What may be logically presumed is not what my survey of the literature indicates. On the contrary, my survey suggests that these studies do not provide scholarly information on magazines that is consistent with current norms of our culture. The question then is what types of studies have been performed using international magazines, and what, if any, are their importance to advancing scholarship in magazine research.

Methodology

A limited number of studies have been performed on magazines published outside the United States, and few are accessible to American scholars. This paper will attempt to first describe some of these research studies and their methodologies. Thirty-four studies have been surveyed as representative of world-wide studies during the period 1980-1993. The parameters of the survey are as follows: only studies using periodicals published outside the U.S. are included, with the exception of comparative studies that also include U.S. magazines; dates investigated were 1980 to present; sources of inquiry began with the *Social Science Index, Humanities Index, Communications Abstracts, Journalism Abstracts, Carl Uncover,* MLA Index, ERIC, Dissertations Abstracts, Paine and Paine's *Magazines: A Bibliography for Their Analysis, with Annotations and Study Guide*; and no studies are included that use U.S. magazines covering foreign events, people, or issues.

Second, the paper reviews articles I found to be important in discussing international magazines. These articles, I would argue, come closer to the norms of scholarship that currently operate in our culture. Third, I offer some suggestions of types of studies that could be performed and why.

The Study: Part One

The significance of evaluating what has been written on magazines is that it identifies gaps which scholars can begin to fill to provide a better understanding of our global patterns of communication. The scholarly journals have already recognized this pattern of globalization in the case of print news media. It is my view that the scholarship on magazines needs to develop an awareness of corresponding patterns of globalization.

As literacy increases, as radio and TV broadcasts dominate the immediacy of the news, magazines are being forced to adapt their pages to provide in-depth coverage of news events. Magazines confirm and expand what people have heard in other media. Whereas the circulations of daily presses have remained about the same for 10 years, circulations of magazines and startups of magazines have increased. This is not to say there are no problems. Throughout the world, the cost or even availability of newsprint is an important obstacle to magazine production.[1] These difficulties are further compounded by the loss of advertising revenue to radio and TV, the reluctance of the public to pay what a newspaper costs, high illiteracy, lack of printing presses, inaccessible rural areas, and a variety of languages besides the official language. All of these factors contribute negatively to the growth of magazines. However, magazines are highly significant in terms of the reproduction of what has been called consumer culture.[2] They provide a unique combination of pictorial and popular literary expression that is not found in either newspapers or broadcast.

With regard to the study of magazines as vehicles for ideas, understanding, and reader service, the work of Paine & Paine has been path breaking.[3] They have advanced and brought more up-to-date the important bibliographic work of Schacht[4] on magazines. In their work, Paine & Paine suggest that magazines may be examined from many different perspectives and offer the following categories as examples:

a. Writing, editing, design, and production
b. Business management & money making
c. Advertising in them or buying space
d. Distribution, display, and sales
e. Selection and access by librarians
f. As a vehicle of sociological study
g. As a popular culture medium
h. History (contemporary or general)
i. Law, ethics, free press in a democracy
j. Use in educational institutions
k. Innumerable magazine content categories
l. Types of specialized magazines

Of the studies identified for this survey, the categories that match Paine & Paine's examples include advertising (c), culture (g), and history (h). The readership and trend studies fall into the business management category (b).

Advertising studies made up 34 percent of the survey. Three of these studies were gender-related studies. One was a Norwegian study which used content analysis to examine a "general gender stereotype model" which treats women's and men's roles as opposites on an abstract continuum. The two-part study analyzed advertisements in three Dutch magazines published from 1965 to 1973 and then Norwegian magazines published between 1965 and 1976.[5] A German study also used content analysis but used *Time* and the West German news magazine *Stern* between 1969 and 1988 to examine how advertising reflects changes in social reality using depictions of gender roles. Jobs, activities, interactions, and situations were used as items of gender role depictions, but posture, gestures, and facial expressions were added as a special feature.[6] A Hong Kong study used six magazines to illustrate through a content analysis the restrictive and distorted nature of gender images in advertising.[7]

There was some degree of methodological sophistication in the German study. A substantial time period was covered, but I felt in spite of this that the information that came out of this was basic at best. Counting images in advertisements to prove gender bias cannot be a strong method of argument to initiate change.

Other advertising studies used Resnik and Stern's typology for classifying advertising, such as a 1983 British study of women's magazines,[8] a Thai study looking at 24 U.S. and Thai magazines, and the cultural differences found in advertisements,[9] and a Chinese study of 349 magazines examining the use of performance and quality in advertisements.[10] None of these studies offered new theory, they only confirmed existing information. The Chinese study, although it used 349 magazines, only reported on a total of 472 advertisements. It was by far closest to useful information in that it proposed that advertisers entering this market should use performance and quality appeals rather than symbolic advertising.

Subjects varied in the remaining advertising studies. There was an Australian study using content analysis of 36 magazines to examine product prices in advertisements,[11] a Canadian study using eight magazines to examine how older people are portrayed in advertising,[12] and a study examining humor in advertisements of U.S., British, and German trade publications.[13] These three I found interesting due to their unusual twists in looking at a question.

Two studies in this survey looking at advertisements expanded the content analysis methodology. A follow-up study by de Kluyver examined eight women's magazines by using a mean-variance analysis as an alternative to existing media planning and scheduling approaches for advertising.[14] A Swedish study used a longitudinal content analysis from 1935 to 1980 and then compared that data with similar U.S. data on advertising trends.[15]

Historical articles made up 38 percent of the survey but were disproportionately represented due to *Punch's* 150th anniversary. Six British studies focused on *Punch* as follows: (1) a profile of Douglas Terrold as *Punch's* first star writer,[16] (2) *Punch* as political satire using Thackeray's writings to illustrate the move from political to moral radicalism in 1847,[17] (3) John Tenniel's cartoons,[18] (4) use of full-page engraving in early *Punch* issues,[19] (5) *Punch's* first 10 years,[20] and (6) representation of the Irish in Victorian Britain through *Punch*.[21] These articles were largely celebratory, since they were all published in the same volume of a special issue of the *Journal of Newspaper and Periodical History*.

Another British study used four historical magazines: *Penny Magazine*, the *London Journal, Reynold's Miscellany*, and *Casell's Illustrated Family Paper* as a group to illustrate how photographic reproduction as art was introduced to the lower and middle classes in 1832-1860.[22] A Canadian study examined the history of Canadian magazines as one that mirrors the Canadian cultural experience. The Canadian magazines and culture were seeking the same kind of independence and protection from American influence as other cultural media in Canadian society.[23] Along similar lines of protection was an Irish study on the *Bell*. As a literary magazine, it began attacking the Censorship Board and raised public awareness on censorship issues.[24] A Chinese study examined the *Beijing Review* and how that magazine has been used "to influence the global balance of power and highlight the mercurial mixture of China's domestic and international political posture."[25] These four articles provided a much needed basis for historical perspective around the world: Britain, Canada, Ireland, and China. All were involved in raising the public awareness to innovative ideas: photographs as art, maintaining cultural sovereignty, censorship issues, and political posturing of the press. These are articles on which other scholars can build their research.

Two studies, both German, focused on historical photographs. The *AIZ* (Arbeiter-Illustrierte-Zeitung) publication was examined along with other illustrated mass circulation magazines in Weimar Germany for "use of photomantages as weapons with which to contradict the truth-claims of photos in Bourgeois magazines by using these same photos."[26] The other German study also examined popular magazines of the 1920s in Weimar Germany as photos became representative of ersatz dreams. Its thesis was that the magazine industry built its success on the curiosity of readers about the world in a fictional context.[27] These studies reminded me of old German movies that had no plot, only images, and I, as the viewer, needed to interpret the meaning.

Cultural studies were more varied than the history and advertising studies, comprising 16 percent of the survey. They also included new countries such as Israel and India. One study looked at the presentation of social roles in two Israeli children's magazines, *Ha'aretz Shelanu* and *Mishmar Li Tyladin*, for sources of abstract and symbolic modeling.[28] The stories were coded and analyzed as to main protagonist, protagonist's role, familiarity, life span, evaluative presentation, protagonist's sex, protagonist's age, journalistic context, and conflict. An Indian study used a qualitative methodology along with a content analysis to examine three Indian magazines with three U.S. magazines for cross-cultural perspectives of the Bhopol disaster.[29] This article used a variety of theories on which to base the study, such as conflict and consensus theories. Then the authors proceeded to use media accounts to test their hypotheses. The study was extremely detailed and resulted in finding little cross-cultural consensus concerning the definition of the Bhopal incident in India and the United States. It was my opinion that both of these studies were so heavily designed for their own purposes that the sum was greater than the parts.

Three other cultural studies were all British. One was a study using the four historical magazines that Anderson used in the study on photographic reproduction as art: *Penny Magazine*, the *London Journal, Reynold's Miscellany*, and *Cassell's Illustrated Family Paper* (1790-1860). In this study he proposed to show the initial development of a modern mass culture. Anderson's thesis suggested the audience was not passive, rather that the new pictorial magazines represented society's long-held values.[30] The second cultural study was on the "post-feminist development" in Britain. This was examined using 1980 women's magazines.[31] Finally, a case study of *Sportsweek* was used to compare sports magazines with the press industry in the U.S., Europe, and the United Kingdom.[32] This study posited that sports magazines were ignored by academic media research. It is my opinion that this study tried to do all: posit an economic picture, compare the industries in the U.S., Europe, and the U.K., and then toss in the case study on the magazine.

Readership studies made up only 9 percent of the survey. A Nigerian study used a model of media exposure and appraisal to examine readership surveys.[33] In the model three independent variables—editorial tone, communication potential, and utility—are posited to determine exposure and appraisal. In another readership study by Bar-Haim, a survey and interview format was used to examine how Romanians were living in Israel.[34] The magazine, *Revista Mea*, was used as a commentary on the community's cultural orientations with respect to those of other communities. The argument was that a magazine retains its popularity only when there is a direct correspondence between the contents and the readers. The study used four cultural orientations to profile the readers: cosmopolitan-continuity, localism-continuity, cosmopolitan-newness, localism-newness. Again, I feel that most of this information was something we already know.

A final readership study was a Dutch study performed on a feminist magazine and its readership.[35] Since the magazine *Opzij* was the only general-audience feminist publication in the Netherlands, the authors focused on both the reception and the content of the magazine. Though the number of issues examined was impressive, 10 volumes (1981-1990), only 14 readers were interviewed and these were ones who had responded to an advertisement in the magazine.

Finally, there was one study identified as a trend study. A British study examined three features of changes in the magazine industry.[36] These were the continued market dominance of the large publishing groups, the trend toward multimedia ownership, and the growth of international publishing. The study concluded that large publishing groups have consolidated their dominance over magazine markets. Absolutely nothing was new here.

The Study: Part Two

Whereas the articles in the first part of the study may illustrate basic types of magazine research, the articles chosen for the second part of the study illustrate finer scholarship and offer tie-ins with existing theory or builds on existing research. These articles illustrate the three areas of defining magazine scholarship: ideas, understanding, and reader service.

Buckman's article on "Cultural Agenda of Latin American Newspapers and Magazines: Is U.S. Domination a Myth?" is an example of how magazine scholarship can use research to develop ideas.[37] Buckman uses dependency theory to anchor his argument on the cultural flow between the U.S. and Latin America. He defines dependency theory in its broadest context as a tool for analyzing the disequilibrium between developed and developing countries. This theory originated from economic theory but has evolved into cultural theory. He then defines cultural dependency as a condition in which the measurable coverage assigned to the domestic culture in the nonadvertising space of a newspaper or magazine is equal to or less than the coverage assigned to the culture of another country or region. He then uses basic magazine assumptions that "any society's tastes are reflected in its newspapers and magazines, and in an age when literacy is rising in Latin America, these media have acquired a mass appeal akin to their U.S. and European counterparts."[38] Buckman posited two hypotheses: one, that measurable U.S. cultural coverage in the sample newspapers and magazines is significantly greater than the coverage of the domestic culture; and two, that measurable U.S. cultural coverage is significantly greater than measurable European cultural coverage. Both hypotheses were tested at the .05 level of significance, applying the chi-square method to the frequency of cultural articles. Buckman used samples of magazines from 1949 and 1982 to examine changes in the Latin American cultural agenda over a third of a century. These were chosen to compare the changes of agenda before and after the advent of television. The sampling procedure was well documented for both newspapers and magazines. Eleven magazines were used in the study. Reliability of the coding was tested by five faculty members and graduate students at the University of Texas. The sampling was impressive: 6,397 cultural articles from newspapers were coded and 2,950 articles and vignettes pertaining to culture were coded for the magazines. Both hypotheses were rejected. The domestic cultural coverage was significantly greater than the U.S. coverage in all three samples.

Where Buckman's article excels is not only in the data gathering but in the qualitative assessment. He gleaned seven basic generalizations as a result of his study. These were as follows: the cultural triangle and the preoccupation with Europe, the Hollywood monoculture of the United States, cultural newcolonialism: the fascination with La Madre Patria, the growth of intraregional influences, national cultural protection, national cultural projection, and the "mixed" category and the hybridization of culture. Buckman ends his piece by tying his discussion back into dependency theory with a look at whether the flow of culture is still somewhat lopsided. He uses a quote from novelist Vargas Llosa to address the issue of cultural borrowing and hybridization:

> The way for a country to fortify and develop its culture is to throw its doors and windows wide open to all intellectual, scientific, and artistic currents, stimulating the free flow of ideas, wherever they many come from, in such a way that its own tradition and experience are constantly put to the test, corrected, finished, and enriched by those who, in other countries and languages, share with us the miseries and greatness of the human adventure. Only by submitting to this challenge and encouragement will our culture be authentic, timely, and creative—the best means of our social and economic progress.[39]

Buchman's article was a good blend of theory, quantitative methods, and qualitative research. He furthered the research on how to develop scholarly ideas.

The second article in my review advances the scholarship of magazine research in the area of understanding. Grube and Boehme-Duerr look at "AIDS in International News Magazines."[40] They base their study on a 1965 Galtung and Ruge study for factors valid in selecting foreign news: frequency, geographical, political and/or cultural closeness, surprise and/or unexpectedness, involvement of elite persons and/or nations, personalization and negativism.[41] Their study compared how five leading news magazines used these news factors in the case of a life-threatening and long-lasting event like AIDS. They tested five hypotheses with variations of each hypothesis. They examined *Der Spiegel*, the *Economist*, *L'Express*, and the European editions of *Time* and

Newsweek. Their results revealed that not all of Galtung's and Ruge's news factors hold true. No straightforward relationship was found between the number of AIDS infections in a country and the space/number of articles devoted to AIDS in that country. In conclusion, the authors suggest that their study should be replicated with other news magazines in other countries and at another period of time. Grube and Boehme-Duerr give a solid description of a social problem and how news magazines are handling it. Their findings were revealing. Whereas *Time* and *Newsweek* carried most of the articles on AIDS, *L'Express* carried none. This article is a start on how scholars should view research on social problems portrayed in the media.

The third article in my review advances magazine scholarship in the area of reader service. Frith and Wesson[42] ask the question: should advertising be standardized around the world, aiming at homogeneous buyers, or should advertising reflect individual cultural differences? The authors base their study on the arguments for standardized advertising posed by other scholars who down-play cultural differences and treat the world as if it were one homogeneous market.[43]

Frith and Wesson compare the cultural values in British and American print advertising. They used the Sunday magazine supplements: the *London Sunday Times Magazine* and the *New York Times Magazine* as well as *Harper's and Queen* and *Town and Country*. The findings in the study suggest the following:

> While the United States and Great Britain are superficially similar in that they are both urbanized, industrial, politically stable, and English-speaking, there are underlying ideological, cultural and communication differences between these two countries.[44]

Even though there were problems with the study, like choosing elite magazines to study homogeneity and the fact that the countries were so similar, the findings of the study indicate that if there are cultural differences between these two using these four elite magazines, then what else is out there to find?

Discussion

When we examine the type of scholarship being published about international magazines, several conclusions emerge. First, there seems to be little linking of data to theory. Second, there seems to be little research on how to disseminate ideas. And third, there seems to be a real void in many areas of magazine publishing.

Theory is not that hard to use in magazine scholarship. Since the print media has established a series of theories that have been tested in the scholarship, magazine scholars should use these as starting points. Examine the print theories as to how they may fit magazines. What kinds of changes have to be made to use them? Which ones are most applicable to the needs of the magazine industry? We need to move past crude empiricism and take numerical data and use it to test more substantive theory.

Ideas are a major part of magazines. How then can scholarly research avoid the editorial content needed to keep magazines alive? More research needs to be conducted on magazine ideas and on content categories. If we are indeed moving in a more global manner with magazines, what ideas are transferrable across cultures? Which will help relationships across cultures? Take for example, the censorship issues of restricting the import of magazines, as Singapore has done recently with the London-based *Economist*.[45] How does these affect globalization of magazines? Which ideas are taboo? Which ones can be combined for countries to give new perspectives to old problems? Which ones have been used too much? Too little? Not at all? For an example of how to research magazine ideas, I found an interesting article on magazine design. Hall writes that magazine design is a new British explosion.[46] He suggests that as the economy downturns, a reaction against the status quo has resulted, and the only place for these new ideas is the underground. Now a lot of techniques in magazine design are emerging from the underground presses in Britain. There are Half-Way House magazines using half print, half electronic to get the message across to the reader. There are magazines that use themes in their issues. There are a lot of ideas in content that can be developed into academic research. Idea research needs to be expanded to make magazine scholarship more useful.

Voids exist in magazine research. Just in Paine & Paine's categories alone,[47] according to my survey for this review, only four of the 12 categories had articles for the time span analyzed. There is still a lot of work that can be done. Magazines can be looked at as vehicles of sociological study, examined for their content categories, and investigated for types of specialized magazines.

There are publications all over the world and studies produced which are not easily accessible to the American scholar. I know of Romanian studies by Virginia Gheorghiu and Yolanda Staniloiu that I cannot obtain easily. And studies that I cannot read because of language problems, like some of Fernando Reyes Matta's work and Ariel Dorfman's. Even with distribution or language problems, there are areas of the world where magazine research can begin as new publications start. One area opening up to the magazine market is the Caribbean Basin. Cuba has had several publications including *Bohemia* and *Cuba*. Jamaica has a number of magazines and so do Barbados and Trinidad. Now there is a regional magazine, *Caribbean Beat*, that is distributed by BWIA. This magazine records and projects the ideas, events, art, sport, music, books, food, and fashion of the region.[48] Regional publications in the Caribbean are only one area of growth in the world for magazines. This is only the beginning. As magazines grow, magazine research needs to grow too.

Notes

[1] Newsprint is only produced in 36 countries and only six produce enough to export: Canada, Finland, Sweden, Norway, USSR, and New Zealand, according to World Communications: A 200-Country Survey of Press, Radio, Television and Film (Gower Press, Unipub: The Unesco Press, 1975), 3-10.

[2] Consumer culture: See Theodore Peterson, "Magazines, 1900-64—An Assessment," Magazines in the Twentieth Century (Urbana, Chicago, London: University of Illinois Press, 1964), 441-451.

[3] Fred K. Paine and Nancy E. Paine, Magazines: A Bibliography for Their Analysis, with Annotations and Study Guide (Metuchen, NJ & London: The Scarecrow Press, Inc., 1987).

[4] J. H. Schacht, A Bibliography for the Study of Magazines (Urbana, IL: College of Communications, University of Illinois, 1979).

[5] M. Flick, "Invisible or Lovely: Women in Advertisements," Media Information Australia 34 (November 1984): 23-34.

[6] H. B. Brosius, N. Mundorf, and J. F. Staab, "The Depiction of Sex Roles in American and German Magazine Advertisements," International Journal of Public Opinion Research 3:4 (Winter 1991): 366-383.

[7] Eva Leung, "A Study of the Portrayal of Women in Magazine Advertisements in Hong Kong," (Masters thesis, Ohio University, 1992).

[8] D. B. Taylor, "The Information Content of Women's Magazine Advertising in the UK," European Journal of Marketing 17:5 (1983): 2832.

[9] Chanporn Jiramongkhollarp, "A Comparative Content Analysis of U.S. and Thai Magazine Advertising," (Master's thesis, Oklahoma State University, 1990).

[10] M. D. Rice and Z. Lu, "A Content Analysis of Chinese Magazine Advertisements," Journal of Advertising 17:4 (1988): 43-48.

[11] D. K. Round, "Price-Informative Advertising and Market Performance," Media Information Australia 37 (August 1985): 35-40.

[12] N. Zhou and M. Y. T. Chen, "Marginal Life After 49: A Preliminary Study of the Portrayal of Older People in Canadian Consumer Magazine Advertising," International Journal of Advertising 11:4 (1992): 343-354.

[13] L. S. McCullough and R. K. Taylor, "Humor in American, British, and German Ads," Industrial Marketing Management 22:1 (February 1993): 17-28.

[14] C. A. de Kluyver and F. T. Baird, "Media Selection by Mean-Variance Analysis," European Journal of Operational Research 16:2 (May 1984): 152-156.

[15] K. Nowak, "Magazine Advertising in Sweden and the United States: Stable Patterns of Change, Variable Levels of Stability," European Journal of Communication 5:4 (December 1990): 393-422.

[16] M. Slater, "Douglas Terrold: Punch's First Star Writer," Journal of Newspaper and Periodical History 7:2 (1991): 25-32.

[17] A. Sanders, "Thackeray and Punch, 1842-1847," Journal of Newspaper and Periodical History 7:2 (1991): 17-24.

[18] F. Morris, "Tenniel's Cartoons: The Pride of Mr. Punch," Journal of Newspaper and Periodical History 7:2 (1991): 64-72.

[19] A. J. Doran, "The Development of the Full-Page Wood Engraving in Punch," Journal of Newspaper and Periodical History 7:2 (1991): 48-63.

[20] R. D. Altick, "Punch's First Ten Years: The Ingredients of Success," Journal of Newspaper and Periodical History 7:2 (1991): 5-16.

[21] R. F. Foster, "Paddy and Mr. Punch," Journal of Newspaper and Periodical History 7:2 (1991): 33-47.

[22] P. Anderson, The Printed Image and the Transformation of Popular Culture, 1790-1860 (New York and Oxford, UK: Oxford at the Clarendon Press, 1991).

[23] J. P. Desbarats, "The Special Role of Magazines in the History of Canadian Mass Media and National Development," in B.D. Singer, ed., Communications in Canadian Society (Scarborough, Ontario: Nelson Canada, 1991), 50-66.

[24] Jacqueline Mulhern, "The Bell on Censorship: An Irish Literary Magazine's Fight For Freedom of Expression in Ireland," (Master's thesis, Ohio University, 1992).

[25] R. L. Terrell, "The First 25 Years of the Beijing Review, An Official Propaganda Organ of the Communist Party of the People's Republic of China," Gazette 37:3 (1986): 191-220.

[26] R. E. Kuenzli, "John Heartfield and the Arbeiter-Illustrierte-Zeitung," Journal of Communication Inquiry 13:1 (Winter 1989): 31-42.

[27] H. Hardt, "Pictures for the Masses: Photography and the Rise of Popular Magazines in Weimar Germany," Journal of Communication Inquiry 13:1 (Winter 1989): 7-30.

[28] Chaim H. Eyal, "Sources of Abstract and Symbolic Modeling: The Presentation of Social Roles in Two Israeli Children's Magazines," Gazette 37:1-2 (1986): 103-122.

[29] Michael J. Lynch, Mahesh K. Nalla, Keith W. Miller, "Cross-Cultural Perceptions of Deviance: The Case of Bhopal," Journal of Research in Crime and Delinquency 26:1 (February 1989): 7-35.

[30] P. J. Anderson, "A Revolution in Popular Art: Pictorial Magazines and the Making of a Mass Culture in England, 1832-1860," Journal of Newspaper and Periodical History 6:1 (1990): 16-27.

[31] J. Winship, "The Impossibility of Best: Enterprise Meets Domesticity in the Practical Women's Magazines of the 1980s," Cultural Studies 5:2 (May 1991): 131-156.

[32] J. Horne, "General Sports Magazines and TCap'n BobU: The Rise and Fall of Sportsweek," Sociology of Sport Journal 9:2 (June 1992): 179-191.

[33] J. D. Johnson, "Media Exposure and Appraisal: Phase II, Tests of a Model in Nigeria," Journal of Applied Communication Research 12:1 (Spring 1984): 63-74.

[34] G. Bar-Haim, "Revista Mea: Keeping Alive the Romanian Community in Israel," in S. H. Riggins, ed., Ethnic Minority Media: An International Perspective (Newbury Park, CA: Sage Publications, 1992).

[35] J. Hermes and V. Schutgens, "A Case of the Emperor's New Clothes? Reception and Text Analysis of the Dutch Feminist Magazine Opzij," European Journal of Communication 7:3 (September 1992): 307-334.

[36] S. Driver and A. Gillespie, "Structural Change in the Cultural Industries: British Magazine Publishing in the 1980s," Media, Culture & Society 15:2 (April 1993): 183-201.

[37] Robert Buckman, "Cultural Agenda of Latin American Newspapers and Magazines: Is U.S. Domination a Myth?" Latin American Research Review 25:2 (1990): 134-155.

[38] Buckman, 134-136.

[39] Buckman, 154.

[40] Anette Grube and Karin Boehme-Duerr, "AIDS in International News Magazines," Journalism Quarterly 65:3 (Autumn 1988): 686-689.

[41] Grube and Boehme-Duerr, 686.

[42] Katherine Toland Frith and David Wesson, "A Comparison of Cultural Values in British and American Print Advertising: A Study of Magazines," Journalism Quarterly 68:1/2 (Spring/Summer 1991): 216-223.

[43] See Richand Ransey, Michael Hyman, and George Zinkhan, "Cultural Themes in Brazilian and U.S. Auto Ads: A Cross-Cultural Comparison," Journal of Advertising 19 (1990): 30-39; Theodore Levitt, "The Globalization of Markets," Harvard Business Review 61 (May-June 1983): 92-101; and Arthur Fatt, "The Danger of `Local' International Advertising," Journal of Marketing 31 (January 1967): 60-62.

[44] Frith, 223.

[45] Philip Shenon, "2 Faces of Singapore: Censor and Communications Center," The New York Times, 4 August 1993, A-7.

[46] Peter Hall, "New British Magazines," Print, September/October 1992, 58-64, 120.

[47] See Paine and Paine

[48] Pat Ganase, "The Magazine Business," Trinidad Guardian, 1 December 1993, 6.

13

Research Review:
City and Regional Magazines

Ernest C. Hynds

ABSTRACT

City magazines comprise what appears to be an under-developed, under-researched segment of the U.S. magazine industry. Many editors and publishers have explored city magazines' potential as information, entertainment, and advertising mediums, but relatively few have explored their vast potential as agenda setters, investigative reporters, and advocates of improved cities. Research on city magazines to see what their full potential might be and how best to develop it has been limited. This article traces the historical development of city magazines, reviews the limited amount of research that has been done in the field, and suggests research approaches that the magazines could use to expand their services to readers, advertisers, owners, staff members, and communities.

Introduction

City magazines comprise what appears to be an under-developed, under-researched segment of the United States magazine industry. Many of the 74 city magazines identified in a 1993 survey are making money by providing information, entertainment, and advertising for affluent readers in their suburbs. But far fewer magazines, perhaps no more than a third, are truly exploring their seemingly vast potential as agenda setters, investigative reporters, and advocates of improved cities. City magazines that successfully mix serious reporting and commentary with guides to leisure-time fun can exert influence and provide service far beyond their numbers, which together comprise less than one percent of the nation's magazines. Moreover, they could provide models for entrepreneurs in hundreds of cities that currently do not have city magazines of their own but whose residents and visitors could benefit from such publications.

As the 21st century approaches, many of the nation's cities, especially the larger ones, are facing major economic and social problems. They need mass media assistance in defining problems, recommending solutions, and building consensus for action. Print media may provide the best vehicles for such service, and in some communities, local newspapers are seeking to meet the need. Magazine involvement is needed, too, and city magazines appear best suited to help. City magazines can complement the reporting of the newspapers and provide an alternative voice on how best to effect solutions. *New York*, *Philadelphia*, *Atlanta*, the *Washingtonian*, and others have at times demonstrated the investigative potential of city magazines. *San Diego* has provided an alternative voice to that of the local newspapers in its community. Many city magazines have encouraged the development of business and industry, especially the tourism industry. All of these are appropriate topics to pursue along with the lifestyle coverage that has dominated the pages of many city magazines.

If city magazine editors, publishers, and owners invest adequate time and money in research, as some appear to be doing, their publications can provide leadership for their communities as well as produce revenue for owners, improve sales for advertisers, and offer information and entertainment for readers. Journalism educators can help city magazines realize their potential in all of these areas by contributing research, by critiquing the research that is being done, and by prodding the magazines to cover issues as well as celebrities. Educators can also use these magazines as models for developing research approaches to other types of magazines and magazines in general. In so doing, they can perhaps expand the types of research applied to magazines and encourage wider dissemination of information about existing magazine research by publishers, trade associations, and others.

With these goals in mind, this article will review the history of city magazines, especially since their renaissance in the 1960s, and describe the status of the genre in the 1990s. Subsequently, it will explore the development of research about city magazines in scholarly journals, papers presented at scholarly meetings, theses and dissertations, consumer magazines, trade and professional publications, and books. Finally, it will suggest other research approaches that might be applied to help city magazines improve and expand their service to readers as individuals and as members of communities.

Evolution of City Magazines

The city magazine idea can be traced back at least to the late 19th century. Ben Moon in his study of city magazine origins suggests that *Town Topics*, founded by Colonel William Mann in New York City before 1900, was perhaps the first American magazine whose editorial content focused primarily on a city. *Town Topics* contained gossip and general light news of interest to its New York society audience.[1] It ceased publication in 1932 when its publisher was charged with having blackmailed persons into buying stock.[2] Prior to that, in the middle of the 19th century, publications called "urban weeklies" discussed urban problems but concentrated more on the fine arts, fashion, music, literature, poetry, humor, gossip, and sports.[3]

An even better prototype of the modern city magazine was founded in 1925 by Harold Ross, who said his *New Yorker* magazine would be a reflection in word and pictures of metropolitan life. It has provided that and more. Cartoons, profiles, plotless short stories, and other features have made the *New Yorker* difficult to classify. It has demonstrated characteristics of the literary magazine, the humor magazine, and the public affairs magazine, and it has gained considerable circulation in communities, often large but sometimes small, outside of New York. Nevertheless, offerings such as "Goings on About Town," which lists theaters, movies, concerts, and myriad other activities in New York City, give it a distinctly city magazine flavor. Such lists have become staples of most city magazines.

In part as a result of the *New Yorker's* success, a number of city-oriented magazines were started throughout the country in the 1920s, 1930s, and 1940s. They included the *Parade* in Cleveland, the *Bulletin-Index* in Pittsburgh and *Town Tidings* in Buffalo as well as the *Philadelphian*, the *Bostonian*, the *Chicagoan*, the *New Orleanian*, the *San Franciscan* and others. Most of the emulators never achieved large circulations, and their failure rate was high. Some lacked editorial quality and a clearly defined editorial format. None were especially successful.[4] Theodore Peterson in his study of American magazines suggests many may have failed to hold readers because they tried too hard to transplant the *New Yorker* into their own localities instead of developing as indigenous products.[5]

San Diego, started in 1948, has been labeled the last major precursor to, or the pioneer magazine in, the modern city magazine movement that evolved in the 1960s. Edwin Self and a partner started the publication that year and merged it three years later with *Point Newsweekly* to provide a liberal voice in a community that had been dominated by conservative newspapers since the death of the Democratic *San Diego Journal*.[6]

Renaissance Begins in the 1960s

Various factors converged to provide the impetus for the development of city magazines in the 1960s. After World War II, the nation's population expanded at a rapid rate and became increasingly concentrated in urban and especially metropolitan areas. By 1960, 70 percent of the population was urban and 63 percent was metropolitan. Increasing numbers of African-Americans joined the melting pot of ethnic groups in the large cities, and all struggled to meet the challenges produced by rapid growth and an accelerated tempo of technological and social change. Conflicts and tensions evolved as local governments created in the 18th and 19th centuries sought to accommodate the rapidly changing needs and attitudes of the 20th. Many inner cities deteriorated as more affluent residents, often white, moved to the suburbs.[7] The human rights movement, the conflict in Southeast Asia, and other developments prompted social unrest and change. In addition, cities became increasingly competitive for business, industry, and tourism.

City magazines developed in response to these and related changes. Many such as *Atlanta* were started by chambers of commerce to promote business and tourism development. A few were developed to provide alternative voices, and some were started as survival manuals for city dwellers, usually upper middle class residents whose readership could attract advertising. Many were started to serve the growing number of affluent persons that settled in the suburbs. It appears that few were started to address city problems such as overcrowding, unemployment, pollution, crime, and creeping decay or even suburban problems such as poor transportation, overcrowded educational and recreational facilities, and restricted tax bases. But in time some came to deal with these problems because they prompted increasing interest and concern among their readers.

The number of city magazines grew rapidly in the 1960s. In 1967 *Business Week* reported, "Some sixty magazines have sprouted up in cities across the land, many of them slick, provocative, and aimed at an affluent audience."[8] In 1968, John Tebbel, writing in the *Saturday Review*, said that with the emergence of *New York* in true magazine format every major American metropolis had a city magazine and the medium had come into its own. "The business press," Tebbel wrote, "was first to notice last year that a kind of publishing which had long been dismissed as self-serving Chamber of Commerce propaganda had changed significantly and was not only a growing medium, offering a new market to advertisers, but one whose magazines had begun to act more like civic gadflies than tame publicity purveyors."[9] *New York* had been published as a Sunday supplement in the *Herald Tribune* before that newspaper ceased publication. *Newsweek* magazine suggested that same year that some city magazines had been started in search of a shortcut to status. "Every red-blooded American city craves a symphony orchestra, a civic center, a major league baseball team and other monuments of civilization," the magazine wrote. "But these days a city can take a shortcut to status with a city magazine."[10]

Emphasis Patterns Emerge and Persist

City magazines continued to grow in importance in the early 1970s, both because of their editorial content and their potential as an advertising medium. The types of articles ranged broadly, but personality profiles and interviews appeared to be the most popular. Industry spokesmen expressed optimism about the future, but noted problems in building circulation, finding good editorial material, acquiring advertiser support, and meeting the challenge of rising costs. Establishing a strong local identity appeared to be the key to success.[11] In subsequent years the magazines sought to overcome their problems by using research to identify readers' interests, increasing their educational efforts to win advertisers, promoting their magazines on radio and televison, increasing special interest sections, and staying alert to local trends.[12]

Emerging content patterns in the 1970s were not always encouraging to those who see city magazines as catalysts for solving community problems and meeting community needs. By the end of the decade it appeared that lifestyle reporting had become the dominant interest of most city magazines. A survey in the late 1970s found that most editors regarded pointing out local problems and needs as important and that some encouraged aggressive journalism, including investigative reporting. It also reported that approximately half of the magazines saw themselves as possible alternative voices to local newspapers. But the survey also found that almost all city magazines regarded providing information about lifestyles and living in the city and providing information about food, travel, and entertainment as important functions. About half reported that promoting business, including tourism, was important. This survey also determined that while most city magazines in the 1960s had been owned by chambers of commerce, most in the late 1970s were independently owned.[13]

David Shaw, who writes about the media for the *Los Angeles Times*, said in 1976 that city magazines had attracted a sophisticated status-conscious audience that buys new cars, stereo equipment, and fine clothes and is highly attractive to advertisers. He suggested that the audience was successful but not content, that it was concerned about achieving. "Crime, inflation, congestion, and competition are the four horsemen of this audience's imminent apocalypse," Shaw wrote. "City magazines cater to those concerns—telling their readers how to protect their homes against burglary, where to shop for bargains, how to beat rush-hour traffic, where to go for psychoanalysis, transcendental meditation, or crash-dieting." He said it seems that most persons read city magazines "either to learn how to cope with their environment or to enjoy, vicariously, the success that others more wealthy and fortunate than themselves have had in so doing."[14]

A partial replication of the late 1970s study completed in 1993 found that lifestyle information was still a major component at most city magazines. As in the 1970s, more than 90 percent of the editors said they provide information about living in the city, lifestyles, food, travel, and entertainment. But the study also found that reporting on community problems and needs was still important to most and that an increasing percentage of the magazines were willing to take stands on local issues through editorials, columns, or other labeled commentary. Almost a third (32 percent) in 1993, as compared with 13 percent in the 1970s, said they often took such stands. About the same percentages, 27 percent in 1993 and 24 percent in the 1970s, said they took stands occasionally. The number of city magazines has not changed dramatically in recent years. Sixty-five were identified as city magazines and included in the 1970s study, and 74 were identified and included in 1993. Both studies have distinguished city magazines from the broader category of city, state, and regional magazines in which they are often listed. The shift to independent ownership was confirmed as more than 90 percent of the publications in 1993 were privately owned.[15]

Review of Research on City Magazines

It seems certain from comments by editors and others that research plays as important a role in determining the editorial content and advertising in city magazines as it does in determining such matters at other magazines. But it appears, as suggested by Thomas Jacobson in 1988, that information about research practices at magazines is "largely diffused throughout the industry, possessed by individual research directors of publishing companies and trade associations."[16] Jacobson, who studied research practices in magazine publishing, said few reports on magazine research practices had been published. He said that most academic research had addressed either magazine content or magazine advertising effects and that little, if any, had described the role of research within magazine publishing companies. He said trade press articles are the most frequent source of information on current research practices, but said they tend to provide anecdotal accounts of how research is used for a particular application and stick close to a single theme or topic.[17]

Jacobson's study involved an assessment of academic research on magazines, a series of meetings with leading researchers in magazine publishing companies and trade organizations, and a mail survey of publishing company personnel involved in the conduct or use of research. He found that 89 percent of consumer magazines and 70 percent of business magazines used research; that 28 percent had independent research departments, and that 22 percent relied to some degree on research activities of centralized corporate research departments. Reader profiles, market studies, buying influence and attention studies, surveys for article and feature ideas, and editorial effectiveness studies were among the most common types of research reported in his study.[18]

Most of the magazine research cited in the book reviews and bibliographies published in *Journalism Quarterly* during the three decades of the modern city magazine movement has centered on general magazines such as *Reader's Digest*, news magazines, and women's magazines. Those types of publications got most of the attention in the books on magazines published during the period and were the subjects of most of the articles in both scholarly and popular publications. There are several books that deal specifically with city magazines, and there are a few dissertations and theses about them cited in *Journalism Abstracts* or other sources. Most of the limited number of articles on specific city magazines have been on publications in large cities such as New York, Chicago, and Los Angeles.

Scholarly Contributions

Sam G. Riley, professor and former head of the department of communications studies at Virginia Tech, has been a major contributor to city magazine research, especially through his work as an editor for Greenwood Press in Westport, Conn. Most recently, in 1991, Riley and Gary W. Selnow, also a faculty member at Virginia Tech, edited a 418-page volume on *Regional Interest Magazines of the United States*. The book, published by Greenwood, includes entries on *Chicago*, *Philadelphia*, *Atlanta*, and many other city magazines. Each entry describes the magazine's founding, development, editorial policies, and content and provides data on information sources.[19] Three years earlier, in 1989, Greenwood published an *Index to City and Regional Magazines of the United States* compiled by Riley and Selnow. More than 900 general-interest consumer magazines are listed in this valuable reference book.[20]

Magazine and other historians are also indebted to Professor Riley for two other substantial works published by Greenwood in 1986. *Magazines of the American South* provides profiles of magazines of general appeal published in the South between 1794 and 1982.[21] *Index to Southern Periodicals* provides two indexes, one with an alphabetical list of periodical titles and one with the periodicals arranged by states and years.[22] Riley's research into Southern magazines also led to scholarly articles in *Journalism Quarterly* on "Specialized Magazines of the South," in 1982 and "Southern Magazine Publishing, 1764-1984," in 1988. The former, based in part on a questionnaire, provides valuable information about city, state, and regional magazines in the region.[23] The latter, done in conjunction with Selnow, does not deal specifically with city magazines. It divides the periodicals discussed into academic/ professional, trade/technical, leisure, and *other* categories. The article argues that the region's magazines do not support the popular myth about the South being a monolith.[24]

It appears from checking the *Journalism Quarterly* indexes and bibliographies and other sources that fewer than a dozen scholarly journal articles have been published about city magazines since the rebirth of the genre in the 1960s, and some of these have not dealt exclusively with city magazines. Most have employed surveys of editors and publishers as a primary means of gathering information, and most have appeared in *Journalism Quarterly*. Alan Fletcher and Fletcher and Bruce G. Vanden Bergh used surveys to collect information for the articles in *Journalism Quarterly* cited earlier (see notes 11 and 12). In addition to reporting data, both articles made extensive use of quotations. Ernest C. Hynds also used a survey to collect data for his *Journalism Quarterly* article cited earlier (see note 13).

Some insights about city magazines can, of course, be obtained by reviewing articles that deal with broader topics. In 1981, John P. Hayes, also using a survey, examined the growth of city/regional magazines and how they obtained their editorial content.[25] Hayes said the magazines' popularity could be attributed to such things as local pride, the failure of some daily newspapers to excite local readers, leisure time, and the upwardly mobile, credit card-carrying adult readers who attract advertisers. He reported that the magazines used a lot of free-lance material but generally did not pay well and paid on publication.[26] Madeline M. Muecke's 1967 article in *Journalism Quarterly* on the ownership of regional magazines didn't deal specifically with city magazines but did include area-of-a-city, city, metropolitan, area-of-a-state, state, and inter-state magazines in its definition of regional.[27] Gene Burd's 1973 article in *Journalism Quarterly* didn't deal specifically with city magazines either, but it did provide useful background information for their study as it explored articles about urban areas in various magazines.[28] Anthony McGann and Judith and J. Thomas Russell touched on regional and metro magazines in their 1983 study of advertising pricing, but their primary focus was on metro editions of national magazines.[29]

Papers, Dissertations, and Theses

City magazines have been the subjects of occasional papers presented at scholarly meetings, a number of master's theses, and at least one doctoral dissertation during the past several decades. Gene Burd and Dianne C. Young reported on "Criticism of News Media in City Magazines" at the 1978 meeting of the Association for Education in Journalism and Mass Communication in Seattle. After studying 420 articles obtained in a survey of city and regional magazines, they concluded that these magazines had adopted media criticism as a standard editorial practice. Most of the articles concerned local media performance and power. Common criticisms were that newspapers were inaccurate, sensational, and without substance; that they boost and protect "sacred cows" rather than criticize, that they ignore problems and issues out of self-interest; and that they allow advertising and class pressures to influence the news.[30]

Alan D. Fletcher and Bruce G. Vanden Bergh presented a paper on growth and problems among metropolitan magazines at the 1981 meeting of the Association for Education in Journalism and Mass Communication in East Lansing, Mich. Their paper, based on the findings of a questionnaire sent to publishers and editors, indicated that community pride was the biggest reason for the rapid increase in popularity of local magazines. They also noted the fact that advertisers are drawn to the magazines in an effort to reach their affluent and educated audiences.[31]

Rob Wiley discussed "The Literature of City Magazines" at the 1987 meeting of the Association for Education in Journalism and Mass Communication in San Antonio, Texas. He suggested that the research literature on city magazines could be divided into five primary sources: books on magazines, popular magazines/journals and newspapers, business magazines, scholarly journals, and unpublished theses.[32]

Vicki Hesterman explored the impact that advertisers have on the content and mission of city and regional magazines in a paper presented to the 1989 meeting of the Association for Education in Journalism and Mass Communication in Washington, D.C. It was titled "A Delicate Balance: Communication Between Editorial and Advertising Departments at Local (City and Regional) Magazines."

Ernest C. Hynds has presented three papers on city magazines to meetings of scholarly groups. He mentioned city and regional magazines in his discussion of "The Recent Rise of Southern Magazines" at the 1982 meeting of the Association for Education in Journalism and Mass Communication in Athens, Ohio; he provided a brief history of *Atlanta* magazine at the 1984 meeting of the American Journalism Historians Association in Tallahassee, Fla.; and he discussed the diverse roles and potential of city magazines at the 1993 meeting of the Association for Education in Journalism and Mass Communication in Kansas City, Mo. He employed historical and qualitative methodology in the first two papers mentioned and a survey of city magazines in the most recent one.[33]

Vicki Hesterman provided a summary of the literature of city and regional magazines and offered specific conclusions and recommendations regarding the practices and policies of these magazines in her 1988 doctoral dissertation,

"Ethical Standards of American Magazines: The Practices and Policies of City and Regional Publications." Much of the information reported in the dissertation was obtained from a questionnaire that was mailed to the magazines. Unfortunately, she found that only a few of the magazines reported having formal or written ethical guidelines. "Some," she said, "saw a need for such standards; others regarded their publication as profit-oriented, boosterish, and not in need of rules guiding other magazines in the genre." She reported that more than 50 percent accepted free tickets, more than 60 percent lacked policies on conflicts of interest, and more than 75 percent said editorial decisions were influenced by advertising concerns. Hesterman concluded that "it is time that magazines in general, and city and regional magazines in particular be scrutinized as carefully as are other media."[34]

Various aspects of city magazines are covered in the dozen or so master's theses completed in recent decades. Fairly typical are Candace Hughes's content analysis of nine selected city magazines for an M.S.J. at Ohio University in 1988, Anita Grant McGraw's study of the role of city and regional magazines and their publishers for an M.A. at the University of Mississippi in 1982, and Patricia A. Kurtz's study of the relationship between metropolitan magazines and locally edited Sunday newspaper supplements for an M.A. at California State University, Fullerton in 1982.[35]

Books, Trade Journals, Consumer Magazines, Newspapers

City magazines are specifically treated in several books on magazines; they are at least mentioned in most general books on magazines and books on the mass media; they are dealt with indirectly in books on magazine advertising, economics, typography, free-lance writing and other topical subjects; and they are the topic of many articles in trade journals, journalism reviews, consumer magazines, and newspapers. City magazines are the subject matter of Sam G. Riley and Gary W. Selnow, eds., *Regional Interest Magazines of the United States* discussed earlier. A number of city magazines are profiled in Alan and Barbara Nourie, eds., *American Mass-Market Magazines*, published in 1990; and a number of them are discussed in William H. Taft, *American Magazines for the 1980s*, published in 1982; and John Tebbel and Mary Ellen Zuckerman, *The Magazine in America, 1741-1990*, published in 1991.[36]

Trade journals and some members of the popular press have been principal sources of information about the continued development of city, state, and regional magazines in the late 1980s and early 1990s. Trade publications such as *Folio*, *Advertising Age*, and *Marketing and Media Decisions* have provided extensive coverage of the field. *Columbia Journalism Review* and similar publications have run articles occasionally. Consumer magazines such as *Time*, *Newsweek*, and *Business Week* have provided frequent coverage, and newspapers such as the *New York Times*, the *Wall Street Journal*, the *Chicago Tribune*, and the *Christian Science Monitor* have provided continuing coverage, especially of city magazines in their areas.

Other Sources for Research Information

Researchers can get information about city magazines from organizations such as the Magazine Publishers of America, the City and Regional Magazine Association, and the American Society of Magazine Editors. They can look for new magazines in Samir Husni's *Guide to New Magazines* [37], *Gale Directory of Publications and Broadcast Media, U.S. Regional Publications Directory, Standard Rate & Data*, and *Ulrich's International Periodicals Directory*. They can also look in basic bibliographies such as Eleanor Blum and Francis Wilhoit, *Mass Media Bibliography: Reference, Research, and Reading*[38], *Journalism Abstracts*, and *Communication Abstracts*.

Suggestions for Future Research

Individual city magazines most likely have engaged in the types of research identified by Jacobson in his study of "Research Activity of Magazine Publishers" discussed earlier. According to him the top ten types of research conducted by magazines included reader profiles, used by 79 percent; market studies, 58 percent; buying influence and intention, 57 percent; marketing and circulation, 53 percent; editorial effectiveness, 51 percent; surveys for article ideas and competitive publication analysis, each 50 percent; competitive readership analysis, 47 percent; syndicated readership studies, 40 percent; and reader traffic studies, 34 percent.[39] City magazines, as other magazines, probably should pursue these kinds of research to help determine who their readers are, what they want, and what types of advertising they will support.

Most academic research of city magazines has involved surveys of editors and publishers, and many of these studies can be updated periodically to get a fresh picture. Surveys also can be used to explore new topics such as what types of research are conducted by city magazines. Surveys are a relatively inexpensive way of obtaining information about the magazines and those that produce or use them. Readers and non-readers can be questioned along with magazine personnel to get a clearer picture of what the magazine is accomplishing.

Focus groups and reader panels might provide even more effective ways for city magazines to interact with their readers and determine what they like and don't like about their magazines. Focus group participants could be asked about community projects and issues in which the magazine is interested as well as about headlines, columns, features, graphics, layout, and other aspects of the magazine itself. Reader panels could rank articles or other materials on a number of scales to ascertain levels of interest, readership, and usefulness.

Agenda-setting would also appear to be a worthwhile area for research about city magazines. Agenda-setting theory suggests that the media in their selection of what to talk and write about help set the agenda for public discussion. Presumably if the media give attention to something, their consumers assume that it is important. Agenda-setting research looks at the relationship between what the media think is important and what their audiences think is important. Many interesting questions can grow out of this. Do city magazines see agenda setting as one of their functions? To what extent, if any, are they seeking to encourage public discussion and action on issues? If they are seeking to set agendas, how are they going about it? How much influence are they exerting and in what areas?

Content analysis, which has been used in a few city magazine studies, also appears to be a good outlet for additional study. Researchers can study content to see how city magazines compare with each other or how a particular city magazine's content has changed over the years. Such studies could document, or at times perhaps disprove, the assertions of staff members answering questionnaires concerning what the magazine is doing. Content analysis could suggest trends in a particular magazine or city magazines generally. It would, for example, be interesting to determine if magazines that have been cited for investigative reporting in the past are as involved in it today or if magazines such as *San Diego* that have been cited as alternative voices to local newspapers in the past are as effective today in providing that choice.

Since research on city magazines to date has been limited, the possibilities for future research appear almost limitless. Potential researchers can find many trails to pursue by looking through one or more of the good media research books available. They might start with *Mass Media Research: An Introduction* by Roger D. Wimmer and Joseph R. Dominick. It's now in its third edition.[40] All types of research that can help city magazines serve their readers, owners, employees, advertisers, and communities more effectively should be considered. The potential of city magazines to serve as catalysts for positive change in their communities should be pursued along with their potential as entertainers and purveyors of advertising and general information. City magazines that successfully mix serious reporting and commentary with guides to leisure-time fun can exert infuence and provide service far beyond their numbers. Research can help them find the right mixtures for their markets.

Notes

[1] Ben L. Moon, "City Magazines, Past and Present," Journalism Quarterly 47:4 (Winter 1970): 711.

[2] Theodore Peterson, Magazines in the Twentieth Century, 2nd ed. (Urbana, IL: University of Illinois Press, 1964), 79.

[3] Herbert Fleming, "Magazines of a Market Metropolis," (Ph.D. diss., University of Chicago, 1906) cited in Gene Burd, "Urban Magazine Journalism Thrives During City Crises," Journalism Quarterly 50:1 (Spring 1973): 78.

[4] Moon, 712.

[5] Peterson, 320.

[6] John Tebbel, "City Magazines: A Medium Reborn," Saturday Review, 9 March 1968, 103.

[7] For a complete look at population changes, see the U.S. Census Reports for 1960 and 1970. A good summary of the changes discussed here may be found in the "Cities and Urban Affairs" section of Britannica Book of the Year 1969, 204.

[8] "City Magazines Are the Talk of the Town," Business Week, 18 February 1967, 184.

[9] Tebbel, 102.

[10] "A Shortcut to Status," Newsweek, 2 September 1968, 44.

[11] Alan D. Fletcher, "City Magazines Find a Niche in the Media Marketplace," Journalism Quarterly 54:4 (Winter 1977): 740-743, 749.

[12] Alan D. Fletcher and Bruce G. Vanden Bergh, "Numbers Grow, Problems Remain for City Magazines," in Journalism Quarterly 59:2 (Summer 1982): 313-317.

[13] Ernest C. Hynds, "City Magazines, Newspapers Serve in Different Ways," Journalism Quarterly 56:3 (Autumn 1979): 621-622.

[14] David Shaw, "List Grows: Magazines of the Cities, A Success Story," Los Angeles Times, 5 April 1976, 3.

[15] Ernest C. Hynds, "Today's Diverse City Magazines Have Many Roles, Much Potential," Paper presented to the Association for Education in Journalism and Mass Communication annual meeting in Kansas City, MO, 1993.

[16] Thomas Jacobson, "Research Activity of Magazine Publishers," Journalism Quarterly 65:2 (Summer 1988): 511.

[17] Ibid.

[18] Ibid., 512-513.

[19] Sam G. Riley and Gary W. Selnow, eds., Regional Interest Magazines of the United States (Westport, CT: Greenwood Press, 1991), 418.

[20] Ibid., comps., Index to City and Regional Magazines of the United States (Westport, CT.: Greenwood Press, 1989), 130.

[21] Sam G. Riley, Magazines of the American South (New York: Greenwood Press, 1986), 346.

[22] Ibid., comp., Index to Southern Periodicals (Westport, CT: Greenwood Press, 1986), 459.

[23] Ibid., "Specialized Magazines of the South," Journalism Quarterly 59:3 (Autumn 1982): 447-450, 455.

[24] Sam G. Riley and Gary Selnow, "Southern Magazine Publishing, 1764-1984," Journalism Quarterly 65:4 (Winter 1988): 898-901.

[25] John P. Hayes, "City/Regional Magazines: A Survey/Census," Journalism Quarterly 58:2 (Summer 1981): 294-296.

[26] Ibid.

[27] Madeline M. Muecke, "Ownership Forms of Regional Magazines," Journalism Quarterly 44:3 (Autumn 1967): 560-561.

[28] Gene Burd, "Urban Magazine Journalism Thrives During City Crises," Journalism Quarterly 50:1 (Spring 1973): 77-82, 108.

[29] Anthony F. McGann, Judith F. Russell, and J. Thomas Russell, "Variable Pricing in Advertising Space For Regional and Metro Magazines," Journalism Quarterly 60:2 (Summer 1983): 269-274, 322.

[30] Gene Burd and Dianne C. Young, "Criticism of News Media in City Magazines," Paper presented at the annual meeting of the Association for Education in Journalism and Mass Communication, Seattle, WA, August 1978.

[31] Alan D. Fletcher and Bruce G. Vanden Burgh, "Metropolitan Magazine Boom Continues, but Problems Remain," Paper presented at the annual meeting of the Association for Education in Journalism and Mass Communication, East Lansing, MI, August 1981.

[32] Rob Wiley, "The Literature of City Magazines," Paper presented to the annual meeting of the Association for Education in Journalism and Mass Communication, San Antonio, TX, August 1987.

[33] Ernest C. Hynds, "The Recent Rise of Southern Magazines," Paper presented to the annual meeting of the Association for Education in Journalism and Mass Communication, Athens, OH, July 1982; "'Only the Best for Atlanta': A Brief History of Atlanta Magazine," Paper presented to the annual meeting of the American Journalism Historians Association in Tallahassee, FL, October 1984; see also note 15.

[34] Vicki Hesterman, "Ethical Standards of American Magazines: The Practices and Policies of City and Regional Publications," (Ph.D. diss., Ohio University, Athens, OH, 1988).

[35] Candace Hughes, "A Content Analysis of Selected City Magazines," (Master's thesis, Ohio Univesity, 1988); Anita Grant McGraw, "The Role of City and Regional Magazines and Their Publishers in Society Today," (Master's thesis, University of Mississippi, 1982); and Patricia A. Kurtz, "A Study of the Relationship Between Metropolitan Magazines and Locally Edited Newspaper Supplements," (Master's thesis, California State University, Fullerton, 1982).

[36] Alan and Barbara Nourie, eds., American Mass-Market Magazines (Westport, CT.: Greenwood Press, 1990), 611; William H. Taft, American Magazines for the 1980s (New York: Hastings House, 1982), 382; John Tebbel and Mary Ellen Zuckerman, The Magazine in America, 1741-1990 (New York, Oxford: Oxford University Press, 1991), 434; see also note 19.

[37] Samir Husni, Samir Husni's Guide to New Magazines (University, MS: University of Mississippi Department of Journalism, 1988).

[38] Eleanor Blum and Francis Wilhoit, Mass Media Bibliography: Reference, Research, and Reading (Urbana, IL: University of Illinois Press, 1990).

[39] Jacobson, 511.

[40] Roger D. Wimmer and Joseph R. Dominick, Mass Media Research: An Introduction (Belmont, CA.: Wadsworth, Inc, 1991).

14

Regional Consumer Magazines and the Ideal White Reader: Constructing and Retaining Geography as Text

Katherine Fry

ABSTRACT

U.S. regions are both physical and cultural constructs. The unique identities of vernacular regions are perpetuated in popular representations, many of which circulate in the mass media. This paper is an examination of representations of nature and culture in the consumer magazines *Midwest Living*, *Southern Living*, and *Sunset*. Distinct patterns of signification employed in each construct the Midwest, South, and West as cultural/geographic texts. Such patterns also reinforce historic domination of non-white races. However, because each magazine targets an overwhelmingly white readership there exists a virtual eradication of racial politics. The magazines' emphasis on advertising and tourism both obscures and commodifies racial repression while constructing regions as unique places of consumption.

Introduction

United States regions are physical geographic entities as well as meaningful cultural constructs. The vernacular West, Midwest, and South are meaning-filled places which rely not on fixed political boundaries but on culturally produced representations to separate them and to perpetuate their distinctions in relation to each other. An array of region-specific representations of landscape features, population groups, artifacts and historic events are diffused throughout popular culture, and particularly the mass media. Consumer magazines *Southern Living*, *Midwest Living*, and *Sunset* contain a broad range of regional representations in both written text and photographs. The compilation of representations that appear on the pages of these regional magazines construct three separate regional identities.

Drawing on communications and cultural geography, this study examines collective identity construction in recent issues of the three geographically targeted magazines. Results indicate that, despite their similarities, each magazine employs its own unique pattern of representation which serves to reinforce regional difference. Yet at the same time, all three imply an ideal readership. The similar emphases on white settlement as regional heritage and the context in which whites and non-whites appear in text and photographs suggest the interpellation of an all-white readership. Representational patterns and the ideal readership of all three magazines recall and reinforce power relations that are foundational to U.S. regional identity. When that identity is offered from a consumer's framework, the region as a cultural entity becomes, for the preferred reader, a place of consumption.

Geographic Place and Power Relations

Place is as much a socially constructed phenomenon as it is a physical, material entity. A social place construction centers on the meanings attached to it and the types of relations operating within it; these are the substance of its identity. The term *identity* implies a relationship of insiders and outsiders,[2] and identity formation is an ongoing process whereby dominant persons or groups work to maintain the distinction between insiders and outsiders. Here it is a matter of determining distinct geographic groups whose identities are constructed and reinforced in cultural discourse. Place meanings which emerge out of popular cultural discourse are filters through which inclusion and exclusion are determined.

Geography, a discipline once focused on landscape description and how landscapes determine human behavior, has branched into sub-disciplines which recognize both the material and the social aspects of geographic places, and the processes whereby place is both generator and product of meaning and behavior.[3] The intersection of geography and critical social theory in particular allows us to examine the way landscapes shape social formations and vice versa. Specifically, Soja examines the way formations of geographic space are actually shaped by relations of domination and subordination.[4] Geographer Robert David Sack suggests a relational framework for analyzing the nature, meaning, and social relations underlying unique place constructions in the broader "world of consumption."[5]

Theorizing place as both physical and cultural has captured interest within communications and cultural studies as well. Grossberg calls for a spatial model of culture and power.[6] He implores cultural studies practitioners to examine the geographies of power, and particularly to "see culture as an active agent in the production of places and spaces."[7] Burgess and Gold examine the ideology of place constructions, and particularly the role of the mass media in hegemony maintenance through place representation.[8] Similarly, Hay analyzes the power of the mass media to create perspectives on place which "result from, generate and gradually transform relations of power and status."[9]

This study integrates geography and cultural studies, focusing on mediated constructions of U.S. regional identity. Textual and photographic representations in regional consumer magazines *Southern Living, Midwest Living* and *Sunset* draw on the past to create distinction through representations of nature and culture, and by comparison with other places. Prevalent in these magazines are patterns of race representation, both historic and contemporary, which suggest power relations and the struggle of non-white groups which are signified in what are essentially reconstructions of Eurocentric regional heritage.

U.S. Regionalism and Representation

The West, the South, and the Midwest are vernacular regions, which means they have strong local and national identification.[10] Vernacular regions are not consensually defined as states are. That is, they do not have clearly marked political boundaries, but are ambiguous, shifting in time and according to purpose.[11] For marketing, census, and cartographic purposes, regions are convenient organizing concepts.[12] But regions also retain separate cultural identities which may be traced back to the earliest patterns of effective settlement during the 18th and 19th centuries.[13] Zelinsky points out that there are five major U.S. contemporary cultural regions: New England, Midland (MidAtlantic), South, Middle West, and West.[14] The West, South, and Midwest are the largest and, it is argued here, the most ambiguously bounded regions of the country because in many instances it is contested which states comprise any one of the three. Their boundaries shift depending upon who is defining them. States such as Missouri and Texas are considered the province of more than one region. However, despite a lack of consensus as to the boundaries of the South, the Midwest, or the West, the phenomenon of regionalism is retained in cultural discourse.

Geographer Earl Shaw argues that regions construct and retain strong beliefs, social viewpoints, and memories through regional iconography, the vast network of culturally shared representations of regionalism.[15] For example, the prairie, the rolling wheatfield, and the small town oftentimes represent the Midwest; the cowboy, the rugged frontier, and the Gold Rush represent the West. These icons of regionalism, here referred to as regional representations, are similar to Barthes' signifiers.[16] Signifiers as components of larger semiological systems—or cultural myths—reflect and reproduce cultural meaning. Regional representations construct and retain the larger myths of regionalism in cultural discourse.

Regional representations circulate within the mass media, identifying insiders and outsiders while at the same time calling up the region's intangible characteristics around which we "form emotion-filled value judgments."[17] The discourses of regionalism—the West, South, and Midwest—exemplify the continual practice of place construction in mediated popular culture. Mediated regional signification is but one of a range of discursive practices which create and retain shifting geographies as texts.[18]

U.S. Magazine Industry

Region-specific consumer magazines represent a growing trend in the U.S. magazine publishing industry—service journalism targeting a market niche through geographic identification.[19] Though geographically specialized magazines have been around for a very long time,[20] geography as a tool of market segmentation is a publishing trend of the Post WWII magazine industry. City magazines were the first geographically targeted service journalism magazines.[21] *Philadelphia Magazine* and *Texas Monthly* are early examples of two such specialized periodicals. Specifically situated urban areas, sites of varying styles and consumption patterns, proved viable advertising markets.[22]

Regional consumer magazines are products of that same geographic targeting concept. Both *Southern Living*, first published by Southern Living Publications, Inc. in 1966, and *Midwest Living*, a Meredith, Inc. periodical in publication since 1987, have always been primarily organs for service journalism or leisure enhancement. *Sunset* magazine, in publication since 1898, has changed owners and formats as the consumer magazine industry has changed, but today it is a glossy conduit of national advertising similar to *Southern Living* and *Midwest Living*. Contemporary regional magazines such as these represent one of the most dynamic sectors within the magazine industry,[23] and all three, *Southern Living*, *Midwest Living*, and *Sunset*, have enjoyed growing circulations.[24]

The demographics of the subscriber readership of each of the three magazines are also similar.[25] Generally speaking, the readers are more often women than men (roughly a 60:40 ratio); they have some college education, and many have earned at least an undergraduate degree (about 45 percent); annual household income is, on average, between $42,000 and $79,000; and in most households the wage earner(s) hold professional/managerial postions (up to 67 percent).[26] While the readership statistics obtained from each magazine do not specifically indicate the race or ethnicity of readers/subscribers, it is argued here that the majority are Caucasian. Since the goal of consumer magazines publishing is to deliver a specialized audience to its advertisers,[27] editorials and advertisments must strive to reflect the interests and demographics of the majority readership. Class and race analyses of the representations in these three magazines suggest the subject postion of an ideal reader is white, middle- to upper-middle income. The interpellated subject identifies with European heritage, and possesses enough disposable income to reinforce that identification through consuming.

While these three magazines are similar to each other in publishing format and readership demographics, they each employ a unique representational strategy. Regional identity construction through the use of geographically and historically specific representations varies among the magazines and makes each a unique repository of regional signification attractive to the ideal regional readership, encouraging geographic distinction, hence cultural separation.

Consumer magazines have a history of being powerful tools of cultural, political and social issues.[28] Kozol's examination of the family as depicted in Post WWII *Life* magazine's photojournalism "legitimated dominant social relations and political policies at a time of tremendous change."[29] The respect magazines have garnered within the landscape of media forms, and the powerful cultural role they have played, indicates that representations in consumer magazines are fertile loci of cultural construction.

Patterns of Regional Representation

A content analysis of 1,089 articles from a total of 12 regional magazine issues published in 1992—four each of *Southern Living*, *Midwest Living*, and *Sunset*—revealed patterned similarities and differences in representational practices.[30] While the numerical frequencies of representations are not included here, results of the quantitative analysis indicated that, in all of the magazines, representations can be grouped into three main types: "natural" representations, "cultural" representations, and relationships with other places. Natural representations are actual physical characteristics including land formations and water bodies that are included in the magazine and connected with the region. Cultural representations are population groups—racial, ethnic, and religious groups—as well as architecture, foods, and other artifacts which can be traced to these population groups. Finally, the region is constructed in each magazine through references to other places. Specifically, this means that each magazine to a certain extent defines relationships, or compares itself, with other U.S. regions, the United States as a whole, and/or foreign cities or nations. At times a single type of representation will be the focus of a given article; more often, combinations of the three types appear together in such a way that they form a unique pattern, the magazine's means of regional identity construction. Below is a discussion of the qualitative content analysis which delineates the way in which representations work together in context to construct regional distinction.

Representations of Nature and Culture
in Identity Construction

Each regional identity in these magazines ultimately springs from the physical characteristics of the region. The representational patterns emphasize characteristics of land and water bodies especially. Cultural representations build on these physical characteristics. Representations of groups, activities, and events unique to the region are situated in relationship to natural resources. *Sunset* magazine's depictions of mountains, canyons, desert, and forest are represented both textually and photographically as spectacle, often with ties to the mystical or spiritual. In *Midwest Living* the land is not typically represented as wild; rather, as utilitarian, with an emphasis on tamed "country" or agricultural land, often as nostalgia. The magazine includes numerous representations of lakes and rivers in several contexts. In *Southern Living*, as in *Midwest Living*, representations of nature are closely tied to the past. Most references to land and water are described less on their own terms, and more in terms of specific people and events in Southern history. In addition, the majority of photographs in all three magazines are outdoor shots, indicating the overall importance of natural, physical characteristics in defining a region. Below are specific examples of how representations work together in magazine articles to form three distinct regional ideals.

The Rugged Frontier West

Sunset magazine reinforces the West as Frontier, an ideal constructed via the magazine's unique representations of nature and culture. Western land in particular is large, open and rugged. Physical features of the Western landscape are oftentimes either the main topic of an article in the magazine, or they are used to introduce or frame another topic. Throughout the magazine, physical land, water, and other natural phenomena are described in words and depicted in photographs in a manner that suggests their breadth, beauty, and spiritual qualities, all suggesting a rugged Western Frontier.

The front section of each month's issue, Travel and Recreation, contains articles about places to see in the West. Many of these articles are about large, awe-inspiring physical features, including mountains and canyons. In the October issue, the article "California's Ultimate Sea of Sand" (pp. 21-29), about the Nipomo Dunes in coastal south central California, describes a virtual contemporary wilderness. The dunes, we read, cover so much area that hikers can get lost in 18 miles of uninhabited, isolated sand that eventually opens onto the "wild coastline" of southern California. The area reaches beyond the horizon. Three photographs of the dunes offer three different scenic views; each includes two or three hikers who are lost in the sheer size of the area framed within the shot. One shot, a sea of sand spread across both pages, includes two tiny hikers in the top left-hand corner. They seem to be walking along the horizon where the sand meets a thin band of blue sky. All of the photographs reinforce the remote, uncivilized nature of the area. Efforts of groups such as The Nature Conservancy, which has dubbed the land "one of the last great places in America" (p. 22), have successfully kept the dunes free from enterprise. This activism has helped the Nipomo Dunes retain their metaphysical aura.

The article refers several times to a possible spiritual force loose in the land. That force is partly generalized and uncontained. "The dunes' mystical quality can hit visitors at any time. For some, the trigger might be the yips of coyotes over the crashing of waves. For others, it's the finely etched line of dune scarp at dawn." (p. 29) The spiritual force might also be associated with specific sources or groups. "The dunes have been a private altar for locals and a cathedral for dreamers, like the Dunites, a group of intellectuals who created a dune utopia here in the 1930s." (p. 22) In keeping with the overall spiritual theme, the article closes with a remark by a nearby resident who sums up the area residents' shared perception of spirituality in this Western landscape. "I guess it goes back to the old belief in Gaea, Mother Earth...It just seems like there are some places more open to get that feeling." (p. 29)

The rugged and mystical landscape is also cultivated in another feature article about the wild, coastal area in California called Big Sur, situated on the Monterey Coast of northern California. "Big Sur Forever" (April, pp. 88-97) describes an area that is miles of mountains, forest, and rocky coastline. Here again, the two-page photograph which opens the article is an aerial shot of the coastline's rocky cliffs, grassy hills, and Pacific ocean. In this photo cars and trucks traveling across a bridge connecting two cliffs are dwarfed by the awesome nature surrounding them. According to the text, Big Sur, or "Paradise," as it is called, is a religious experience in itself.

> It is easy to slip into New Age burbling when talking about Big Sur, but if
> any place can be said to possess an aura, it is this one...It has a motto, coined
> some years ago when local artist Ephraim Doner stood at a public meeting
> and proclaimed "Big Sur is where you go to launder your Karma." (p. 90)

These two articles and many like them in *Sunset* magazine reflect an overall effort to retain the idea of the original rugged Frontier West, while adding
an aura of mystery, the metaphysical connected to the physical. The idea of the
West as frontier was first formally developed in Frederick Jackson Turner's
Frontier Thesis in 1893.[31] According to Turner, the Great West was free
land, a primitive wilderness settled by enterprising Americans. But it was also
simplicity and fluidity of life, qualities which "furnish the forces dominating
the American character."[32] While the idea of the rugged West, ripe for settlement by individualistic, hearty Americans of European descent, has been reinforced throughout American history and is continuously recreated in the mass
media,[33] *Sunset* magazine adds another element, a version of the Native
American perspective. The metaphysical, or spiritual, connection to the land
as it is often described in the magazine reflects a more contemporary "take" on
the Western frontier, one that accommodates a multi-cultural, albeit White,
perspective. It is not surprising to see a magazine about the West embrace
contemporary New Age mysticism to reinforce the traditional notion of Frontier.[34]

Sunset's cultural representations are usually situated in conjunction with
natural representations. That is, groups associated with the region are often
depicted as subordinate to the larger forces of nature. Gold seekers and cowboys exemplify the Western ideal of rugged individualism meeting the Frontier landscape. The April article, "Cowboys Then and Now—and in Hologram"
(p. 15), tells readers about a new museum opened by the Cattlemen's Heritage
Foundation, called Cowboys Then & Now. At the museum "a detailed time
line traces cowboy history from the first hands—Indians taught to care for
livestock by California mission padres—to modern cowboy poets." This description, in one sentence, depicts the idealized history of the West, including
the groups considered most relevant to Western settlement.

Sunset magazine, of the three, includes the largest percentage of articles
which contain textual references to foreign cities or nations, and by comparison few articles which refer to the United States as a whole or other U.S.
regions. Most foreign references function to establish relationships. In the April
issue, "The Essence of Fruit...Eau de Vie" (p. 176) is a typical example of how
Sunset establishes a relationship with a foreign place. The article discusses a
method of fermenting fruit previously practiced only in Europe. California
winemaker Randall Grahm describes his efforts to bring that tradition to the
United States. According to the article, the frustration for Grahm and other

Western winemakers was that they seemed to be "voices in the wilderness" because of U.S. unfamiliarity with the method. But these Western winemakers forged ahead anyway.

References to the U.S. as a whole or other U.S. regions are rare in *Sunset*. The August article, "To Columbus, In Honor of Columbus" (p. 50), includes a reference to the Midwest. This brief article in the gardening section begins, "Few Western gardeners think of Columbus, Ohio, as a travel destination, but there's a good reason to visit now." Oftentimes references to other regions takes the form of a reference to one particular place or city as representative of the region. In this case, the Midwest is represented in the reference to Columbus, Ohio. It is apparent from these kinds of comparisons that the Westerner is already in the ultimate region; there's really no need to travel elsewhere in the country, least of all the Midwest. In *Sunset* the pattern of references to places outside the region, like the representations of nature and culture, reinforces the notion of Western autonomy; the West is the final frontier destination.

The Agrarian Midwest

Representations of nature and culture in *Midwest Living* magazine construct an identity very different from the West. The pattern of signification in this magazine reinforces the "Heartland" ideal, or nostalgic rural Midwest.

Nature in *Midwest Living* is gentler than nature in *Sunset*. Here the land and water are represented in a way that emphasizes utilitarianism through traditional activities, especially farming. Most of the descriptions of land and water suggest accessibility instead of awesome spectacle. The Midwest prairie, country, lakes, and rivers are often the back-drops for other nostalgic activities. Textual descriptions match photographic displays of activities and groups from a simpler past. The rural Midwest is captured in the magazine's many references to prairie and countryside. For example, the open prairie of South Dakota is one of the "Easy Outdoor Adventures" feature of the August issue (pp. 50-51). This prairie, we read, "rolls like a green sea for miles." The horses on the prairie "step daintily through a gurgling stream that splices a meadow bobbing with black-eyed Susans." The ease of this landscape is also captured in the accompanying photographs. In the main shot, a trail of horseback riders wanders across the page along an expanse of tall grass, a gently sloping hill sparsely covered with pine trees fills the background. Bringing up the rear of the train of riders is a horse-drawn chuck wagon. In this photograph the sun is shining, the sky is blue, and the air is calm, matching the description of the prairie.

An enduring representation of land in the magazine is the cultivated landscape. Farmland and farming activities are nostalgically depicted. A special photo feature in the April issue includes a series of photographs of various

Midwest settings. Of the ten photographs in the "Reflections of the Heartland" photo essay (pp. 101-106), five are depictions of agriculture. One shot is a wide angle photo of an Iowa farm in the early morning. Endless rows of tall green corn extend to the horizon on either side of a narrow winding trail which leads to the white wooden farmhouse, barn, and corn bin. This shot, and the adjacent shot of a cluster of old-fashioned grain elevators in Carson, North Dakota, are idealized depictions of single family Midwest farms.

Waterways are also important physical characteristics of the Midwest. The August issue features a story about Hannibal, Missouri, located on the banks of the Mississippi River. "Mark Twain's Missouri" (pp. 37-44) is about the recreated boyhood home of Samuel Clemens, or Mark Twain. The entire city of Hannibal revolves around the famous author. What Twain, hence Hannibal, is best known for is the romance of the mighty Mississippi River. Today the River is celebrated by the residents of Hannibal and by 250,000 visitors each year. Daily sightseeing cruises on old fashioned red-white-and-blue-decked paddleboats add to the "magnetic attraction of the River." The Mississippi River was once a major thoroughfare filled with steam-powered paddleboats for shipping. It served as a link between Hannibal's industry and its national markets. Now, as illustrated in this article, it has itself become the town's major industry.

Small towns such as Hannibal, the gentle countryside and farmland epitomize the natural agrarian Heartland of *Midwest Living*. Of all three magazines, the largest percentage of articles in *Midwest Living* include rural-wilderness and/or small town settings in the text and photos. Both are the agrarian ideal. The natural resources of the Midwest, represented here as gentle and accessible, depict a time in the past when the land and water were direct means by which many Midwesterners made a living. The Norman Rockwellesque image of the Midwest cultivated in *Midwest Living* suggests a still-yearned-for connection with the land and important waterways such as the Mississippi that connects the Midwest with the South, and, during early European settlement, acted as a gateway to the Western Frontier.

Cultural representations in the magazine include European immigrants and religious groups that comprised the nostalgic landscape. The April Celebrations section lists the Celtic Music Festival in Missouri (p. 36), a "salute to the Ozarks' early Irish, Welsh, and Scottish settlers," as well as the St. Joseph's Day Celebration in Cedar Rapids, Iowa, which includes a Czech Village (p. 32). The August issue lists a German Fest (p. 22) where Milwaukee residents "roll out the barrel for three days of schnitzels and tortes, yodeling, contests, and German dancers and bands." Many of the Germans who originally settled the Midwest came for religious reasons. The August feature article, "Amish Sojourns" (pp. 87-93), describes contemporary Amish communities in Ohio and Indiana. *Midwest Living* represents the Amish life as a perfect present-day past. The photographs—outdoor shots, mostly of farmland and farm work—are unusual in that they are among the only ones in all four issues of the magazine that actually depict farm labor. One photograph is a wide-angle view looking down on a barn-raising, another shows a farmer in his hay field as he "tackles the harvest," baling hay with an old-fashioned horsedrawn baler. This particular photograph captures the essence of connection to the land in a "simpler" time. The Amish authentically represent what the magazine as a whole wants to recreate.[35] They are the quintessential agrarians, providing all the trapping of nostalgia crucial to the *Midwest Living* version of the Midwest.

Midwest Living's references to other places focus on other regions and the United States as a whole. The context of these references belies a regional self-consciousness, a need to defend and define itself, and to compare its resources with those of the rest of the country. The April issue's letter from the editor at the front of the magazine, entitled "Thanks for the Midwest Memories!" (p. 6), looks back at the first five years of the magazine's publication, and in doing so defines the Midwest as well as other regions.

> If nothing else, my 5-plus years as editor of *Midwest Living* have confirmed what those New Yorkers and Californians keep telling us: Midwesterners are the kind of people you want next door—all-American good neighbors endowed with abundant honesty, humor, warmth, and can-do optimism.

This letter is representative not only of how directly *Midwest Living* magazine characterizes itself, but also how often it defines its strong points and it needs, sometimes in defensive comparison with other places in the country. Comparison is crucial to identity construction in *Midwest Living*. Many of the comparisons and characteristics in the text draw on perceived attributes of Midwesterners that are rooted in a sense of strong moral values, community, and simplicity, values associated with nostalgic agrarianism.

The Old/New South

In *Southern Living* magazine, representations of nature and culture reinforce the ideal of the genteel Old South, a South with its own natural beauty which is tied closely to wealth and social status. Even articles about the contemporary urban South in this magazine hearken to events of the past which have afforded the South's distinction within the country.

Unlike *Sunset* and *Southern Living*, *Midwest Living* does not describe the land and other natural resources with great detail in the text, although many such features are included in accompanying photographs. Here the physical resources are represented as meaningful because of, and secondary to, the people, activity, and history that they hold. To a large extent, the land is privately owned. The October issue's "A Feast From the Land of Tides" (pp. 64-69) is about the marshlands, or Lowcountry, along the southern coast of South Carolina. This area is "the land of shrimpboats, where egrets flash white against the sky and the air smells of sulfur and marshlands. It is a place of mystery and wonder, diversity and sameness" (p. 65). Following this brief initial description, the article emphasizes the people who have lived in the Lowcountry for generations, including 10,000 African Americans freed after the Civil War who introduced recipes and cooking styles that made use of foods grown and caught in the Lowcountry marshlands. Three generations of a white family appear in a photograph accompanying this article. All of the accompanying photos highlight food and social gatherings around meals. As this article illustrates, the Lowcountry is significant because of its residents, its history and its foods.

The plantation is a landscape in *Southern Living* magazine comparable to the farm in *Midwest Living*. Like a Midwestern farm, a Southern plantation is a culturally defined space of land, used as an economic as well as natural resource. On a symbolic level, both serve another historic purpose in these magazines. While in *Midwest Living* the farm represents a closeness to the land and a simple lifestyle, in *Southern Living* the plantation is representative of an elegant, genteel lifestyle. The restored plantations featured here focus on the grand homes restored to their original antebellum luxury. The December article "Columbus Welcomes Christmas" (pp. 68-71) features several such homesteads in Mississippi. "These antebellum houses embody a part of the culture and social history of the South, the same type of thing as the English country estates" (p. 68). These mansions were the centerpieces of plantation life; wealth was a prominent feature. Other private spaces of land included in the magazine are gardens. In *Southern Living*, public and private gardens, filled with magnolias, dogwood, cypress, and Spanish moss, are included in numerous photographs. Private property of this sort is a featured item in both the rural and urban settings of *Southern Living*.

The qualities of the land, water, and fauna are represented here mostly as back-drops for history, people, and recreational activity. This representational strategy suggests that the South has a more removed identification with nature than either the West or the Midwest. Some of the settings in *Southern Living* are rural, reminiscent of the Old South;[36] but there are fewer rural settings in *Southern Living* than in either *Sunset* or *Midwest Living*. The urban South as it is often represented in this magazine moves just slightly away from the rural plantation ideal, but still retains the emphasis on wealth and leisure. Essentially, the "New" South is an extension of the myth of the Old South.

Cultural representations also reinforce the Old-South-as-New-South ideal. Like the other two magazines, *Southern Living* constructs a Southern heritage of European settlers, while including uniquely Southern foods and architecture, as illustrated earlier. The French are a particularly well-represented group in the magazine. In the April issue several articles describe the French heritage of the South. "Celebrating All Things French" (p. 16) is about the annual tribute to the French-speaking world, held in Lafayette, Louisiana. The Cajun community of Louisiana, the text explains, is descended from French Canadians who settled in the South. But this article includes representations of the French influence from all over the world, including Polynesia and Africa. "They are all cultural cousins, sharing a common bond in their French connection." As for contemporary French influence, "The Old World Flavor of New Orleans" (pp. 137-174) describes brunch, "New Orleans' most traditional yet most innovative culinary experience." Each one of the individual articles in this section introduces a New Orleans French Quarter resident who regularly prepares an elaborate brunch for guests, most eaten outdoors in enclosed private gardens. French-influenced foods are highlighted in each article. The photos of lavish brunch displays in these private backyards feature a bounty of tastefully arranged foods and flower displays, fine china, silverware, and well-dressed (White) guests. "The Art of the Brunch" is perfected as a Southern tradition, particularly here in New Orleans, the heart of French heritage in the South.

The essential ingredient to Southern identity is the Civil War which, as an identity marker, is constructed most effectively in relationships to other places. The Old South is blatantly reconstructed in not only the references to antebellum plantation homes and a few brief references to freed slaves, but also in defined relationships with the North and references to the Civil War. The October issue contains an article that refers to, and subtly ridicules, the North. "Autumn 'Dawg' Days in Athens" (pp. 32-33) is about University of Georgia football. The author recounts a typical football Saturday in Athens, Georgia, spent with an unidentified 'friend' from the North. According to the article, the football cheer "Sic 'em, Dawgs!" confused the Northerner. "How do you explain the University of Georgia's football cheer to someone who's never been below the Mason-Dixon line?" Although the tone of the article is light, the implication is that Southerners are a closed group, a group with its own culture, vocabulary, and sense of understanding. The Northerner (read "Yankee"), is constructed as a cultural outsider. A contemporary reminder of regional distinction such as this one will not directly refer to the Civil War, but articles that deal with Southern history of any sort will refer to the Civil War by name, as well as use the terms antebellum, Union, Confederate, and Yankee as nouns and modifiers in many contexts. The Civil War, referred to directly or indirectly, is pervasive in *Southern Living*.

So important is the War to this magazine's construction of the South, even an article about a foreign nation is framed by Civil War memories. "The Confederate State of Bermuda" (April, pp. 3234) concerns contemporary St. George, a city in Bermuda that was, during the War, home to Confederate blockade-runners. In the article are many references to the War, and many historic re-minders in St. George, including the Confederate Museum which portrays the story of Dr. Luke Blackburn, a man who eventually became governor of Ken-tucky.

> Dr. Blackburn...hatched a Civil War plot to spread deadly yellow fever to northern cities. He came to Bermuda, where an epidemic was raging, and gathered up blankets and clothing of victims to ship to the North, thinking they would contaminate anyone who touched them. (p. 34)

Other reminders of that period are the antique-laden homes of "distin-guished Bermuda families that played a part in southern life." References to the Civil War era, whether direct as above, or veiled as in the Athens, Georgia article, not only identify the South, but also identify the North and the rest of the country. In *Southern Living* the Civil War as identity marker continually distinguishes the South; such distinction is quintessential Old South.

Regional Identity and Race

Power relations, specifically racial tension, are encoded in popular repre-sentations of regional identity. Many of them are materially rooted in forms of repression. For example cowboys, European settlers and Gold Rush pioneers represented in both *Sunset* and *Midwest Living* magazines obscure the histori-cal phenomenon of dominant groups invading and reassigning the cultural place of indigenous people. Similarly, restored plantations in *Southern Living* maga-zine obscure the struggles of slavery. Indeed, the overall patterns of significa-tion which result in the construction of regional ideals—the Western Frontier, the Agrarian Midwest, and the Old South—belie the struggles of Native Ameri-cans and African Americans. The magazines each draw on a dominant narra-tive of white settlement which implies group repressions. However, that re-pression is virtually erased here because of readership demographics and the overriding framework of consumption.

The standard race in all three magazines is Caucasian. When non-White groups are included in the text or photos of magazine articles they are often represented in service positions to whites, or are represented only via artifacts of their culture, without discussion of their own history, development, or expe-rience. The article about French influence in *Southern Living* focuses on French culture throughout the world, a blatant acknowledgement of historic wide-spread French colonialism. In the South it is still celebrated annually. Included in this article is a photograph of Polynesian dancers and drummers performing on stage for an all-white audience. Similarly, an article in the August issue of *Sunset* (p. 32) features native Hawaiians in grass skirts performing a hula dance. In both cases the "natives" are offering something for the implied tourists, the white onlookers who are also the white readers. The native people are constructed as objects meant for what Urry calls the white tourist gaze. They are commodified for white buyers.[37] In all three magazines other races appear only as the artifacts of their cultures.

Midwest Living includes many listings of festivals where one can purchase American Indian artifacts or can see an authentic Indian Powwow, but for a price. The *Southern Living* article on the South Carolina Lowcountry refers to the foods of the area, introduced by the freed slaves who settled there. However, blacks are not included in the photographs accompanying this article. These examples, and many more like them, illustrate an insidious use of racial difference as historic racial repression is erased completely or is obscured as a commodity.

Portrayals of African Americans and Native Americans here are stereotypes not unlike those which have appeared in television, film, and other popular forms of entertainment. The frequencies of and changes in racial portrayals in mainstream mass media, especially film and television, have been examined by many scholars.[38] Race representations in the media have evolved, yet have retained a one-dimensional quality. This is in large part because the media institutions out of which they emerge are white, male-dominated corporations controlling representations with an eye toward sales.[39] Bottom line mentality often translates into images which maintain white as standard or status quo. The potential for opposition is often stifled, but it is not completely suppressed. Yet while the politics of race representations in television and film is an ongoing, sometimes fierce public debate, a discussion of racial inequity in regional lifestyle magazines is practically nonexistent.

The unique patterns of representation ultimately define a white, upper middle-class ideal readership. The magazines, while constructing regional identity, are first and foremost consumer magazines whose main objective is selling audiences to advertisers. They engage in creating what geographer Sack calls places of consumption, constructed for ideal white readers and serving to perpetuate the dominant, Eurocentric history of each region while offering it as commodity.[40]

Eradication of racial politics, then, is easily achieved because the subject matter—tourism, leisure, and products for living enhancement—is seemingly benign and the audience is, for the most part, homogeneous. Without a potential voice of opposition within the targeted white readership, and because the majority of content is advertising, the regions themselves turn into commodities, a string of places of consumption. Race difference as a representation of regional identity authenticates places of consumption while suppressing real historic struggles of African Americans and Native Americans.

Racial domination, or commodification of the racial "other" in representation, is not fixed and does not go completely uncontested in all popular forms. The inability to achieve a totalizing effect is the work of hegemony.[41] For example, in the broader culture, various minority races have attempted to bring their own historic perspectives to public attention, most often in "alternative" publications, but in other public forums as well. The recent nationwide protest of the celebration of the 500th anniversary of Columbus' voyage is an example of how voices from the margins are struggling to reinsert their place in the reconstruction of U.S. history. However, their voices are still muted within some mainstream media, and particularly in regional consumer magazines.

Regional identity, then, is formed in these magazines vis-a-vis representations of power. Addressing specifically national identity, Richard Dyer and Toni Morrison point out that the ideals of American identity, including freedom and individualism, are white patriarchal ideals dependent upon their opposites, slavery and subordination, which are embodied in other than white races, or what Morrison calls the "Africanist" presence.[42] In other words, race is foundational to the core of American identity. It is suggested here that race is also foundational to more particularized regional identities.

Analyzing the power relations implied in representations of regional identity is, perhaps, one means by which to explain their cultural construction. It also provides one response to Hay's suggestion that postmodern geographies consider the myriad complexities of cultural processes behind the mediated production of place.

Regional consumer magazines are but one type of mediated repository wherein representations communicate and construct geographic regions and, in doing so, perpetuate tensions among and within regions. Future research might analyze regional representation in other media in order to extend the discussion of how regional identities, built on group repression, circulate in the national discourse, perpetuating mythic American identity which often draws on inter-regional distinctions and tensions. This tension is, arguably, the very substance of American national identity.

Notes

[1] Edward Soja, Postmodern Geographies: The Reassertion of Space in Critical Social Theory (London: Verso, 1989).

[2] Phillip Schlesinger, Media, State, and Nation: Political Violence and Collective Identities (London: Sage, 1991).

[3] William Norton, Explorations in the Study of Landscape: A Cultural Geography (New York: Greenwood Press, 1989). See also Robert David Sack, Place, Modernity, and the Consumer's World (Baltimore: The Johns Hopkins University Press, 1992).

[4] Specifically, Soja cites extensively the works of Giddens, Henri Lefebvre, Michel Foucault, Fredric Jameson, Nicos Poulantzas, and David Harvey.

[5] Sack, 206.

[6] Lawrence Grossberg, We Gotta Get Out of This Place, (New York: Routledge, 1992).

[7] Grossberger, 26.

[8] Jacquelin Burgess and John R. Gold, Geography, the Media and Popular Culture (London: Croom Helm, 1985).

[9] James Hay, "Invisible Cities/Visible Geographies: Toward a Cultural Geography of Italian Television in the 90s," Paper presented at the annual meeting of the International Communication Association, Miami, FL, May 1992.

[10] Norton, 1989.

[11] For a list of the various purposes for which the United States is divided into, as well as a range of perspective on, regions, see Andersen et al, "Regional Patterns of Communication in the United States: A Theoretical Perspective," Communication Monographs 54, (June 1987): 128-144.

[12] Harm J. de Blig, Geography: Regions and Concepts (New York: John Wiley & Sons, Inc., 1971).

[13] Wilbur Zelinsky, The Cultural Geography of the United States (Englewood Cliffs, NJ: Prentice Hall, 1973).

[14] Zelinsky's regional boundaries do not coincide with the marketing boundaries set in Sunset, Southern Living, and Midwest Living. See Zelinsky, 118.

[15] Earl B. Shaw, Fundamentals of Geography (New York: John Wiley & Sons, Inc., 1965).

[16] Roland Barthes, Mythologies, Annette Lavers, Trans. (New York: Hill & Wang, 1972).

[17] John F. Kolars and John D. Nystuen, Human Geography: Spatial Design in World Society (New York: McGraw-Hill, 1974), 197.

[18] Hay, 1992.

[19] Service journalism means magazine journalism which provides reference information along the lines of "how-to, when-to, and where-to." Each is a reference of places to go and things to do within the region. See Sam G. Riley and Gary W. Selnow, "U.S. Regional Interest Magazines, 1950-1988: a Statistical Overview," Paper presented at the annual meeting of the Association for Education in Journalism and Mass Communication, Washington, DC, August 1989.

[20] William H. Taft, American Magazines for the 1980s, (New York: Hastings House, 1982).

[21] Here geographic magazines and service journalism are used in the post-WWII sense. Geographically specialized magazines were published in the late 19th and early 20th centuries, but the strategy of market specialization in the industry unique to the era after the War led to a more narrowly conceived notion of geographically targeted magazines using service journalism.

[22] Leonard Mogel, The Magazine (Englewood Cliffs, NJ: Prentice-Hall, Inc., 1979).

[23] Riley and Selnow, 1989.

[24] Although the three magazines do not have equal circulation figures, all three have grown steadily since first publication. Current paid circulation figures, according to Standard Rate and Data Service, Consumer Magazine and Agri-Media Source, November, 1993, are: Midwest Living 777,447; Southern Living 2,374,530; and Sunset 1,428,725.

[25] These figures obtained by telephone interview with research analyst Ray Petsche at Sunset magazine; from the 1991 Subscriber Profile published by Southern Living magazine; and by telephone interview with Dave Johnson in the Research Department of the Meredith Corporation.

[26] The break-down of readership demographics by magazine is based on information available in 1991. However, the researcher notes that while they may have changed slightly by 1994 they still delineate the same targeted demographic population sector.

[27] See Jay Black and Jennings Bryant, Introduction to Mass Communication, Third Edition (Dubuque, Iowa; Wm C. Brown 1992), p. 161.

[28] Frank Luther Mott, A History of American Magazines (Cambridge, MA: Harvard University Press, 1938).

[29] Wendy Kozol, Documenting the Public and Private in Life: Cultural Politics in Postwar Photojournalism (Philadelphia: Temple University Press), in press.

[30] This paper does not provide the quantitative data, i.e. numerical frequencies, of representations in each category in all three magazines. Rather, the focus here is descriptive analysis of representations in context as they appear in various sample articles.

[31] Turner first proposed his frontier thesis in a speech in Chicago in 1893. It has since been referred to by American historians to explain the European influence on U.S. development. See Frederick Jackson Turner, "The Significance of the Frontier in American History," in Gary Colombo, Robert Cullen, and Bonnie Lisle, eds., Rereading America: Cultural Contexts for Critical Thinking and Writing (New York: St. Martin's Press, 1989).

[32] Turner, 21.

[33] The Western as a film and television genre has been around as long as both media have been in the United States. For a history of the Western as a media genre, see Rita Parks, The Western Hero in Film and Television: Mass Media Mythology (Ann Arbor, MI: UMI Research Press, 1982). A recent trend back to Westerns across the media is evident in the surge of new Hollywood films such as "Unforgiven" and 1993 fall season television shows such as "Dr. Quinn, Medicine Woman", "The Adventures of Brisco County, Jr." and "Harts of the West." Numerous lay theories circulate to explain this renewed trend, yet simple observation suggests that the Western frontier is still a significant identifying representation in the national mind.

[34] Several media scholars have explored contemporary Native Americans in the mass media. The relatively recent interest in Native customs is also reflected in the New Age mysticism embraced by many non-Natives. For a discussion, see Annette M. Taylor, "Television's Native Americans: A Search for Identity," Paper presented at the annual meeting of the International Communication Association, Washington, DC, May 1993.

[35] In this case Midwest Living is imitating perceived authenticity by reifying it as a mass produced image, thus rendering it a part of material culture, which is, ironically, a culture rejected by the Amish people. For a discussion of the historic tension between imitation and authenticity in the United States, see Miles Orvell, The Real Thing: Imitation and Authenticity in American Culture, 1880-1940 (Chapel Hill: University of North Carolina Press, 1989).

[36] Steven Smith, Myth, Media and the Southern Mind, (Fayetteville, AR: The University of Arkansas Press, 1988).

[37] John Urry, The Tourist Gaze (London: Sage, 1990).

[38] For discussions and histories of race stereotypes in the mass media see the following volumes: George Hill and Sylvia Saverson Hill, Blacks on Television: A Selectively Annotated Bibliography (Metuchen, NJ: The Scarecrow Press, Inc., 1985); J. Fred MacDonald, Black and White TV: Afro-Americans in Television Since 1948 (Chicago: Nelson-Hall Publishers, 1983). Nancy Signorielli, Role Portrayal and Stereotyping on Television: An Annotated Bibliography of Studies Relating to Women, Minorities, Aging, Sexual Behavior, Health, and Handicaps (Westport, CT: Greenwood Press, 1985); Jessie Carney Smith, Images of Blacks in American Culture: A Reference Guide to Information Sources (New York: Greenwood Press, 1988).

[39] According to S. Robert Lichter, Stanley Rothman, and Linda S. Lichter, the most powerful media moguls are predominantly white (95%), male (79%) college grads (93%), with a personal annual income up to and exceeding $50,000. See their book, The Media Elite, (Bethesda, MD: Adler & Adler, 1986), pp. 21-23.

[40] Sack, 1992.

[41] Antonio Gramsci, Selections from the Prison Notebooks, Quintin Hoare and Geoffrey Nowell Smith, Trans. (New York: International Publishers, 1971).

[42] See Richard Dyer, "White," Screen 29 (1988): 44-64. See also Toni Morrison, Playing in the Dark: Whiteness and the Literary Imagination (Cambridge, MA: Harvard University Press, 1992).

Acknowledgements

The author would like to thank Barbie Zelizer and Paul Swann, both of Temple University, for their help in developing this article.

V

Magazines as Literature, Magazines as History

15

Research Review:
Magazines and Literary Journalism,
An Embarrassment of Riches

Thomas B. Connery

ABSTRACT

Although a few booklength studies of literary journalism have appeared over the past ten years, literary journalism as a form of nonfiction prose remains largely unexplored by scholars. A number of reasons are probably responsible for the neglect, but the result is that the field is largely wide open for research. Even the most basic areas of identification and recovery, particularly in regard to magazines, remain to be done. But as the nature and extent of literary journalism over time becomes more firmly established through additional research, the most fruitful investigations will explore literary journalism's role as a form of cultural expression, its tendency and ability to depict, or express, life being lived at a specific moment in a specific place. This article recommends a number of questions that researchers might pursue, and briefly investigates what it means to explore literary journalism as a cultural form.

Introduction

More than twenty years ago, *Esquire's* esteemed editor, Harold Hayes, noted the literary journalistic gold still to be dug from magazines: "The wealth to be found from mining magazine journalism somewhat prior to the day before yesterday is embarrassing—or should be to historians of the New Journalism and others who persist with the term."[1] Hayes' comment was part of a widespread reaction to the new journalism of the 1960s and 1970s and Hayes was suggesting not just that precursors existed, and therefore the word "new" was quite inappropriate, but also that scholars and historians might find an unacknowledged tradition should they take the time to dig.

Although considerable progress has been made since Hayes made his remark—not the least of which has been the slow jettisoning of the term "new journalism"—the field of literary journalism remains largely underexplored by scholars.[2] And, despite Hayes' call to mine magazines, the surface has just been scratched. This should not be surprising. Literary journalism may no longer be in that "twilight zone that divides literature from journalism," as Edwin Ford put it in 1937, but its boundaries remain imprecise and consequently it is somewhat of an academic orphan with no clear ancestry or home.[3]

Those interested in literary journalism come from several academic disciplines: American Studies, media studies, journalism, mass communication, communication and English. None of these has a journal that would be naturally or automatically receptive to research and discussion of literary journalism.[4] Dwight MacDonald's unfortunate description of the New Journalism as a "bastard" form has been convincingly refuted, but within academic circles literary journalism seldom is considered legitimate material for scholarly consideration.[5] Furthermore, when scholars submit literary journalistic research for publication or presentation within one of the traditional academic disciplines, it is unlikely that truly knowledgeable referees will be assessing the work because those most knowledgeable are few and scattered about the disciplines.

Similarly, because the interest is scattered among several disciplines, and mass interest for the most part is absent, major publishers are less likely to be interested. Significantly, three of the half dozen books on literary journalism that have been published in the past ten years have been published by Greenwood Publishing Group. Of course, none of this has prevented literary journalistic research, but merely is offered as probable reasons for the lack of great progress in delineating and assessing the field.

But perhaps just as limiting as the traditional academic boundaries has been the tendency of scholars to round up the usual suspects for analysis. For instance, the most recent (1993) volume on literary journalism, *Literary Selves: Autobiography and Contemporary American Nonfiction* by James N. Stull, joins two previous books, Barbara Lounsberry's *The Art of Fact: Contemporary Artists of Nonfiction* (1990) and Chris Anderson's *Style as Argument: Contemporary American Nonfiction* (1987) in focusing on Tom Wolfe, Norman Mailer and Joan Didion. Stull and Lounsberry look at the work of John McPhee as well, while Anderson adds Truman Capote, Lounsberry adds Gay Talese, and Stull includes Joe McGinniss and Hunter Thompson. If these three books were merely three among many, their focus would matter less. With the exception of McGinniss, however, this group of writers has been the focus of just about all of the extended discussion of contemporary literary journalism.[6]

All three of these works contribute to the literary journalistic discussion. But by focusing on the same group of writers such research does little to expand the discussion, either in terms of the time period—most of the writing considered in these three books was written twenty to thirty years ago—or in regards to less famous writers doing the same thing. Consequently the extent and impact of such writing as cultural forms of expression is more easily overlooked by literary and cultural historians, and media studies scholars.[7]

In contrast, *Literary Journalism in the Twentieth Century* (1990), edited by Norman Sims, contains a collection of essays that mixes approaches and perspectives and clearly indicates the range of literary journalism, in the process demonstrating the many ways that the field can be explored and defined.[8] Sims' own essay on Joseph Mitchell has been described by one critic as "a fascinating hybrid that borrows from three modes of discourse" and a model of how the field might be explored.[9] But essays on Hemingway and John Steinbeck, and one on W.E.B. Du Bois, James Agee, Tillie Olsen, and Gloria Anzaldua are exemplary as well. They not only provide readers with rich and unconventional interpretations of unjustly overlooked writing, but also yield much for other scholars to expand and build upon.

While *Literary Journalism in the Twentieth Century* expands the boundaries of the literary journalistic scholarly conversation, its content reveals how many avenues remain to be explored. These are worth listing. It should be noted, however, that a historical and bibliographical essay comprises much of the introduction to *A Sourcebook of American Literary Journalism*. So rather than repeat what already is in print, including advice for conducting research in literary journalism, what follows are recommendations that specifically relate to literary journalism in magazines.

Uncovering Riches

The boundaries of fiction and conventional journalism became so fixed in the twentieth century that literary journalism became distinguishable and distinct, later becoming an antidote to the conventional forms of both magazine and newspaper style. But until late in the nineteenth century, journalism was more literary and stylistically varied than it would become in the following century. As the twentieth century advanced, newspapers in particular developed a restricted and confining narrative form. Consequently, it is far more likely that in this century literary journalism will be found in magazines.

When Harold Hayes urged historians to search magazines, he specifically noted the *American Mercury*, *Vanity Fair*, *Harper's*, and the *New Yorker* as possible sources, saying these magazines "could produce encyclopedias on variations of the form currently defined and designated as New Journalism."[10]

Later, he acknowledged his own publication, *Esquire*. Yet it was the *Saturday Evening Post* that published Joan Didion's literary journalism in the early 1960s, and in the 1950s the *Post* had published other pieces that might qualify, including "Death on M24" by John Bartlow Martin and "They Give the Kids a Chance" by Morton W. Hunt, both published in 1952. Although John Hersey's work is commonly associated with the *New Yorker*, he wrote works of literary journalism for *Life* in the 1940s, and James Agee's "Havanna Cruise" was published in *Fortune*.[11] Thus the size of the lode is even larger, and more extensive, than Hayes realized.

Similarly, it is clear that *Esquire* since the early 1960s, the *New Yorker* since the late 1930s, and *Rolling Stone* from its birth, but particularly in the 1970s, all regularly published works of literary journalism. Yet all three of those publications merit much closer scrutinizing and analysis. Other publications and writers also need to be identified and recovered, not just in the sixty years or so prior to Hayes' comment, but over the past fifteen years, when literary journalism has become less unusual if not more common. Most of us would not recognize the names of writers regularly producing literary journalism, but other writers, such as Tracy Kidder, Richard Rhodes, Calvin Trillin, and Jane Kramer, to name a few, are better known but have not yet been studied and placed within the literary journalistic context.

But the overall role of magazines needs to be assessed as well, including why one publication might be more open to literary journalism than another. Here, the researcher deals with the cultural use and function of the publication, as well, perhaps, as economic necessity, and the questions asked begin to get more complex and challenging. Except for certain works and publications of the 1960s and 1970s, however, the most basic of questions remain unanswered: (a) Who wrote literary journalism? (b) Where was literary journalism published? (c) What connected the topics? (d) What connects the writers? Not just topics and style, but an attitude or philosophy as revealed in letters, diaries, essays, interviews, or their literary journalism, and (e) What was accomplished that was not accomplished in other prose forms? In other cultural forms?

It only follows that if the basic questions have not yet been answered sufficiently, then neither have the more complex questions that should be asked once the work is identified. Here are some questions or research areas that merit further consideration:

a. In what way does literary journalism provide a more personal account of people, issues, and events rather than an institutional one?

b. Does a specific type of publication yield a specific type of literary journalism?

c. How has economics been a factor? Are publications less established in the mainstream, or, facing serious competition for readers and advertising dollars, more likely to break from formula writing?[12]

d. In its blurring of traditional boundaries, is recent literary journalism an expression of a postmodern sensibility, or is it an expression of a human desire for a story-telling narrative style, one once common to nonfiction prose?

e. How is literary journalism not just an expression of culture, but of community? By "community" I mean the sense of identity and familiarity that comes from readers entering the narrative with the narrator, either as participant or observer, but in either case in a subjective sense.

f. The relationship between literary journalism and autobiography needs further exploration, building on what has been done in several essays in the Sims collection, and expanding on Stull's work in *Literary Selves* and Lounsberry's in *The Art of Fact*, particularly her Talese analysis.[13]

g. It would appear that there are three distinct periods in which literary journalism is more common than at other times. Why? What connects the periods? It would seem, for instance, that each period (1890-1910, 1930s-1940s, 1960s-1970s) was a time of tremendous change and reform, periods in which progressive ideas come to the front, wars are fought, big changes in media occur.[14]

h. It also seems that literary journalism has continued to play an important role beyond the most recent period, and the form has become less raucous and less of a personal performance. Is that true and why is it true?

i. In *Literary Journalism in the Twentieth Century*, John Pauly's essay makes a case for the political nature of the new journalism. Would Pauly's contentions apply to literary journalism of previous periods? Is there a way to consider the literary value of this work and not dismiss its supposed political nature? Obviously, this topic would be connected to the question regarding periods.

Perhaps a clearer understanding and appreciation of literary journalism might be accomplished by making connections between writers of quite different periods. Some examples might include:

a. One might make a case for Mark Twain as our first "Gonzo" journalist and writer, comparing his tone, technique, and approach to those of Hunter Thompson, ultimately demonstrating some of their differences as cultural influences.

b. Lafcadio Hearn's offbeat yet lush portrayals could be compared to those of Truman Capote.

c. Agee's *Let Us Now Praise Famous Men* (rejected by *Fortune*) could be contrasted to Michael Herr's *Dispatches* (much of which ran in *Esquire*). Both writers distrusted conventional journalism's ability to adequately and accurately capture reality, and Agee had lost faith in fiction's power as well. Both Herr and Agee attempt to create their own prose form, primarily by making their accounts intensely personal so that the experience depicted becomes quite strange and foreign. Shelley Fisher Fishkin's "The Borderlands of Culture" in Sims' collection might serve well as a jumping-off point for this type of analysis or exploration.

Further understanding and appreciation of literary journalism might also be gained not just by searching for new theories and approaches, but by attempting to apply those that already exist to different writers and periods. For instance, Pauly's notions have already been mentioned. Other examples are the ideas of David Eason or Joseph Webb.

Webb explained and defined new journalism by developing the notion of the Romantic Reporter, a journalist who rejects the rationalism and scientific realism that underlie modern journalism's belief in objectivity. For Webb new journalism, or literary journalism, is a move away from realism and the principles that inform it. Both the goal of reporting and the process are different for the Romantic Reporter.[15]

Eason's attempts to make sense of the new journalism and particularly his "The New Journalism and the Image-World: Two Modes of Organizing Experience," revised for the Sims' collection, give researchers a model to apply to other writers and other periods. Eason identifies two types of literary journalism, realist and modernist, and his ideas can be expanded and modified.[16]

A very significant aspect of Eason's work is that while it recognizes new journalism as a literary act, it also treats it as a cultural construct. Researchers need to move away from analyzing literary journalism primarily as literary art, and see it more as a cultural way of knowing, as a number of essays in the Sims collection do. Christopher Wilson has observed that all professional writers are "cultural mediators in the most literal sense," and that certainly applies to literary journalists.[17] But that doesn't quite capture the significance of saying literary journalism is a cultural way of knowing. Warren Sussman's notion helps us here. As Sussman puts it, "The search for culture was the search for meaningful forms, for patterns of living."[18] Literary journalism—indeed any literary or journalistic form—participates in that search and is itself a "meaningful form" that contributes to our cultural meaning-making.

As researchers examine literary journalism as a system of meaning, an interpretation of reality, a cultural form of expression, it is essential that they not divorce the text under consideration from the cultural context, including the social milieu that created the work. That cultural context could include as well the personal history of the writer or even the history and role of the publication in which it appeared.

In other words, to partially understand a literary journalistic text on its own terms is to assess it in the tradition of a type of nonfiction prose narrative, reflecting certain literary traditions and conventions. But to thoroughly assess its meaning and impact, it must be placed within the media framework of its time and in light of the cultural forces of the moment as well.

Magazines journalistically inform readers, but they also are cultural repositories that maintain certain rituals and attitudes of the culture. Like all journalism, literary journalism helps tell us who we are, signifies how we define and constitute ourselves. Like other cultural forms of expression, literary journalism interprets and reaffirms common values, but it also, by its subjective/interpretative nature, challenges those values and versions of reality. To borrow from Michael Schudson's language regarding journalism, literary journalism demonstrates another way that "the stories we tell ourselves and circulate among ourselves serve as reminders of who we are and what we're about."[19]

For instance, to simply read John Hersey's "Joe Is Home Now" as it appears in his collection *Here To Stay* is to separate the piece from its cultural genesis and its media context, which further explain and define the piece. "Joe Is Home Now" appeared in *Life* magazine and deals with the adjustment problems of returning WW II GIs.[20] The text is framed by a bold headline and deck, by an editor's commentary, and two photographs. The editor's note explains the seriousness of the Hersey article, scolding Americans for not doing enough to assure a smooth transition for GIs wounded emotionally and physically. The note calls for "human reconversion" or "the process of turning those casualties back into normal civilians." It also explains that the article's main character, Joe Souczak, is a composite of 43 different returning soldiers interviewed by Hersey.

One of the photos, on the same page as the article's beginning, is of two women leaning against a car and the caption says, "His sisters wait for him in the station square." A full-page photo of a returning GI with one arm takes the page opposite the text, and photos accompany the text on the remaining pages.

Hersey's article, which mixes fact and fiction in an attempt to depict a part of American life and behavior, was just one of many depictions of returning GIs presented to Americans, and probably just one of a number of articles that dealt with the "problem" of adjustment. Furthermore, *Life* had its own culture and history that would further define Hersey's article, as would the other articles and photos in this issue of *Life*. Whatever had been Hersey's motivation in writing the article, Henry Luce's "mind-guided camera," as he referred to *Life*, used the article to call attention to a potential problem by presenting it in an entertaining way yet with an authority guaranteed by the editor's note and the photographs. Together, Hersey and *Life* presented a version of reality that contained a different meaning and significance than when the article is just one of many in a book. "Joe Is Home Now" doesn't necessarily transcend its medium, rather it melds with it, is of it, is part of a larger meaning-making vehicle, a mass circulation magazine of the 1940s, that itself is a form of cultural expression.

What this type of research in literary journalism would do is provide an overriding interpretative or research frame in which all sorts of theories and approaches might be employed, but it also would go a long way toward demonstrating the cultural nature of literary journalism. Combined with investigating the questions previously posed, we will obtain a much better understanding of literary journalism's connection to magazines, as well as magazines' distinct use of this form of expression.[21]

We will, perhaps, also see that literary journalism has been and remains a way to obtain what Raymond Williams calls "this felt sense of the quality of life at a particular time and place." We might recognize that literary journalism can be a means to answer the question James Carey says should be answered by cultural historians: "How did it feel to live and act in a particular period of human history?"[22] It all has the potential of a far richer treasure hunt than even Harold Hayes envisioned.

Notes

[1] Harold Hayes, "Editors's Notes on the New Journalism," in Ronald Weber, ed., The Reporter as Artist: A Look at The New Journalism Controversy (New York: Hastings House Publishers, 1974), 261.

[2] A number of books are rather standard when considering literary journalism, including a handful of books that deal with the New Journalism of the 1960s-70s. All of these books contain bibliographies. A good starting point would be the bibliographies in Thomas B. Connery, A Sourcebook of American Literary Journalism (Westport, Conn: Greenwood Press, 1992); Norman Sims, Literary Journalism in the Twentieth Century (New York and Oxford: Oxford University Press, 1990); Barbara Lounsberry, The Art of Fact: Contemporary Artists of Nonfiction (Westport, Conn.: Greenwood Press, 1990); James N. Stull, Literary Selves: Autobiography and Contemporary American Nonfiction (Westport, Conn.: Greenwood Press, 1993); Chris Anderson, Style as Argument: Contemporary American Nonfiction (Carbondale and Edwardsville: Southern Illinois University Press, 1987); Chris Anderson, Literary Nonfiction: Theory, Criticism, Pedagogy (Carbondale and Edwardsville: Southern Illinois University Press, 1989). For a bibliographical discussion of many of the books and articles assessing literary journalism, see Connery, Sourcebook, 19-28. Discussions of literary journalism regularly appear in works on magazine writing, such as Theodore A. Rees Cheney's Writing Creative Nonfiction (Berkeley: Ten Speed Press, 1991). A more recent example is Patricia Westfall, Beyond Intuition: A Guide to Writing and Editing Magazine Nonfiction (New York: Longman, 1994), which includes a lengthy discussion of John McPhee.

[3] Edwin H. Ford, A Bibliography of Literary Journalism (Minneapolis: Burgess Publishing, 1937), i.

[4] The first issue of a new journal, Creative Nonfiction, edited by Lee Gutkind of the University of Pittsburgh, was published in Fall 1993. Gutkind alludes to new journalism and

literary journalism in his "From the Editor" note, but the journal's content consists of original nonfiction, some of it literary journalism, and an interview with John McPhee.

[5] Dwight MacDonald, "Parajournalism, or Tom Wolfe and His Magic Writing Machine," in Weber, ed., Reporter as Artist, 223.

[6] At least a half-dozen significant works on the New Journalism focus on several of these writers. They are discussed in Connery, Sourcebook, 22-23. Of these familiar "suspects," John McPhee is the odd figure because he was never mentioned as a new journalist and was not included in the discussions and studies done at the time of the new journalism.

[7] To be fair, it should be said that when critics and scholars consider the same writers, they often discuss different works and, for the most part, use very different approaches that often reach very different conclusions. With some writers, however, such as Truman Capote or Norman Mailer, it's rather common to discuss In Cold Blood or Armies of the Night respectively.

[8] It may seem to those familiar with the Sims book that my comment is merely a way for me to pat myself on the back because I have an essay in this collection. Nothing is farther from the truth. My essay is the least of the book, and merely designed to provide historical context, to in effect set up what follows it.

[9] Michael Robertson, review of Literary Journalism the Twentieth Century in American Journalism 8 (Fall 1991): 275.

[10] Hayes, "Editor's Notes," 261.

[11] Selected bibliographies of Hersey's and Agee's literary journalism are in Connery, Sourcebook. John Bartlow Martin, "Death on M-24," Saturday Evening Post, 5 April 1952, 22-24, 114-117. Morton W. Hunt, "They Give the Kids a Chance," Saturday Evening Post, 10 May 1952, 24-25, 59-65.

[12] S.M.W. Bass and Joseph Rebello, for instance, have suggested that changes in Esquire in the early 1960s might have been due to competition from Playboy. See their paper, "The Appearance of New Journalism in The Sixties Esquire: A Look at the Editorial Marketplace," Paper presented at the American Journalism Historians Association annual meeting, St. Paul, MN, Fall 1987.

[13] In the Talese chapter, for instance, Lounsberry makes a case for all of Talese's work being informed by the idea of fathers and sons, fathers and families, by Talese having been "the unnoticed son of an immigrant Italian tailor." Lounsberry, The Art of Fact, 3.

[14] I explain these three periods in the Preface to A Sourcebook of American Literary Journalism, xii-xiii.

[15] Joseph M. Webb, "Historical Perspective on the New Journalism," Journalism History 1 (Summer 1974): 38-42,60. It would be particularly worth re-examining Webb's ideas in light of the research and discussion over the past fifteen years regarding authenticity and the nature of realism.

[16] David Eason, "The New Journalism and the Image-World: Two Modes of Organizing Experience," Critical Studies in Mass Communication 1 (March 1984): 51-65. In this article, Eason called the two modes ethnographic realism and cultural phenomenology. In Sims, Sourcebook, 191-205, Eason calls the two realism and modernist. In one mode, literary journalism believes that reality can be made sense of and captured in narrative; in the other mode, literary journalists find reality incomprehensible and therefore are unable to depict it.

[17] Christopher P. Wilson, The Labor of Words: Literary Professionalism in the Progressive Era (Athens: University of Georgia, 1985), xi-xii.

[18] Warren I. Susman, Culture as History: The Transformation of American Society in the Twentieth Century (New York: Pantheon Books, 1984), 188.

[19] Michael Schudson, "Preparing the Minds of the People: Three Hundred Years of the American Newspaper," in John B. Hench, ed., Three Hundred Years of the American Newspaper (Worcester: American Antiquarian Society, 1991), 427.

[20] John Hersey, "Joe Is Home Now," Life, 3 July 1944, 68-80.

[21] Although a few of the essays in the Sims collection, Literary Journalism in the Twentieth Century, can be considered cultural interpretations, the best models of such research might be found in other, related, areas. See for instance, Michael Robertson, "Cultural Hegemony Goes to the Fair: The Case of E.L. Doctorow's World's Fair," American Studies 33 (Spring 1992): 31-44, and Richard Wightman Fox and T.J. Jackson Lears, eds., The Power of Culture (Chicago: University of Chicago Press, 1993).

[22] James Carey, "The Problem of Journalism History," Journalism History, 1 (Spring 1974): 4. Carey used the Williams quote. Raymond Williams, The Long Revolution (New York: Harper and Row, 1966), 47.

16

The Reform Years at *Hampton's*: The Magazine Journalism of Rheta Childe Dorr, 1909-1912

Agnes Hooper Gottlieb

ABSTRACT

Rheta Childe Dorr has been remembered as a war correspondent and an advocate of women's equal rights. Dorr's career, however, took several other distinct twists, and her reform writing, while certainly less glamorous than her high-profile forays to Russia, today provides an important example of the type of "social" muckraking that was being written 80 years ago. For it was as a writer for *Hampton's* Magazine that Dorr wrote extensively of the importance of municipal housekeeping, that is, the idea that a woman's home extended beyond her own four walls and included a need to keep her city safe, clean, and uncorrupt. In articles for *Hampton's*, Dorr publicized the plight of the poor, promoted educational reforms, and highlighted the activities of women's organizations.

Introduction

When Rheta Childe Dorr's obituary appeared in the *New York Times* in 1948, she was remembered as a war correspondent and an advocate of women's equal rights. The newspaper chronicled her work as an eyewitness reporter of fascinating news stories during nine trips to Europe. Her five books were listed: *What Eight Million Women Want* (1910); *Inside the Russian Revolution* (1917); *A Soldier's Mother in France* (1918); the autobiography, *A Woman of Fifty* (1924); and the *Life of Susan B. Anthony: The Woman Who Changed the Mind of a Nation* (1928).[1]

The newspaper, however, never mentioned the important writing Dorr did as a social reformer for the crusading *Hampton's Broadway* Magazine in the early years of the twentieth century. In fact, Dorr's career took several distinct twists, and her reform writing, while certainly less glamorous than her high-profile forays to Russia, today provides an important example of the type of "social" muckraking that was being written 80 years ago.

It was as a writer for *Hampton's* that Dorr wrote extensively of the importance of municipal housekeeping, that is, the idea that a woman's home extended beyond her own four walls and included a need to keep her city safe, clean, and uncorrupt. Articles by Dorr and other women journalists of the period, especially those writing about women's clubs, can be seen as an extension of municipal housekeeping. Using the power of their pens, these writers, including such journalists as Boston author Helen M. Winslow, club pioneer Jane Cunningham Croly, and Baltimore editorial writer Louise Malloy, promoted a wider sphere for women by advocating their involvement in municipal reforms.[2]

Dorr herself sometimes saw it necessary to carry a picket sign, but her most effective reform work was her writing. In articles for *Hampton's*, a reform publication with muckraking aspirations, Dorr publicized the plight of the poor, promoted educational reforms, and highlighted the activities of women's organizations. As journalism historian Frank L. Mott noted, Dorr's concerns fit well with the muckraking era, but she concentrated specifically on social, rather than political or economic, reforms.[3]

Historical and Biographical Review

Like the *Times* obituary, historical essays about Dorr concentrated on other aspects of her career and skimmed over her two-plus years spent at *Hampton's* or overlooked the time period altogether. Most historians have focused what little they wrote about Dorr on her sensational trip to Russia during the Revolution there. Marion Marzolf in *Up from the Footnote* noted that as a reporter for the *New York Mail* in 1917, Dorr went to Russia and interviewed the sister of the Czarina and others involved in the struggle.[4] Journalist Ishbel Ross in the 1936 volume *Ladies of the Press* wrote about Dorr's early career, her work for suffrage, and her trip to Russia, but skipped right over the years she spent crusading at *Hampton's*.[5]

More recently, historian Zena Beth McGlashen studied Dorr as a reformer, but investigated only her writing for the *New York Evening Post*. Noting that Dorr herself counted her writing from the Russian Revolution and World War I as her most significant journalism, McGlashen argued: "This bias on the part of Dorr is understandable in light of the value given the male role model. By

covering a war—which was clearly what men were assigned to do—Dorr saw
herself engaged in 'real' journalism."[6] McGlashen persuasively argued that
her writing from Russia was "simply part of the biased reporting" of those
who witnessed the beginning of the Revolution. Dorr's writing about women
workers, however, carries more weight from a historical perspective. Reform
writing by Dorr and others can be studied today as examples of the outlets
available to professional women during the Progressive Era. A study of the
more than 20 articles she wrote during her tenure at *Hampton's* illustrates effectively and colorfully the specific reform activities she believed important
and demonstrates how she tried to sway other women, specifically club women,
to take these projects on as their "causes."

McGlashen concentrated her study of Dorr's work on the writing she did
as a newspaper reporter for the *Evening Post* in the first few years of the twentieth century. McGlashen noted that Dorr used the newspaper's women's section to give a platform to the reform activities of women's clubs. Dorr's recognition of the importance of women's roles in reform activities laid the groundwork for her writing on social issues. It was as a magazine writer for *Hampton's*,
however, that Dorr found a significant national audience for her reforms.

Dorr, born in Omaha, Neb., in 1866, lived her life committed to bettering
the lives of the poorest and the weakest members of society, namely women
and children.[7] Like other women of her day, she married young and had a
child. However, similarities to typical Victorian women end there—Dorr realized that she could not conform to the strict sense of maternity and house-
wifely duties expected by her husband, so she took their young son and headed
for New York in 1898. She joined the *Post* staff in 1902 to write for the women's
section, but after four years, she wanted to move on. She had begun to hate
newspaper writing, while she became more and more interested in social issues. As her reform activities intensified, her work relationships faltered. When
she asked her managing editor what future she had on the paper, she was told
she had none, other than the job as women's editor which she held. She was
not suited to the job of editorial writer, she was told, because her radical ideas
contradicted the *Post* tradition.[8]

Meanwhile, she began to live the life of a dedicated reformer. She had
moved with her young son to the lower East Side of New York both because it
was cheap and because she could see first hand the difficult living conditions
of the impoverished. Dorr slowly began identifying with the plight of the immigrants who surrounded her. She picketed for the shirt-waist workers, de-
fended beaten women strikers in court, and worked within the Women's Trade
Union League for "minimum wage-laws, the eight-hour-day, and what I thought
even more essential, woman suffrage."[9]

She left the paper in the summer of 1906 and traveled to Europe where
she covered the coronation of King Haakon of Norway, visited Russia for a

glimpse of revolutionary rumblings, and covered the International Woman Suffrage Association quinquennial meeting in Copenhagen. She was inspired by a visit to England and meetings with the suffragists there to use her writing talent for specific causes.

Back in the United States, however, her strategy to write about the plight of poor women and children met with difficulties. A story about the difficult job of a department store clerk was rejected by the women's magazines, which relied heavily on department store advertising for profits.[10] In preparation of another series on the plight of working women, she worked as a seamstress in a corset factory, a trousers plant, a coat factory, and a muslin underwear factory. She took volumes of notes on the conditions and treatment of workers in each factory and prepared for an explosive series of articles in *Everybody's Magazine*, a monthly published by department store magnate John Wanamaker that mixed fiction and non-fiction by well-respected authors.

When the time came for the articles to be written, however, Dorr had a falling out with her male editors. She said they had little interest in the expose material about factories around New York. What they wanted instead was a series of article about women invading male bastions of work. The editor then assigned a writer, William Hard, to collaborate with Dorr. While she continued her investigation, the plan was for Hard to shape the material into twelve printable articles. Dorr was to be listed as co-author. As tension increased between Dorr and her editor, she finally took legal action when she read in the magazine that the "series of the year" would begin publication in October. Titled "The Woman's Invasion," which Dorr herself had suggested, the advertisement said the series was written solely by William Hard. Dorr secured a woman attorney who obtained an injunction against the magazine and, ultimately, the series appeared in print under co-authors' bylines.

The victory won, Dorr remained unsatisfied with a whitewashed treatment of her explosive information. "...[I]n the truest sense the articles were not mine. The title was mine, the idea was mine, most of the material was mine, but the intent and meaning of the whole thing was distorted beyond recognition," Dorr wrote.[11] The series was a great success in publishing, but to Dorr, a "nightmare."[12]

She was a reformer without a voice, a writer without an audience, until she joined forces with *Hampton's Broadway* Magazine, where her reforming tendencies were appreciated. Dorr met publisher Benjamin B. Hampton when he accepted for publication an article she had submitted about woman's suffrage. He forced her to rewrite the piece, but then offered to print anything else that was as good as "The Women's Invasion." At that point, Dorr poured out the long history of that magazine series to him. Hampton agreed to help her write the stories she had so passionately wanted to tell. In fact, she later credited him with turning her into a writer. At *Hampton's*, she was "given unlimited opportunity to express my own ideas in my own fashion" and the results were a series of articles that promoted better working and living conditions for women and children.[13]

That Dorr found a forum in *Hampton's* was not surprising. The magazine first was published under the title *Hampton's Broadway* Magazine in 1907 during the muckraking period. During subsequent years it underwent a name change to simply *Hampton's* Magazine, but under both titles it provided a middle ground between investigative magazines like *McClure's* and the popular literary periodicals. Dorr described the goal of *Hampton's* to be a forum for "constructive social criticism, big news stories and great fiction."[14] In his Pulitzer Prize-winning *The History of American Magazines*, Frank Luther Mott noted that *Hampton's* uncovered instances of "public abuses which form a kind of postscript to the muckraking movement."[15]

During Dorr's years at *Hampton's*, the magazine's circulation soared from 125,000 in 1908 to 450,000 in 1910.[16] Dorr herself stated that she was allowed "a certain authority in directing the magazine's policy."[17] Dorr said that all articles about women, children, suffrage, and education were referred to her. Dorr's writing at *Hampton's* was representative of the municipal housekeeping tasks tackled by women journalists. Dorr wrote more than 20 articles— all of them relating to municipal housekeeping topics: education, the condition of children, the need for a juvenile court, and the working conditions of women.

Mott argued that within this forum, Dorr had "a field all her own."[18] She has been described as a "woman's muckraker." In other words, her writing exposed the ills of society that were of concern to women.[19] Her subjects, however, actually were broader than women's interests only. Dorr's articles described in detail the plight of women and children, but also the urban, political, and social ills that were at the root of their woes. Mott believed that Dorr's articles nicely complimented "the expose tone of the magazine, they were not precisely muckraking forays, but challenging discussions of important social problems, bolstered with fact."[20]

"The Wreck of the Home," one of her earliest pieces at *Hampton's*, described women's double bind as wage-earners and mothers. Dorr reminisced years later that she herself understood this double burden because she was forced to work to support herself and her son. She often felt pangs of guilt that she had not remained in her marriage for the sake of her son. And she wondered when she read of a teenage boy who had turned to crime if he was the child of a working mother.[21]

For a 1909 *Hampton's* article, Dorr used her experiences in the factories to illustrate her argument and related a series of anecdotes that described her points. Locked in dull, mindless jobs for want of training, women and homemakers were ruined, Dorr asserted. An editorial note before "Give the Working-Girl a Chance," stated that the article should be read as a plea for special industrial training for girls:

> We have been letting our girls, at the age of fourteen, take up mechanical, dreary, detached tasks at which they have automatically worked for many years, only to find themselves on the human scrap heap, broken down and worn out. One woman irons one side of your collar day in and day out for all the fresh young years of her life. Gradually she becomes physically incapable of even that sordid task. She sees nothing, comprehends nothing, attempts nothing, except that one side of that collar. If it isn't ironing a collar, it is feeding a machine, or folding a piece of paper, or putting mucilage on a piece of cloth. Such dumb tasks, pursued year after year by our millions of working women, are stultifying, stupefying, stunting, and ruining millions of our mothers and home-makers. Mentally they become cramped, apathetic, narrow, timid, dependent; physically they become weak, anaemic, diseased, broken. It is time we gave our working-girls a chance, and Mrs. Dorr points the way.[22]

To further her arguments, Dorr adopted a strategy typical of the municipal housekeepers of her day. She argued that routinized work forced upon women was "destroying the home by taking away from the workers the power to make homes."[23] Repeatedly, Dorr argued in one article that unskilled labor forced upon a young girl made her "less skilled, less intelligent, less independent than she was when she entered the trade" and, above all, left her "incapable of making a home!"[24] Arguing that the "unskilled worker is a human machine," Dorr warned, "The only way to preserve the home is to conserve the home-makers."[25] Appealing to her middle-class readers, who believed in an ideal version of the American home, Dorr suggested the only viable solution was to provide training in trades for young women who were forced to work.

Dorr's writing technique employed anecdotes to make her points and so the reader learned through numerous examples. She illustrated, as one of many examples, the plight of two sisters, Annie and Jennie, whose lives were transformed by enrollment at the Manhattan Trade School. Again appealing to the maternal instincts of her readers and the middle-class ideal of domesticity, Dorr concluded her article by noting that society could not afford "to have citizens born of brutalized and degraded mothers" and she warned that society would not want the type of homes these women were able to create.[26] "Would it not be better to acknowledge that women are equally with men the workers of the world, and give them the training which instead of preventing them from becoming home makers will rather help them in that mission?" she asked.[27]

Her next article, which focused on the need for pure milk for babies, suggested that women's clubs should promote the cause of clean milk for babies and education for impoverished mothers who did not know much about caring for their children.[28] In another article, Dorr described how a wealthy member of a woman's club sold her stock in cotton mills because she worried about children being employed there. She then pressed her women's club to generate an investigation of child labor.[29]

Dorr passionately believed that women's clubs were appropriate forums for municipal reforms. A series of articles for *Hampton's* focused on the reform responsibilities of the women's club movement. She argued that it was one of the most important movements of the twentieth century and that its real importance began when clubs started studying citizenship issues instead of literature. Her three-part article, "What Eight Million Women Want," was later the title chapter of her book about the reforming activities of American women. The eight million women cited referred to the fact that there were eight million American women and also eight million members of the International Council of Women, which was actively attempting to improve the social order.[30] The magazine article, which claimed that the women's club was the "parent" of civic reform, noted that one-tenth of the eight million American women— 800,000 women—belonged to active civic clubs. "Remember that this one-tenth of the woman population is the educated, intelligent, socially powerful tenth," she wrote, referring to the make-up of most women's clubs.[31]

Dorr wrote that although the club movement had begun initially for studying and self-improvement, this phase was "doomed" because women were not in the habit of doing things for themselves. She stated that women had served society for so many generations that they preferred service to idle study. Most of the work of these women consisted of projects that related to children, public schools, and the home, topics dear to Dorr herself and ones that fell under the municipal housekeeping blanket. Through these municipal reform activities of what she termed average women, Dorr believed that the club movement could wield an "immense power."[32]

In Part Two of the article, Dorr combined her two favorite interests— municipal housekeeping and women's rights. She wrote about elderly women whose livelihoods were threatened by property laws that were unfair to wives. She publicized the cruelty of wife beating and argued that once again it was the work of women's clubs to investigate laws that discriminated against women and to lobby for their abolition. The series concluded with a description of the plight of working women and a plea for the continued involvement of women's organizations in lobbying for protective legislation. Dorr argued that industrial committees of the women's club movement were a "thorn in the flesh" of the manufacturing industry. She appealed to employers, noting that women's club investigations had shown that good working conditions actually fostered increased productivity and, therefore, increased profits.[33]

A later article on women's rights used the women of Colorado, who had been voting since 1893, as examples to show the responsible, reform-minded way women would respond to universal suffrage. Since women obtained the vote, Dorr argued, they had fought for good government and specific reforms. In Colorado, protective legislation had been passed, the best juvenile court system in the country was in place, and women had attained the right to equal property and inheritance laws. "All of these evidences of progressive thought and action were agitated mainly by women and were made into laws chiefly through the influence of women," Dorr asserted.[34] Unlike men, women voted for the good of the state, she contended. Bowing to the social strictures of her day, Dorr argued that women tended to use their votes to assure that moral candidates were elected. "A man may be a capable public official, but if the women decide that they could not receive him in their homes they will refuse to vote for him," she stated.[35]

Dorr argued that the woman's movement of her day was an organized attempt to help women join the human race.[36] She celebrated the work of pioneers, including Mary Wollstonecraft, Charlotte Bronte, and Elizabeth Blackwell, who endured insults and prejudice to open the professions to women. And she applauded the work of Susan B. Anthony, Elizabeth Cady Stanton, and Lucy Stone, who generated the push for universal suffrage. In 1911, Dorr predicted that women would not have to wait much longer for suffrage. Women, by their work and activities, were proving that they had a right to belong to the human race and that "no laws, no policies of exclusion, no selfish discrimination can alter the fact."[37]

While the suffrage question was dear to her, Dorr wrote even more impassioned articles when the subject literally was a matter of life or death. One such article exposed the deadly dangers of fire by portraying the horror of the Triangle Shirtwaist fire in 1911. Dorr used the fire to illustrate the hazards facing factory workers. Dorr vividly described how "doomed creatures" trapped on the upper floors of what was believed to be a fire-proof building shrieked and clawed at each other to escape.[38] "From windows on the eight, ninth, and tenth floors men and women were hurling themselves," Dorr wrote.[39] "They sped downward, turning end on end like manikins. The rapid thud, thud of the bodies on the stone pavement, the crash of flesh and bone on the hard earth, were sounds not to be described in words."[40] One hundred forty-five people, most of them young women, died in the blaze. In the aftermath of the fire, people learned that the doors to the building were locked to prevent late-comers, to keep union agitators out and to keep the workers in. The building itself, with only one fire escape, was a firetrap, and Dorr pointed the blame at municipal laws, which did not cover safety regulations. Just as preventive medicine was the best approach to health, so too were preventive measures the answer to fire safety. Dorr argued that fire fighting had been the focus of reform for too long, "yet we continue to have fires."[41] The only viable solution, she contended, was to focus energy on fire prevention. Fireproof buildings were inadequate; deathproof buildings were needed.

In another article about unsafe working conditions, Dorr lobbied for child labor laws. Again appealing to her middle-class readers, Dorr argued that the future of the race was at stake. Children who were worked to exhaustion, she argued, grew to be worthless adults. These adults threatened the very future of the home. "The race cannot possibly be improved, society cannot possibly progress, if children are to be brought into the world by exhausted and ambitionless parents," she wrote.[42]

Dorr wrote more than 20 long articles during her years at *Hampton's*. The articles were extensively illustrated with touching photographs of working women, children in factories, unsafe factories, and women carrying picket signs. The writing style that she developed relied heavily on anecdotes to further her points. Readers learned, for example, in an article about delinquent girls of the reform activities of Maude E. Miner, who rescued young women from the streets and brought them to live at Waverly House in New York.[43] An article about children with learning problems was illustrated by the story of a 16-year-old boy who was just starting school.[44] An article about children's health described the plight of a third grader named Harry who peddled candy at night and then fell asleep during school every day.[45] Dorr outlined another similar story: A young girl named Becky was forced to work every night in the family's bakery and then succumbed each day to the "sleeping sickness" in school.[46]

Another touching story described the life of a 12-year-old son of a drunken, irresponsible father. Young Danny Rosenbecker quarreled with another boy and in the heat of a losing fist fight, picked up a hatchet and struck the opponent on the head. Danny was tried for murder as an adult and sentenced to 20 years of hard labor in Ohio State Penitentiary in 1902, a year when the juvenile court system was just gaining popularity. Dorr described how she tracked down the 20-year-old Danny in 1910, although the juvenile court authorities, firmly entrenched in Ohio in by then, had never heard of him because his case had not been referred to them. Dorr visited Rosenbecker and described how eight years in prison had transformed him from a young boy into a "jailbird."[47] Dorr used the illustration of Danny Rosenbecker to appeal for more humane treatment of children in the court system. The hope for "bad" children, she stated, was the juvenile court.

Dorr also appealed to her readers' altruistic tendencies by describing in detail organizations and societies that were working to improve the urban environments. Women's clubs, settlement houses, and schools were highlighted in an effort to show readers that volunteer activities could make a difference. The roots of the juvenile court, for example, were traced to club women in Chicago. Dorr asserted that club women were responsible for advocating the juvenile court system in every state that eventually adopted it.[48] She repeatedly publicized the club movement and lobbied for continued involvement in reform activities by socially-conscious clubs.

Dorr suggested remedies for social ills by publicizing the work of women who dedicated their lives to settlement houses, schools, and clinics to help unfortunate women and children. By highlighting these individuals, Dorr was able to focus on sweeping reforms that she could prove worked. She argued, for example, that mental deficiency in children often was caused by "poverty, by overcrowded homes, poor food, bad air, lack of playgrounds."[49] The only solution, she advocated, was to "remove the patient from the cause of the evil."[50] Her advocacy for children extended to a concern for their physical health. Here, she argued in favor of preventive health care, a progressive idea at the turn of the century, and teaching hygiene in the schools.

It was tantamount to "race suicide" to neglect the health of children until they actually were ill, she wrote. As was typical of the municipal housekeeper, she appealed through the "race suicide" argument to the sensitivities of middle-class readers, who were at the time debating this question among themselves. Middle-class white people were concerned that fewer and fewer white babies were being born. Fewer women were marrying and women, especially white women of the middle and upper classes, were having fewer children. Dorr's argument suggested that children raised in an unhealthy environment failed to become productive, contributing members of society because they were "slightly damaged goods."[51] She called tuberculosis the "great white plague" because of the effect on city children.[52]

Dorr sketched a portrait of an ideal school, which she said actually existed in Philadelphia. There, the rooms were heated, cleanliness was the rule, big windows let in sunshine and women were prepared for college or business, professional or domestic work. While Dorr conceded that the price for such a school was high, she argued that it was well worth the money because it was graduating "fine, healthy, intelligent women, fit for motherhood."[53] She argued that special attention needed to be given to girls' education, especially physical education, because the future of the race depended upon it. The bodies of the "future mothers of the race" actually needed more physical training than boys, she contended.[54]

Like other municipal housekeepers, Dorr believed that the cities needed to be cleaned up in both the liberal and political senses. She traced the cycle of poverty and the steadily plummeting quality of the lives of children to the growth of urban environments. City life stole the natural outdoor environment away from the "wild young human animal" and changes were needed to rectify this problem. Children needed to play outside, they needed manual training and industrial education and they needed to have their parents educated about the proper way to raise them, she argued.[55]

While some of Dorr's remedies—such as cleanliness, physical education, good hygiene, and preventive health care—seem non-controversial today, she also proposed some radical reforms that have never been implemented. She suggested, for example, that all children under age 16 should be kept in school 12 months a year. During the summer months, parents who could afford to take their children from the city would be permitted to do so, but all other youngsters would go to vacation public school. There, classes in manual training, cooking, sewing, iron work, swimming and sports would be held outdoors. She envisioned a complex system of daycare in which babies would be brought to nurseries and young women students trained to care for them.[56] Although she proposed such training in traditional childcare, Dorr still criticized the fact that public school curricula prepared men for entry into the professional world, while it trained women "for one position only— housekeeper to a man."[57] Such sweeping reforms never came to fruition, although longer school years and expanded daycare facilities are still being proposed today.

Dorr used her writing to constantly push women readers to become increasingly involved in a host of urban activities. She literally preached to her readers and, when necessary, chastised them. When juvenile court systems, pushed through by club women, failed to solve juvenile delinquency, Dorr told her readers it was "because you have done an incomplete work."[58] She told readers they had failed to go far enough in their advocacy and had neglected to insist upon a support system to help the courts deal with juvenile delinquency. "You have established the theory of a court, but you have failed to provide the machinery through which the theory can work."[59] She argued that the court needed help with support services. "The community, that is to say, you and I, must help," she wrote, and she promised that in future articles she would explain why reform work was a civic duty and how volunteers could help solve social problems.[60] She suggested in a subsequent article that tension between the classes needed to be eased and that reform needed to be substituted for punishment. She stated that a "bad" child was the victim of "bad and imperfect social conditions. Instead of punishing him for what we did, we will give him what he really never had before—a chance to be good."[61]

Conclusion

Dorr spent two and a half years at *Hampton's*, but her career there ended when the magazine itself fell upon hard financial times. While circulation soared and advertising poured in, the magazine failed on the stock market. Owner Benjamin B. Hampton sold $700,000 worth of stock to 4,500 readers, but he had trouble raising money and charged that financial difficulties had resulted from editorial policies that offended businessmen.[62] The editors always were short of money, especially for salaries. Dorr once requested a raise and the managing editor replied sarcastically that it made little difference if the publication owed her two hundred dollars or a thousand.[63] Despite delays in being paid, however, the staff stayed on after the magazine was sold in 1911 to St. Louis publisher Frank Orff. Orff consolidated the magazine with another of his publications, Columbian, and it continued as *Hampton-Columbian Magazine* for a few months. Efforts to save it were unsuccessful and the magazine folded in May 1912.[64]

After the magazine failed, Dorr could not find another job that suited her temperament and her personal reform agenda. Her fervor for municipal housekeeping tasks continued, but she had no forum. She wanted to write only about causes she believed in and, thus, had trouble finding a new niche for her style of writing. As she put it: "One of my limitations is that I literally can't do any work unless I like to do it. I can labor but I cannot drudge. And it has been my bad luck that almost every congenial job I ever had, on salary, I mean, I have either outgrown and had to leave, or my newspaper, magazine, or organization has met disaster.[65]

To make ends meet, she worked as a freelance writer and lecturer to earn money. Without a forum to write about municipal housekeeping causes, Dorr sought a new avenue to express herself. She abandoned her municipal reform writing and turned instead to the cause of suffrage because she believed the "suffragists and the feminists...were working towards a definite goal, constructive, progressive and sane."[66] Dorr became the first editor of the militant *Suffragist*.[67] She saw this as a natural extension of her reform writing. In fact, Dorr had been interested in suffrage throughout her years at the *Post* and *Hampton's*. Thus, when *Hampton's* folded and salaried work did not materialize, Dorr moved on to the next stage of her career, which involved "waking women up to feminism."[68]

Notes

[1] "Rheta C. Dorr, 82, Author, Feminist," New York Times, 9 August 1948, 19.

[2] Journalistic involvement in the municipal housekeeping movement is explored in Agnes Hooper Gottlieb, "Women Journalists and the Municipal Housekeeping Movement: Case Studies of Jane Cunningham Croly, Helen M. Winslow, and Rheta Childe Dorr," (Ph.D. diss., University of Maryland, 1992). For a discussion of the municipal housekeeping movement in general, see Karen J. Blair, The Clubwoman as Feminist: True Womanhood Redefined, 1868-1914 (New York: Holmes & Meier, 1980) and Anne Firor Scott, Natural Allies: Women's Associations in American History (Urbana, IL: University of Illinois Press, 1991).

[3] Frank Luther Mott, A History of American Magazines, 1905-1930, vol. 5 (Cambridge, MA.: Belknap, 1968), 149.

[4] Marion Marzolf, Up From the Footnote (New York: Hastings House, 1977), 45.

[5] Ishbel Ross, Ladies of the Press (New York: Harper & Brothers, 1936), 109-116.

[6] Zena Beth McGlashen, "Club 'Ladies' and Working 'Girls': Rheta Childe Dorr and the New York Evening Post," Journalism History 8:1 (Spring 1981): 8.

[7] "Writers and their Work," Hampton's Broadway Magazine, June 1909, 863.

[8] Dorr, A Woman of Fifty (New York: Funk & Wagnalls, 1924), 127.

[9] Ibid., 117.

[10] Ibid., 171.

[11] Ibid., 197.

[12] Ibid.

[13] Ibid., 203.

[14] Ibid., 205.

[15] Mott, History of American Magazines, vol. 5, 149.

[16] Ibid., 151.

[17] Dorr, A Woman of Fifty, 203.

[18] Mott, A History of American Magazines, vol. 5,149.

[19] Louis Filler, The Muckrakers (University Park, PA: Pennsylvania State University Press, 1968), 273.

[20] Mott, A History of American Magazines, vol. 5, 149.

[21] Dorr, A Woman of Fifty, 210.

[22] Editorial Note, "Give the Working-Girl a Chance,"Hampton's Broadway Magazine, January 1909, 67.

[23] Ibid., 68.

[24] Ibid., 69.

[25] Ibid., 73.

[26] Ibid., 77.

[27] Ibid.

[28] Rheta Childe Dorr, "The Square Deal for the Babies," Hampton's Broadway Magazine, April 1909, 514.

[29] Rheta Childe Dorr, "The Twentieth Child," Hampton-Columbian Magazine, January 1912, 794-795.

[30] Rheta Childe Dorr, "The Prodigal Daughter," Hampton's Broadway Magazine, April 1910, 528.

[31] Rheta Childe Dorr, "What Eight Million Women Want," Hampton's Broadway Magazine, August 1909, 175.

[32] Ibid., 178.

[33] Rheta Childe Dorr, "What Eight Million Women Want," Part III, Hampton's Broadway Magazine, December 1909, 804.

[34] Rheta Childe Dorr, "'The Women Did It' in Colorado," Hampton's Magazine, April 1911, 433.

[35] Ibid., 436.

[36] Dorr, "Breaking into the Human Race," 317.

[37] Ibid., 329.

[38] Rheta Childe Dorr, "Deathproof versus Fireproof," Hampton's Magazine, June 1911, 688.

[39] Ibid., 689.

[40] Ibid.

[41] Ibid., 691.

[42] Dorr, "The Twentieth Child," 806.

[43] Dorr, "The Prodigal Daughter," 526.

[44] Rheta Childe Dorr, "Making Over the Backward Child," Hampton's Magazine, June 1910, 814.

[45] Rheta Childe Dorr, "A Fighting Chance for the City Child," Hampton's Magazine, July 1910, 108.

[46] Ibid., 109.

[47] Rheta Childe Dorr, "The Child's Day in Court," Hampton's Magazine, November 1910, 634.

[48] Ibid., 636.

[49] Dorr, "Making Over the Backward Child," 822.

[50] Ibid.

[51] Rheta Childe Dorr, "A Fighting Chance for the City Child," Hampton's Magazine, July 1910, 112.

[52] Ibid., 104.

[53] Rheta Childe Dorr, "Rebuilding the Child World," Hampton's Magazine, October 1910, 495.

[54] Ibid., 496.

[55] Rheta Childe Dorr, "A Fighting Chance for the CityChild," Hampton's Magazine, July 1910, 115-116.

[56] Rheta Childe Dorr, "Rebuilding the Child World," 497.

[57] Dorr, "Breaking Into the Human Race," 325.

[58] Rheta Childe Dorr, "Another Chance for the BadBoy," Hampton's Magazine, December 1910, 801.

[59] Ibid.

[60] Ibid., 807.

[61] Rheta Childe Dorr, "Reclaiming the Wayward Girl," Hampton's Magazine, January 1911, 78.

[62] Mott, A History of American Magazines, vol. 5, 150-151.

[63] Dorr, A Woman of Fifty, 207.

[64] Mott, History of American Magazines, vol. 5, 145.

[65] Dorr, A Woman of Fifty, 209.

[66] Ibid., 219.

[67] Maurine H. Beasley and Sheila J. Gibbons, Taking Their Place: A Documentary History of Women in Journalism (Washington, DC: American University Press, 1993), 140.

[68] Dorr, A Woman of Fifty, 224.

Acknowledgments

This article was the winner of the 1993 Top Faculty Paper Prize awarded by the Magazine Division of the Association for Education in Journalism and Mass Communication at the annual meeting held in Kansas City, MO in August 1993.

17

The Women's Movement in the 1920s: American Magazines Document the Health and Progress of Feminism

Carolyn Ann Bonard

ABSTRACT

Textbooks commonly state that, following women's gain of the right to vote in August 1920, their movement collapsed. However, magazine articles published in the following decade show that the women's movement was a vibrant force that was shaping the beginning of a new social order and preparing women for assimilation into the political system.

Introduction

The women's rights convention held in 1848 at Seneca Falls, New York commonly dates the beginning of the women's movement in the United States. The convention sparked a 72-year struggle for women's right to vote which culminated in the ratification of the Nineteenth Amendment to the U.S. Constitution in August 1920. Twenty-seven million women had gained the right to vote.[1] Thereafter, the women's movement seems to have been cast aside by recorded history. A government textbook states: "Having won its major battle for the right to vote, the women's movement virtually collapsed. Only a few groups continued to work for their cause."[2] A history textbook states that "women's united efforts failed to create an interest group solid enough or powerful enough to dent political, economic, and social systems run by men."[3] What happened to the women's movement in the decade following the adoption of the Nineteenth Amendment? Could magazine articles published in that decade have recorded the pulse of the women's movement, either explicitly or implicitly?

Method

Magazine articles that might answer these questions were located through *Readers' Guide to Periodical Literature.*[4] Fourteen varied headings were selected, some of which reflected the issues of the decade: "Education of Women," "Feminism," "Married Women: Employment," "Woman: Employment," "Woman: Equal Rights," "Woman: Occupations," "Women and Politics," "Woman Suffrage: United States," and "Working Girls and Women." Other headings were more general: "Married Women," "Wives," "Woman," "Woman: Social and Moral Questions" and "Woman: United States."

Magazines were chosen that collectively represented a diversified content and audience: two women's magazines, *Ladies' Home Journal* and *Good Housekeeping*; two general interest magazines that had a similar format and content to the selected women's magazines, *Saturday Evening Post* and *Collier's, the National Weekly*; and three intellectual magazines, *Harper's Monthly*, the *Nation* and *Atlantic Monthly*. The initial step of this study, then, involved locating articles published between August 1920 and August 1930 in seven selected magazines listed under 14 specified headings in *Readers' Guide*.

As a further step, all issues of *Harper's Monthly* and *Ladies' Home Journal* published during this decade were searched. In *Ladies' Home Journal*, seven articles were found through *Readers' Guide*. A complete search of the 120 issues of the decade found two additional articles, which might have been listed in *Readers' Guide* under headings other than the 14 headings selected for this study. In *Harper's Monthly*, eight articles were found through *Readers' Guide*. A complete search of the 120 issues of the decade found four additional articles. The complete searches through these two magazines confirmed that using *Readers' Guide* to locate articles relevant to this study had been a sufficiently thorough method of research. These two steps located 33 articles that might indicate what happened to the women's movement in the decade following the adoption of the Nineteenth Amendment.

Results

Social and Economic Aspects of the W.5omen's Movement

The women's movement, or feminism, was an attitude that emphasized the individual and recognized the importance of the job. In the April 1925 issue of *Harper's Monthly*, Elizabeth Breuer stated:

> In this country feminism, as an organized movement of women in great active groups, is over. But in its place is rising a feminism which is a point of view. This point of view expresses itself not so much in sex-consciousness

as in the personal self-consciousness of women who are trying to straddle two horses and ride them both to a victorious finish. One of these is the Job—through which woman can express herself as an individual in a world of masculine standards; the other is her love life, which she cannot leave behind if she is to be happy as a woman.[5]

Breuer wrapped up her definition of feminism by stating: "The woman who attempts complete fulfillment in both aspects of her life is a feminist."[6]

The women's movement challenged the traditional social order. Ethel Puffer Howes stated in the April 1922 issue of *Atlantic Monthly* that society "tacitly assumed that marriage barred or terminated a career."[7] Why did a woman have to choose between marriage and career? This was an issue that Nancy Barr Mavity addressed in the July 1926 issue of *Harper's Monthly*. She stated: "The choice has no meaning unless marriage implies of necessity the bargain of financial support on the part of the husband for domestic services on the part of the wife."[8] Concerning the attitude of society toward a woman who worked outside the home, Mary Roberts Rinehart, in the April 1921 issue of *Ladies' Home Journal*, stated: "The family pride suffered. It reflected on the pride of the masculine portion of it, as indicating their failure to support their womankind."[9] Mavity suggested the ultimate conclusion to the marriage-career issue in this question: "Is the chance to choose one's work as a person instead of a sex-being worth the long and complex struggle to amend our entire social and economic constitution?"[10]

The women's movement allowed women freedom to seek fulfillment in both the home—marriage and motherhood comprehensively considered—and career or to freely choose either home or career. In the June 2, 1926 issue of the *Nation*, Eunice Fuller Barnard stated:

> The party of the left suggests that women make parenthood and profession coordinate but independent, as men have done; the party of the right that they develop parenthood itself to a professional status. The compromise party believes that along with their major profession of parenthood women may as a minor interest still cherish and develop their individual talents.[11]

In the October 1927 issue of *Harper's Monthly*, Dorothy Dunbar Bromley recognized that the economic independence a woman obtained through a job "spells her freedom as an individual, enabling her to marry or not to marry, as she chooses—to terminate a marriage that has become unbearable, and to support and educate her children if necessary."[12] More picturesquely, in the August 1921 issue of *Good Housekeeping*, Anne Shannon Monroe stated: "Men have cried out in alarm, 'With all this suffrage, with all this entering of professions, with all this throwing wide of the world's doors, women will rush out of the homes!'"[13] Monroe upheld this rush because those women will "find their rightful places, and the home-job will eventually fall to those who should hold it."[14] Women were no longer bound to tradition for tradition's sake. In the August 1920 issue of *Ladies' Home Journal*, Harriet Abbot stated: "Now, our conduct shall be the result of intelligent choice, and when we elect to live according to the older doctrines it shall be because we recognize truth even when it comes to us in some of the shackles of platitudes."[15]

The women's movement overturned the traditional social order. In the November 1921 issue of *Harper's Monthly*, Alexander Black vividly stated one point of view concerning this upheaval:

> The whole theory of taking care of woman involved her occupying a 'place,' so that one who played the part of a showman exhibiting the world might be free to say that over there, in a cage, were the women. But the women broke out of the cage. They roved over the whole picture. This made it exceedingly difficult to go on thinking about taking care of them.[16]

Black added that women have "smashed the tradition of 'place.' They have overrun the forbidden industries and professions."[17] In the May 1929 issue of *Harper's Monthly*, Lillian Symes presented a flip side of this radical change, stating that feminists' "attempts at economic and social emancipation" have put them in the position of "playing both a man's and a woman's part. Instead of achieving freedom, they have achieved the right to carry two burdens, to embrace a new form of servitude." [18] Concerned about the future of the social order, Symes, in the June 1930 issue of *Harper's Monthly*, stated: "Old values are giving way to what seems a loss of all values. Intellectually and socially we are in a chaos of conflict." [19] Similarly, in the March 1929 issue of *Harper's Monthly*, Floyd H. Allport stated: "For while the sophistries underlying our present sex-stereotypes are being exposed, there must arise the question of what is to take their place."[20]

The women's movement emphasized the individual in a new social order. In the December 1925 issue of *Harper's Monthly*, Beatrice M. Hinkle stated: "The great movement which is now sweeping over the land, affecting the women of all classes, carries with it something immeasurable, for it is the destroyer of the old mold which for ages has held women bound to instinct."[21] The emphasis of the traditional order, the "old mold," was on the woman as wife and mother; the emphasis of the women's movement was on the individual. Hinkle stated that women have "cast aside the maternal ideal as their goal and are demanding recognition as individuals first, and as wives and mothers second."[22] The new social order recognized man's as well as woman's individuality, as Hinkle stated:

Women have escaped from the authority and restrictions imposed upon them as the result of the unalterable convictions of man that his wife was his property, and that she must live her life as he wished it. The twain are no longer one flesh—the man being 'the one'—but instead they are two distinct personalities, forced to find a new basis of adaptation to each other and a new form of relationship.[23]

Similarly, in the January 1925 issue of *Ladies' Home Journal*, Ruth Scott Miller stated concerning Joseph Sabath, a county court judge "who holds the world's judicial divorce record with over twelve thousand decisions":

Judge Sabath insists, perhaps more vehemently than most, that the world must recognize the new social order of things; must realize that when a marriage occurs today new relationships are set up that are entirely opposed to those which obtained fifty years ago.[24]

However, the declaration of women's individuality was not the vanguard of the women's movement. In the October 1926 issue of *Harper's Monthly*, R. Le Clerc Phillips stated that women "who were the voices of the feminist movement" concentrated "on rights of citizenship, rights of economic independence, and, above all, on the right to give practical expression to their political opinions," rather than speaking out about their "rights as women."[25] Phillips defined "rights as women" as "their rights to the open expression of their individuality as women absolutely untrammelled by all male preconceptions—and misconceptions—of what that individuality really is."[26]

Women's gain of the right to vote advanced, rather than caused, the new social order. In the September 11, 1920, issue of *Saturday Evening Post*, Elizabeth Frazer stated that:

The woman-suffrage movement...was perhaps the greatest single influence in sharpening and bringing to a point those other more subterranean and unconscious forces that were advancing woman's cause. The whole tide was setting in the direction of the freedom of women; and the suffrage movement called attention to but did not produce that tide.[27]

In the July 20, 1927 issue of the *Nation*, Mary Austin referred to the "forward turn of twentieth-century feminism" and defined this phrase when she stated: "All that votes for women seems to mean at the moment is a marker for the turn at which the redistribution of sex emphasis begins."[28] Austin explained:

Now that the turn is accomplished, and nothing startlingly political or professional seems to be determined by it, what does stand out in the nature of an achievement is the escape not of one sex from the other but of both from a social complex unwholesomely driven and informed by sex distinctions.[29]

These magazine articles indicate that the women's movement in the decade following the adoption of the Nineteenth Amendment was a new attitude that was shaping the beginning of a new social order, not in a determined, organized manner, but as a natural result of women's collective individuality—the individuality of each woman who expressed her uniqueness, independence and equality with man.

Political Aspects of the Women's Movement

This study has examined the social and economic aspects of the women's movement through the more specific aspects of marriage, motherhood, and career. In the February 1921 issue of *Atlantic Monthly*, Mary Van Kleeck stated that feminism's "essence is voluntary choice" in these three aspects as well as in politics.[30] Although women did not organize as a faction, articles disputed women's failure in politics with two points. First, women's right to vote was their right as U.S. citizens. Whether they exercised that right was not, in itself, a measure of their achievement or failure in politics. An editorial in the May 17, 1930, issue of *Collier's, The National Weekly* stated: "Suffrage for women or men was an act of justice which can neither succeed nor fail. Whether men or women vote stupidly or wisely, for good measures or bad, is beside the point. The right to vote is inherent in our kind of government."[31]

Another point that disputed women's failure in politics was that their indifference was gradually being overcome through political education and involvement in politics. An editorial in the August 1930 issue of *Ladies' Home Journal* attributed women's indifference to politics to the fact that "women who were to be given suffrage had not been brought up to use it."[32] Similarly, in the October 1924 issue of *Good Housekeeping*, Ida M. Tarbell stated: "One handles a new subject shyly and awkwardly. One does not know the vocabulary, etiquette, principles."[33] At first, women were not motivated to become involved in politics. In the February 1921 issue of *Ladies' Home Journal*, Elizabeth Jordan stated: "It had not yet occurred to them that they could affect the politics in their local environments. Least of all did it strike them that they needed training as a preparation for their new responsibility."[34] In the September 1922 issue of *Good Housekeeping*, Frazer stated that, initially, women's political influence would be in municipal affairs more than in higher political divisions because "such affairs touch most closely the home,"[35] and this primary area is the "the amoeba of political life."[36]

National organizations educated and involved women in politics. In the April 1922 issue of *Good Housekeeping*, Frazer stated: "In this task of educating the women in the abc of practical, every-day local politics, two agencies, the National Federation of Women's Clubs and the National League of Women Voters, have done yeoman service."[37] In the August 1924 issue of *Ladies' Home Journal*, Frazer quoted Maud Wood Park, president of the National League of Women Voters: "The actual work of the League, the end, for which all the other things are the means, is first of all training in citizenship."[38] Eventually, women's involvement in politics affected legislation even at the national level. In the April 1922 issue of *Ladies' Home Journal*, Charles A. Selden listed the National League of Women Voters and the General Federation of Women's Clubs as the national women's organizations with the largest number of members among the 14 organizations of the Women's Joint Congressional Committee.[39] Concerning the purpose of this greater organization, Selden stated: "When, on occasion, the women organizations see that it is necessary to act unanimously on any measure, as was the case in the [Sheppard-Towner] Maternity Bill fight, they put into action the most powerful lobby that has ever operated on the American Congress."[40]

The women's movement was raising women's political status. In the December 1923 issue of *Harper's Monthly*, Breuer stated that women's political education was a "task leading to the more subtle emancipation of women."[41] In noting that two women had been elected as state governors, Emily Newell Blair, in the October 1925 issue of *Harper's Monthly*, stated:

It shows the way by which a woman can move into office, namely by becoming identified in the public mind with issues of which it approves and by winning that public's confidence as to performance—which is exactly the way by which a man comes into office. It is equality.[42]

Thus, to say that the women's movement failed to dent the political system run by men is to be looking for a women's bloc and not see that, rather than denting the system, women were being assimilated into it as they became sufficiently knowledgeable and capable.

Controversy over the Equal Rights Issue

Within the women's movement, a secondary aspect of women's political education and involvement in politics was the issue of how women could gain equal rights. Van Kleeck, in defining feminism, stated:

Feminism is not, and has not, a definite programme. Like democracy, it is a spirit and not an invention—not an institution, but a changing life within the changing forms of institutions. And feminism, like democracy, busies itself with the issues that the times create.[43]

The main issues for women during the first decade of the Nineteenth Amendment were economic and legal equality. In the June 1924 issue of *Ladies' Home Journal*, Selden quoted Ethel M. Smith, the national legislative representative of the women's trade unions: "It is the economic fight that is the bitterest of all. Men may be quite willing to let women vote, but it is quite another thing to pay them the same wages as men, or allow them to secure a shorter workday." [44] Concerning the married woman's legal inequality, Rheta Childe Dorr, in the July 1928 issue of *Good Housekeeping*, stated:

> She could own no property, real or personal; her wages, if any, belonged to her husband; he was the sole guardian of her children and could give them away if he chose, could apprentice them to trades, forbid their marriages, or force them to marry without the mother's consent. In fact, as the legal phrase had it, a married woman was civilly dead.[45]

The Seneca Falls convention in 1848 drew up demands for equal rights, but, as Inez Haynes Irwin stated in the March 1924 issue of *Good Housekeeping*, the "only right we have gained for all the women of the United States is the right to vote."[46] Likewise, in the February 1926 issue of *Harper's Monthly*, Edna Kenton stated: "The Nineteenth Amendment gave women as a matter of legal fact, just one thing—the power to vote."[47] Women's struggle for equality since they acquired the right to vote had two conflicting strategies. Irwin and Kenton upheld one strategy, the Equal Rights Amendment backed by the National Woman's Party. Breuer, in her 1923 article, stated:

> The Woman's Party is regarded by many women's organizations as their common enemy, being as it is the radical wing of the woman's movement in the United States. This attitude proceeds from the intention of the Woman's Party to remove from the statute books all laws which discriminate for or against women on sex lines, and that destruction accomplished, to create other laws which shall give necessary protection in industry, marriage, and other legal and social relationships, to men and women alike as human beings, regardless of sex, but regardful of the minimum of physical endurance for both. To accomplish this it seeks to tear down the whole body of protective legislation which has been built up through years of painful struggle by the majority of women's organizations, and the women's organizations are therefore fighting its program tooth and nail.[48]

This controversy within the women's movement over how to obtain equal rights indicates that the movement was very much alive.

Conclusion

Magazine articles published during the first decade of the Nineteenth Amendment indicate that the women's movement was a vibrant force, a new attitude that was shaping the beginning of a new social order, and a medium for women's assimilation into the political system. Why these conclusions have not been recorded in history can be explained in two ways: attitude and assimilation are not easily transferred to recorded history, and, furthermore, the women's movement was an undercurrent which historians might have overlooked, concentrating, rather, on the vote and what women accomplished with it.

Notes

[1] "What Do the Women Want Now," Ladies' Home Journal, January 1921, 29.

[2] Richard A. Watson, Promise and Performance of American Democracy, 5th ed. (New York: John Wiley & Sons, 1985), 533.

[3] Mary Beth Norton, David M. Katzman, Paul D. Escott, Howard P. Chudacoff, Thomas G. Paterson, and William M. Tuttle, Jr., A People and a Nation, vol. 2, 2nd ed. (Boston: Houghton Mifflin, 1986), 605.

[4] Elizabeth J. Sherwood, ed., Readers' Guide to Periodical Literature, vol. 5 (New York: H.W. Wilson, 1922); Alice M. Dougan and Bertha Joel, eds., Readers' Guide to Periodical Literature, vols. 6, 7 & 8 (New York: H.W. Wilson, 1925, 1929, 1932). Abbreviated as Readers' Guide in future references.

[5] Elizabeth Breuer, "Feminism's Awkward Age," Harper's Monthly, April 1925, 545.

[6] Ibid.

[7] Ethel Puffer Howes, "Accepting the Universe," Atlantic Monthly, April 1922, 445.

[8] Nancy Barr Mavity, "The Wife, the Home, and the Job," Harper's Monthly, July 1926, 190.

[9] Mary Roberts Rinehart, "A Home or a Career," Ladies' Home Journal, April 1921, 25.

[10] Mavity, 198, 199.

[11] Eunice Fuller Barnard, "Home—Job—or Both? The Woman's Problem," The Nation, 2 June 1926, 601, 602.

[12] Dorothy Dunbar Bromley, "Feminist—New Style," Harper's Monthly, October 1927, 554.

[13] Anne Shannon Monroe, "The Woman Who Should Marry," Good Housekeeping, August 1921, 30.

[14] Ibid.

[15] Harriet Abbot, "What the Newest New Woman Is," Ladies' Home Journal, August 1920, 154.

[16] Alexander Black, "The Truth about Women," Harper's Monthly, November 1921, 756.

[17] Ibid.

[18] Lillian Symes, "Still a Man's Game," Harper's Monthly, May 1929, 684.

[19] Lillian Symes, "The New Masculinism," Harper's Monthly, June 1930, 103.

[20] Floyd H. Allport, "Seeing Women as They Are," Harper's Monthly, March 1929, 407.

[21] Beatrice M. Hinkle, "The Chaos of Modern Marriage," Harper's Monthly, December 1925, 13.

[22] Ibid., 9.

[23] Ibid., 6.

[24] Ruth Scott Miller, "Masterless Wives and Divorce," Ladies' Home Journal, January 1925, 20.

[25] R. Le Clerc Phillips, "The Real Rights of Women," Harper's Monthly, October 1926, 609.

[26] Ibid.

[27] Elizabeth Frazer, "Encore Les Femmes! Woman: A Political Animal," Saturday Evening Post, 11 September 1920, 17.

[28] Mary Austin, "The Forward Turn," The Nation, 20 July 1927, 59.

[29] Ibid.

[30] Mary Van Kleeck, "Women and Machines," Atlantic Monthly, February 1921, 255.

[31] "Ten Years of Woman," Collier's, The National Weekly, 17 May 1930, 94.

[32] "Ten Years of Suffrage," Ladies' Home Journal, August 1930, 22.

[33] Ida M. Tarbell, "Is Woman's Suffrage a Failure?" Good Housekeeping, October 1924, 242.

[34] Elizabeth Jordan, "Education for Citizenship," Ladies' Home Journal, February 1921, 27.

[35] Elizabeth Frazer, "A Political Forecast," Good Housekeeping, September 1922, 161.

[36] Ibid., 159.

[37] Elizabeth Frazer, "Politics Begins at Home," Good Housekeeping, April 1922, 120.

[38] Elizabeth Frazer, "The Rising Tide of Voters," Ladies' Home Journal, August 1924, 132.

[39] Charles A. Selden, "The Most Powerful Lobby in Washington," Ladies' Home Journal, April 1922, 93.

[40] Ibid., 95.

[41] Elizabeth Breuer, "What Four Million Women are Doing," Harper's Monthly, December 1923, 120.

[42] Emily Newell Blair, "Are Women a Failure in Politics?" Harper's Monthly, October 1925, 517.

[43] Van Kleeck, 255.

[44] Charles A. Selden, "Four Years of the Nineteenth Amendment," Ladies' Home Journal, June 1924, 138.

[45] Rheta Childe Dorr, "Free and Equal Citizens," Good Housekeeping, July 1928, 217.

[46] Inez Haynes Irwin, "The Equal Rights Amendment, Why the Woman's Party is for It," Good Housekeeping, March 1924, 18.

[47] Edna Kenton, "The Ladies' Next Step," Harper's Monthly, February 1926, 366.

[48] Breuer, "What Four Million Women Are Doing," 121, 122.

Acknowledgments

This article was the winner of the 1993 Top Undergraduate Paper Prize awarded by the Magazine Division of the Association for Education in Journalism and Mass Communication at the annual meeting held in Kansas City, MO in August 1993.